SECRET SNAKES
AND
SERPENT SURPRISES

SECRET SNAKES AND SERPENT SURPRISES

Dr Karl P.N. Shuker

COACHWHIP PUBLICATIONS
Greenville, Ohio

Secret Snakes and Serpent Surprises, by Dr Karl P.N. Shuker
© 2022 Dr Karl P.N. Shuker
Cover design © Coachwhip Publications: Crested cobra by Steven Bellshaw / background © Iana Kotova

CoachwhipBooks.com

ISBN 1-61646-520-4
ISBN-13 978-1-61646-520-9

Permission to use images from *Cryptozoology,* the journal of the International Society of Cryptozoology, given by the late Richard Greenwell, ISC Secretariat.

Creative Commons licenses included in this title:
    https://creativecommons.org/licenses/by/2.0/deed.en
    https://creativecommons.org/licenses/by/3.0/deed.en
    https://creativecommons.org/licenses/by/4.0/deed.en
    https://creativecommons.org/licenses/by-sa/2.0/deed.en
    https://creativecommons.org/licenses/by-sa/2.5/deed.en
    https://creativecommons.org/licenses/by-sa/3.0/deed.en
    https://creativecommons.org/licenses/by-sa/4.0/deed.en

Fair Use: Any limited use of copyright material (including anonymously published social media pranks) is strictly for the purposes of criticism, comment, education, and research, as detailed by Title 17 of the United States Code (USC Title 17 § 107).

DEDICATION

I wish to dedicate this book to the memory of Steve Moore (1949-2014), one of my first and enduring friends in the Fortean community, who always encouraged and supported my own writings and researches within the fascinating fields of inexplicabilia, including cryptozoology.

Thank you Steve, and may you now know the answers to all of the many ancient historical and mythological riddles (including those associated with Glycon) that you investigated so extensively, and with such zeal, expertise, and wisdom, during a life richly inspired by mystery and wonder.

Steve Moore
(© Paul Sieveking)

ACKNOWLEDGEMENTS

I wish to offer my sincere thanks to the following persons and organisations for providing me with all manner of interesting information and illustrations, as well as for their much-appreciated thoughts and opinions regarding various of the diverse subjects documented in this book, plus their greatly-valued encouragement in recent or earlier times that inspired me to prepare this book.

David Alderton; Maureen Ashfield; Keith Baker; Michael Bassett; Trevor Beer; Michael Bright; Markus Bühler; Centre for Fortean Zoology; Philip Chapman; Marc Clam; John L. Cloudsley-Thompson; Guntram Deichsel; Tim Dinsdale; Jonathan Downes; Omi Draper; Philippa Foster; Richard Freeman; William Gibbons; Michael Goss; Markus Hemmler; David Heppell; Bernard Heuvelmans; Ingo; Philip H. Jensen; Ivan Mackerle; Christopher Mallery; Scott Mardis; Carl Marshall; Colin McCarthy; Robert Michaels; Ralph Molnar; Steve Moore; Tim Morris; Richard Muirhead; Adam Naworal; Michael Newton; Hodari Nundu; Mark O'Shea; Andy Paciorek; Marko Puljic; William M. Rebsamen; Changchang A. Sangma; Robert Schneck; Klaus-Dieter Schulz; Mary D. Shuker; Bob Skinner; Tim Swartz; Nick Sucik; Richard Svensson; Lars Thomas; Robert Twombley; Typhon; Alistair Underwood; Anthony Wallis; Richard Wells; Bruce A. Young.

My especial thanks go to my editor/publisher Chad Arment, who not only has provided me with a great deal of valuable information that I have incorporated into this present book but also shares my enthusiasm for herpetological cryptids, including mystery snakes. He was immediately interested when I first showed him an early version of this book quite a while ago, with a view to it being published when eventually complete. As a result, another long-planned project of mine is now duly prepared and in print—thanks again, Chad!

CONTENTS

DEDICATION	5
ACKNOWLEDGEMENTS	7
INTRODUCTION	13
1: SHERLOCK HOLMES AND THE SPECKLED BAND—AN UNKNOWN SPECIES OF SNAKE?	19
2: ON THE TRAIL OF MEDITERRANEAN MYSTERY SNAKES	35
3: THE HORN SNAKE AND THE HOOP SNAKE—NORTH AMERICA'S MOST (IN)FAMOUS PSEUDO-SERPENTS	45
4: THE CURIOUS CASE OF THE CROWING CRESTED COBRA	57
5: THE SCARLET VIPER—NO LONGER A MYSTERY OF NATURAL HISTORY	81
6: A SELECTION OF SECRET ASIAN AND AUSTRALASIAN SNAKES	99

7: When Two Heads—or More—Are Not
   Better than One! 113

8: Secrets of the Snake-Stones—Charting
   Their Histories and Mysteries 127

9: Giant Anacondas and Other Super-Sized
   Cryptozoological Snakes 141

10: The Mongolian Death Worm—A Shocking
    Surprise in the Gobi? 165

11: Snakes with Wings—And Other
    Strange Things 177

12: Courting the Cobra 195

13: Gooseberry Wives, Hairy Vipers,
    and Hazelworms 217

14: A Bipedal Snake in the Garden of Eden?
    What Did the Pre-Cursed Serpent Look
    Like? 233

15: A Melanistic Mystery Snake? 251

16: Bleating Pythons, Chiming Puff Adders,
    and Other Unexpected Serpentine
    Vocalists 257

17: Kipling and Karait—An Ophidian Bungle
    in *The Jungle Book*? 273

18: Bouncing in the Balkans—The Yugoslavian
    Jumping Snake 287

19: In Search of Serpent Kings 297

20: A Snake with a Head at Each End?
    The Amphisbaena Awakes! 309

CONTENTS

21: Seeking Glycon—The Roman Empire's Blond-Haired (and Human-Eared!) Ophidian Oracle-Utterer — 321

22: Remembering the Beast of Bodalog—Wales's Mystery Water Snake . . . or a Water Vampire? — 339

23: Vanquishing *Bothrodon*—How a Giant Snake was Transformed into a Seashell! — 347

24: In Pursuit of Impossible Snakes—A Further Collection of Pseudo-Serpents — 357

25: Venomous Verses—A Selection of My Serpent-Inspired Poetry — 377

Select Bibliography — 385

Index of Animal Names — 403

About the Author — 411

INTRODUCTION

> A narrow fellow in the grass
> Occasionally rides;
> You may have met him,—did you not?
> His notice sudden is.
>
> The grass divides as with a comb,
> A spotted shaft is seen;
> And then it closes at your feet
> And opens further on.
>
> He likes a boggy acre,
> A floor too cool for corn.
> Yet when a child, and barefoot,
> I more than once, at morn,
>
> Have passed, I thought, a whip-lash
> Unbraiding in the sun,—
> When, stooping to secure it,
> It wrinkled, and was gone.
>
> Several of nature's people
> I know, and they know me;
> I feel for them a transport
> Of cordiality;
>
> But never met this fellow,
> Attended or alone,
> Without a tighter breathing,
> And zero at the bone.
>
>   Emily Dickinson—'Snake'

Few creatures divide human opinion so diametrically regarding their perceived benevolence, or malevolence, as do snakes—the eternally-cursed serpent kind according to Christianity, the most divine and blessed of reptiles according to Hinduism, vilified and venerated, sanctified and demonised, passively protected, actively annihilated, often overlooked, but never deemed not worthy of notice if or when encountered. Thus is our species' complex entwining of fear and fascination in relation to these creatures expressed—an ancient but still extremely relevant, multi-headed monster of instinctive, irrational, and incomprehensible reactions that challenge one another incessantly as they gnaw at the very roots of our own origin on this planet.

For obvious reasons directly linked to self-preservation, it is of course the venomous species of snake that receive most attention from humanity and engender most fear and dread from it, but for those many people worldwide not familiar with which species are venomous and which are not, all of serpentkind is ultimately (albeit unfairly) cast within the shadow of suspicion and terror as to their

Close-up of the magnificent life-sized sculpture by Tim Johnman of a reticulated python at Taronga Zoo in Sydney, Australia, which I visited in 2006 (© Dr Karl Shuker)

likelihood of being potentially dangerous. The same rationale also applies to the giant constricting species, such as the larger pythons, boas, and anacondas.

Fortunately for ophidiophobes everywhere, however, snakes generally feel much the same about us, and tend to be far more elusive than exhibitionist in typical lifestyle. Indeed, even today new species of serpent are still being discovered and formally documented by science, sometimes in remote, little-explored regions but also in more familiar terrain. Nor are these scientific debutants all inconspicuous or nondescript.

On the contrary, they include certain very spectacular examples—such as Kenya's giant spitting cobra *Naja ashei,* the world's biggest such species but officially described only as recently as 2007; a very large and distinctive black-scaled cobra that had existed in plain sight for centuries on the small West African island of São Tomé without any herpetologist realising that it was a separate species undescribed by science until it very belatedly received such recognition, and its own taxonomic name, *Naja peroescobari,* in September 2017; and another sizeable species also hiding in plain sight but this time in Great Britain, one of the world's largest and most exhaustively documented islands, zoologically-speaking, but nevertheless where in August 2017 its grass snakes (genus *Natrix)* were publicly revealed to belong to two discrete species, differing both genetically and morphologically from one another.

Yet even these noteworthy newcomers may pale into insignificance if some of the mystery snakes currently found only within the chronicles of cryptozoology are ever shown to be real and still in existence. As investigated and documented in this present book—providing the most extensive survey of these serpents ever published—they include such extraordinary entities up for consideration as Africa's bizarre crowing crested cobra as well as comparably rooster-mimicking counterparts in the Caribbean island chain and also elsewhere around the world; an elusive pythonesque cryptid in Australia; a potentially dangerous water snake in the Far East, and a putative if much shorter-lived counterpart in Wales, UK; jumping snakes in Central Europe; airborne anomalies in Africa plus the southern USA (and even London, England); and all manner of reports alleging the existence of truly gargantuan anacondas, including some with horns.

Photo-bombed by *Titanoboa!* (© Dr Karl Shuker)

In among such reports are the inevitable hoax contingent, such as the infamous hoop snake and horned snake; the more obscure but no less preposterous snow snake; the telescopic snake; and the Paraguayan barking snake, whose supposed vocal abilities stemmed not from nature but merely from nomenclatural ineptitude.

Having said that, and as will also be examined here, there are many very diverse and extremely perplexing reports on file referring to snakes reputedly capable of vocalising a much greater array of sounds than the sibilant hisses normally associated with these reptiles. Nor is that the only example of contentious behaviour ascribed to snakes. The age-old traditions and rituals of snake veneration and handling practised in Africa and Asia even today are chronicled here too, including some truly incredible, thoroughly mystifying instances when such treatment should have resulted in instant death for the acolytes engaged in it, yet in reality seem not to have provoked the ophidian participants in any way. Also examined is the formerly much-favoured belief that a snake's unblinking gaze can hypnotise its prey, preventing it from fleeing to safety and thereby enabling the snake to seize the hapless victim—a controversial practice known as fascination.

And what about immense amalgamations of snakes dubbed serpent kings; or snake stones that can allegedly draw venom from snake bites and thence save lives; or the extraordinary history of a horse-headed, human-eared, prophecy-voicing snake deity named Glycon on full display and visited by countless visitors in bygone Europe; or snakes with two or more heads, and even some with a head at each of their body; or how the accursed Eden Serpent was once depicted and deemed originally to have been a human-headed

INTRODUCTION

bipedal beast of wisdom and poise; or anguiniform anomalies with hair instead of scales; or the ostensibly shocking presence in the Gobi Desert of Mongolia's deadly death worm; or the true nature of the scarlet adder, St Paul's viper, Kipling's diminutive but deadly dust serpent Karait, and even the daunting, much-dreaded Speckled Band confronted by none other than Sherlock Holmes?

All of these fascinating subjects and many more too can be found here in this unique survey of secret snakes and the many behavioural and cultural surprises presented by the serpent world down through the ages—constituting an exclusive, never previously-assembled compilation of snake-themed writings of mine, expanded and updated from the varied articles and book excerpts in which they originated. So prepare to be fascinated—but only in the most harmless, non-lethal manner!—by the ophidian offerings that I am now about to unveil before you. However, it may be best not to stare too long into the eyes of any of the limbless ones portrayed in the sumptuous collection of illustrations presented here, just in case . . .

1
SHERLOCK HOLMES AND THE SPECKLED BAND—AN UNKNOWN SPECIES OF SNAKE?

It was a singular sight which met our eyes. On the table stood a dark-lantern with the shutter half open, throwing a brilliant beam of light upon the iron safe, the door of which was ajar. Beside this table, on the wooden chair, sat Dr. Grimesby Roylott clad in a long grey dressing-gown, his bare ankles protruding beneath, and his feet thrust into red heelless Turkish slippers. Across his lap lay the short stock with the long lash which we had noticed during the day. His chin was cocked upward and his eyes were fixed in a dreadful, rigid stare at the corner of the ceiling. Round his brow he had a peculiar yellow band, with brownish speckles, which seemed to be bound tightly round his head. As we entered he made neither sound nor motion.

"The band! the speckled band!" whispered Holmes.

I took a step forward. In an instant his strange head-gear began to move, and there reared itself from among his hair the squat diamond-shaped head and puffed neck of a loathsome serpent.

"It is a swamp adder!" cried Holmes; "the deadliest snake in India. He has died within ten seconds of being bitten. Violence does, in truth, recoil upon the violent, and the schemer falls into the pit which he digs for another. Let us thrust this creature back into its den, and we can then remove Miss Stoner to some place of shelter and let the county police know what has happened."

As he spoke he drew the dog-whip swiftly from the dead man's lap, and throwing the noose round the reptile's neck he drew it from its horrid perch and, carrying it at arm's length, threw it into the iron safe, which he closed upon it.

> Sir Arthur Conan Doyle—'The Adventure of the Speckled Band', from *The Adventures of Sherlock Holmes*

During his numerous cases, the famous if fictitious consulting detective Sherlock Holmes, created by Sir Arthur Conan Doyle, encountered a number of extraordinary creatures—the hound of the Baskervilles, the giant rat of Sumatra, an unknown species of worm that sent its observer insane, and an exceptionally venomous, enigmatic Indian serpent referred to obliquely by one of its victims as the speckled band. But does the latter snake truly exist, and, if so, what is it?

HOW SHERLOCK HOLMES DEFEATED THE SPECKLED BAND

First appearing in February 1892 within the *Strand Magazine* as a stand-alone Sherlock Holmes short story, 'The Adventure of the Speckled Band' is one of twelve that were then collected together and republished later that same year within a compilation volume entitled *The Adventures of Sherlock Holmes*. (It was also adapted by Conan Doyle into a stage play called *The Stoner Case*, with the production opening at London's Adelphi Theatre in June 1910.)

This particular story tells of how Dr Grimesby Roylott, a very aggressive medical doctor heavily in debt but with two heiress step-daughters, murdered one of them, Julia Stoner, using a most ingenious, undetectable modus operandi that he was now also secretly attempting to use upon his other step-daughter, Helen Stoner. If successful, he would retain all of their money. Although Helen does not realise that her own life is in imminent danger, she feels sufficiently disturbed by the mysterious death of her sister, who was heard to cry out "It was the band! The speckled band!" immediately before dying, to engage Sherlock Holmes to investigate.

Assisted by his faithful companion Dr John Watson, it is Holmes who then discovers that Roylott had murdered Julia (and

Waxwork of Dr Grimesby Roylott with the swamp adder wrapped around his head, at London's Sherlock Holmes Museum (PD / Wikimedia)

was now seeking to do the same to Helen) using an exceedingly venomous species of Indian snake referred to by Holmes as a swamp adder, whose blotch-patterned body was the speckled band that the doomed Julia's last words had succinctly described. Happily, after hiding in Helen's bedroom they are able to thwart the deadly serpent, which, angered by Holmes's attack upon it with a cane, swiftly flees from whence it had come—back into the bedroom of its owner, Roylott. When Holmes and Watson then enter Roylott's room, they find him dead, with what looks at first like a speckled band wrapped around his head. Upon cautious, closer inspection, however, this proves to be the swamp adder, which in its enraged, still-agitated state had turned upon Roylott, killing him with a single lethal, fast-acting bite.

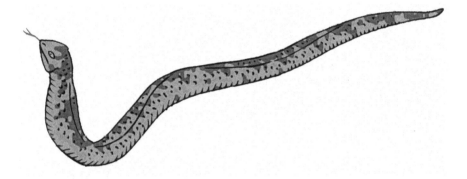

Reconstruction of the likely appearance of the Indian swamp adder, aka the speckled band (© Tim Morris)

THE INDIAN SWAMP ADDER—IN SEARCH OF AN IDENTITY

In the story, the swamp adder was referred to by Holmes as "the deadliest snake in India", but what exactly *is* a swamp adder? No known species of snake in India—or anywhere else, for that matter—is ever referred to by that particular name. Unfortunately, however, the story contains only the sparsest of morphological and behavioural details concerning this enigmatic serpent.

Its body is yellow, patterned with brownish speckles, and probably around 3 ft long but fairly slender if it resembles a band and can wrap itself around a man's forehead. Its own head is squat and diamond-shaped, and its neck is puffed. Its hiss is said to be "a very gentle, soothing sound, like that of a small jet of steam escaping continually from a kettle", but according to Holmes its venom is so toxic that it kills in 10 seconds. Yet its fangs apparently leave such tiny, inconspicuous puncture wounds when it bites its victim that they were not noticed by the coroner who examined Julia Stoner's body. For according to a statement made by her sister Helen to Holmes, no marks had been found upon Julia by the coroner.

Down through the years, this intriguing reptilian mystery has engaged the attention of many scholars, of Sherlockian and herpetological expertise alike, with a number of different identities proposed for the perplexing Indian swamp adder.

IS THE SWAMP ADDER TRULY A SPECIES OF VIPER?

The most popular identity is the very venomous tic polonga or Russell's viper *Daboia russelii*, a large terrestrial species found throughout the Indian subcontinent. Due in no small way to its frequent proximity to human habitation, this infamous species is responsible for more deaths and incidents involving snake-bite than any other venomous snake in the entire region. Up to 5 ft long, its relatively slender, brown-blotched, yellow-tan body does recall the 'speckled band' description for the mystifying swamp adder. Also, as its triangular head is distinct from its neck, when viewed at certain angles its head and the beginning of its neck can collectively yield a diamond shape.

However, like that of all vipers, this species' venom is haemotoxic, which is relatively slow-acting compared to the much more rapid-acting neurotoxin produced by elapids (which include cobras and kraits). And far from being gentle and soothing in sound, its hiss is famously loud—among the loudest hisses produced by any species of snake. In addition, its preferred habit is dry, grassy, open terrain; it actively avoids humid, swampy, marshy areas. Clearly, therefore, the Russell's viper is unlikely ever to be referred to as a swamp adder.

Two other viperid candidates that have been proposed on occasion are the Indian saw-scaled viper *Echis carinatus* (also known as the little Indian viper) and the temple viper, or Wagler's pit viper, *Tropidolaemus wagleri*. However, the former species does not exceed

(T) Russell's viper *Daboia russelii* (Mike Prince, CC BY 2.0)

(B) Saw-scaled viper *Echis carinatus* (Omid Mozaffari, CC BY 2.0)

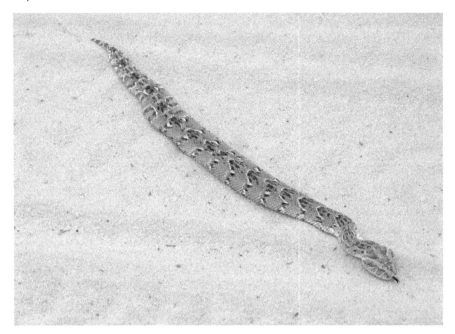

(T) Puff adder *Bitis arietans* (Bernard Dupont, CC BY-SA 2.0)

(B) Rhinoceros viper *Bitis nasicornis* (Bernard Dupont, CC BY-SA 2.0)

32 in (and only rarely exceeds 2 ft), and it does not possess either the speckled patterning or the diamond-shaped head of the swamp viper. Moreover, it is an inhabitant of dry, rocky terrain, not humid swamps.

As for the temple viper: this pit viper species is bigger than the saw-scaled viper, with females growing up to 3 ft long. It also exhibits a range of colour and pattern variations, but none of them includes that of the swamp adder. And, crucially, it is not native to India anyway (its distribution being confined to southeast Asia).

Neither is the African puff adder *Bitis arietans*, yet this too has been suggested by some as a putative swamp adder. Quite apart from its fundamental zoogeographical difference, however, the puff adder is renowned for the loudness (as opposed to the gentleness) of its hiss, and for the savagery of its bite, whose fangs can cause severe physical trauma in addition to their envenoming effects. This is a far cry from the very inconspicuous puncture marks attributed to the swamp adder.

Another exclusively African species that has been considered is the rhinoceros viper *Bitis nasicornis*, named after its instantly noticeable horn-like scales on the end of its nose—features conspicuous only by their absence in the swamp adder's description! Exit the puff adder and the rhinoceros viper.

COBRAS, BOAS, AND OTHER UNLIKELY SWAMP ADDER EXPLANATIONS

The common Indian or spectacled cobra *Naja naja* is a much-touted elapid candidate for the swamp adder's identity, particularly by the late Richard Lancelyn Green and certain other Sherlockian scholars and devotees. Certainly, its neurotoxin would act more swiftly than the haemotoxin of any viper or adder. Nevertheless, it is difficult to conceive how so familiar and distinctive a snake as this one, perhaps the best-known serpent species in all of India, could possibly be one and the same as the mysterious swamp adder. True, the latter's puffed neck may be an allusion to the cobra's hood (or at least a cobra-reminiscent neck expansion), but the Indian cobra lacks the characteristic speckled patterning of the swamp adder, and its head is not diamond-shaped. In fact, it looks nothing remotely like any type of adder or viper.

Indian cobra *Naja naja*
(Pavan Kumar N., CC BY-SA 3.0)

Boa constrictor
(Luis Alejandro Rodriguez J., CC BY-SA 4.0)

Even more implausible ophidian identities that have been raised at one time or another include the New World's decidedly non-venomous, non-Asian boa constrictor *Boa constrictor*; the extremely venomous but irrefutably Australian taipan *Oxyuranus scutellatus*; and a species of krait.

Fundamental zoogeographical differences aside, the boa constrictor notion no doubt stems from a suggestion that Conan Doyle was inspired to write his story after having read a tale entitled 'Called on by a Boa Constrictor: A West African Adventure', which had appeared in *Cassell's Saturday Journal*, published in February 1891. Staying in a ramshackle cabin belonging to a Portuguese trader, the narrator reveals his horror at being woken by a massive snake dangling over him. Paralysed by fear, he cannot cry out, but he spots a bell hanging off a beam within reach. Although the cord to ring it has rotted away, the narrator discloses how he manages to summon help by hitting it with a stick. (Incidentally, as this tale was set in West Africa, if the snake in question were indeed of the constricting variety it would have been a python, not a boa, irrespective of the tale's title.)

Banded krait *Bungarus fasciatus*
(Davidvraju, CC BY-SA 4.0)

Nor is that the only link between the speckled band mystery and a species of constricting snake. In his stage production of this story, *The Stoner Case*, Conan Doyle cast an African rock python *Python sebae* as the speckled band. Unfortunately, this particular snake did not excel in the role. Conan Doyle later wrote:

> We had a fine rock boa [sic] to play the title-rôle, a snake which was the pride of my heart, so one can imagine my disgust when I saw that one critic ended his disparaging review by the words, *"The crisis of the play was produced by the appearance of a palpably artificial serpent."* I was inclined to offer him a goodly sum if he would undertake to go to bed with it.

As for a krait: it is true that certain kraits are Indian, all are venomous (some extremely so), and they may be encountered in damp areas. However, they differ dramatically from the speckle-patterned swamp adder with its squat diamond-shaped head by virtue of their boldly striped markings and their sleek, slender head.

Kraits are also extremely timid, often preferring to conceal their head amid their coils, drawing attention away from it by vigorously twitching their tail instead, thus readily contrasting with the swamp adder's active, undisguised aggression.

Of course, there is the remote, but not impossible, prospect that the swamp adder is not a snake at all . . .

WHEN IS A SNAKE NOT A SNAKE?
WHEN IT'S A LEGLESS LIZARD?

Certainly, there are various peculiar behavioural characteristics claimed for the swamp adder that cause problems when attempting to reconcile it with *any* species of snake. In 'The Adventure of the Speckled Band', the swamp adder reaches its victim, Julia Stoner, by crawling through a ventilation shaft linking her bedroom with that of her murderous step-father Roylott next door, and then down a rope pull hanging directly over the bed in which she is sleeping. After it has bitten her, the snake crawls up the rope again and back through the shaft, in response to Roylott (in his bedroom) having alerted it by whistling to it!

First and foremost: unless it were an exceptionally adept arboreal species, would the swamp adder be able to climb up a vertical length of rope? And secondly: as snakes are famously insensitive aurally to airborne vibrations (although see also Chapter 16), how could it possibly be able to hear Roylott's whistling, especially as he was in a separate room?

Consequently, there has been speculation that the swamp adder is not a snake at all, but conceivably a legless or near-legless species of lizard, belonging to the skink family. There are indeed several species of skink fitting this description, and which therefore do appear remarkably serpentine on first glance, particularly to non-specialist observers. Some such lizards, moreover, are native to India.

Chalcides chalcides, a near-limbless skink (PD/Wikimedia)

And skinks, unlike snakes, can definitely hear airborne vibrations. Whether they are adept at climbing up and down vertical ropes is another matter, but in any case this otherwise ingenious non-ophidian identity is fatally scuppered by the incontestable fact that skinks are entirely non-venomous. Consequently, if a skink bit someone, they would not be poisoned by it.

The only sensible conclusion that can be drawn from this chapter's analysis of the varied candidates on offer is that the swamp adder is an entirely fictitious, invented creature that Conan Doyle created specifically to supply his story with a supremely formidable reptilian opponent for pitting against Sherlock Holmes. Aspects of its appearance may well have been inspired by real snakes, such as

1 | THE SPECKLED BAND

the Russell's viper's body colouration and markings, and the rapid action of the cobra's neurotoxin, but the swamp adder has no basis in reality as a valid, discrete species in its own right.

However, that is not quite the end of this literary serpent's identity crisis. There is still one more identity to consider, the most astonishing of all—not only because of its particular nature but also because of where (and how) it appeared within the scientific literature.

SWAMP ADDER AND MONGOLIAN DEATH WORM—ONE AND THE SAME CREATURE?

Elsewhere in this book (Chapter 10), I document an extraordinary mystery beast said to inhabit the Gobi Desert and known as the Mongolian death worm. According to the nomads inhabiting this vast expanse of sand, the death worm can spit forth a deadly, corrosive venom, and can also kill instantly if touched by a mechanism that sounds uncannily like electrocution. No specimen of this reputedly lethal animal has ever been made available for scientific

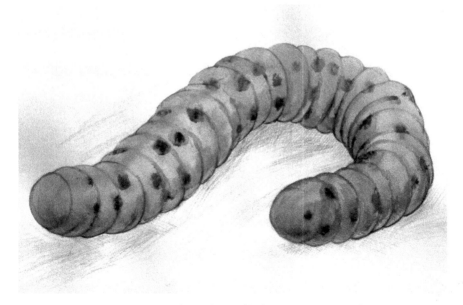

Reconstruction of the likely appearance of the Mongolian death worm (© Ivan Mackerle)

analysis, and it may well simply be folkloric, or even if genuine merely a harmless amphisbaenian or similar reptile whose murderous talents owe more to local superstition than to physiological capability.

In 1956, however, the death worm was sensationally linked to the swamp adder as the latter's bona fide identity. Not only that, it was even given a formal scientific name. The publication in which all of this appeared was a very comprehensive 238-page monograph of the lizard family Helodermatidae, which houses those two famously venomous New World species, the Gila monster *Heloderma suspectum* and the beaded lizard *H. horridum*. Published in no less august a scientific journal than the *Bulletin of the American Museum of Natural History*, and entitled 'The Gila Monster and Its Allies', it was authored by renowned herpetologists Drs Charles M. Bogert and Rafael Martín Del Campo, and as would be expected from such authors writing in such a journal, the paper was totally scientific and serious throughout—or was it?

Tucked away on pages 206-209, in a section entitled 'Hybrid Origin', was a mind-boggling claim that according to a paper by snake authority Dr Laurence M. Klauber, a hybrid creature had been successfully produced in a laboratory in Calcutta, India, by crossbreeding cobras with Gila monsters! Not only that, some of these astounding hybrids had subsequently escaped, with various of their descendants yielding the allegedly highly venomous Indian lizard called the bis-cobra (see my book *The Menagerie of Marvels*, 2014), and other descendants yielding the Mongolian death worm in the Gobi Desert!

Moreover, and equally dramatic, this selfsame hybrid was also claimed to be the identity of the swamp adder in Conan Doyle's Speckled Band story. A quadrupedal lizard with the venomous potency of a cobra would, in the opinion of Klauber, reconcile all of the problems faced when attempting to identify the swamp adder with any of the more traditional identities that have been proposed.

Accordingly, in their monograph Bogert and Martín Del Campo put forward an official binomial name for this hybrid, which was clearly now breeding true and therefore, they felt, fully deserved one. They dubbed it *Sampoderma allergorhaihorhai*—'Sampoderma' combining 'samp' (a Hindustani name for 'snake') and the Gila monster's genus, *Heloderma*; and 'allergorhaihorhai' being a name

1 | THE SPECKLED BAND

Gila monster *Heloderma suspectum*
(Doug Donaldson, CC BY 2.0)

Chiapan beaded lizard *Heloderma alvarezi*,
formerly a subspecies of *Heloderma horridum,* now
considered a full species (Lachesis95, CC BY 3.0)

applied by the Gobi nomads to the death worm. They even included a line drawing of the hybrid's appearance.

Needless to say, however, the concept of successful hybridisation between a cobra and a Gila monster is so outlandish that there was clearly more—or less—to the claims of Bogert and Martín Del Campo than met the eye, as a closer study of this particular section of their monograph soon revealed. (Moreover, the bis-cobra is also a red herring, figuratively if not taxonomically, because in reality it is a harmless varanid that superstitious folklore has conferred all manner of venomous traits upon.) For although Klauber was indeed a real-life herpetological authority and his paper regarding the hybrid also existed, it had not been published in any scientific journal but instead within an issue from 1948 of the *Baker Street Journal*.

This was a periodical devoted entirely to the fictional world contained within the stories of Sherlock Holmes, and included much imaginative and entertaining but entirely theoretical speculation and extrapolation regarding various aspects of these stories' plots, characters, etc. And indeed, in his paper Klauber refers to Holmes, Watson, and the nefarious Dr Roylott as real persons, naming Roylott as the creator of the cobra x Gila monster hybrid. In short, it was all entirely tongue-in-cheek, not to be taken in any way seriously.

As this is instantly apparent from reading Klauber's paper, why, therefore, had Bogert and Martín Del Campo included the fictitious hybrid in a sober, ostensibly factual manner within their otherwise entirely literal, highly authoritative monograph? According to Daniel D. Beck writing in his own major work, *Biology of Gila Monsters and Beaded Lizards* (2005), it was a prank by Bogert that was meant to poke fun at one of his "stodgy" colleagues at the American Museum of Natural History.

Whatever the reason, there is no doubt at all that equating it even in jest with the Mongolian death worm yielded for the dreaded Indian swamp adder (aka the speckled band) an identity so extraordinary that even the great Sherlock Holmes himself may well have been hard-pressed to deduce it!

2
ON THE TRAIL OF MEDITERRANEAN MYSTERY SNAKES

> And when Paul had gathered a bundle of sticks, and laid them on the fire, there came a viper out of the heat, and fastened on his hand.
>
> And when the barbarians saw the venomous beast hang on his hand, they said among themselves, No doubt this man is a murderer, whom, though he hath escaped the sea, yet vengeance suffereth not to live.
>
> And he shook off the beast into the fire, and felt no harm.
>
> Howbeit they looked when he should have swollen, or fallen down dead suddenly: but after they had looked a great while, and saw no harm come to him, they changed their minds, and said that he was a god.
>
> Acts of the Apostles (28: 3-6), from *The Holy Bible*

Down through the ages, a number of mysterious, unidentified forms of snake have been reported from various countries and islands lying on either side of the Mediterranean Sea, including the following selection of examples.

ST PAUL AND THE MYSTERY VIPER OF MALTA

As quoted at the beginning of this present chapter, it is recorded in the Acts of the Apostles (28: 3-6) within *The Holy Bible*'s New Testament that when a ship transporting St Paul and other prisoners to Rome was shipwrecked on the island of Melita (known now as Malta), St Paul was bitten by a viper. What makes this incident memorable not only from a theological but also from a herpetological standpoint, however, is that there is no known species of viper living today on Malta. So how can St Paul's ophidian attacker be explained?

In their biblical commentary *The Acts of the Apostles* (1959), Charles W. Carter and Ralph Earle suggested that just because there are no vipers on Malta today does not necessarily mean that there were none in St Paul's day. Perhaps they died out due to the expanding human population here in later times. However, American cryptozoologist and scriptures scholar Chad Arment has pointed out that there is no physical evidence to confirm that vipers have ever existed on Malta. Nor does the viper family's zoogeographical distribution in this region of Europe provide much support for such a notion.

Consequently, Chad considers it more plausible that Malta's mystery 'viper' was in reality the European cat snake *Telescopus fallax*—a species of venomous rear-fanged colubrid that usually measures up to 2.5 ft long and is native to Malta. As its mouth is too small for its fangs to be used effectively when biting humans (which it will sometimes do if handled), the cat snake is not deemed to be dangerous. However, in cases where a person is allergic to the proteins contained in its venom, anaphylaxia and various complications can occur if not treated rapidly. Bearing in mind that its preferred habitat includes dry stony areas overgrown with low shrubs in which it can climb, this fairly small, lithe snake could easily be picked up with a bundle of sticks (unlike any of Europe's larger, bulkier vipers).

However, this line of speculation takes as granted that the snake which bit St Paul was indeed venomous—but was it? Perhaps St Luke (author of the Acts of the Apostles) and/or the native Maltese islanders mistakenly assumed that it was, when in actual fact it was a harmless species. Certainly, in many parts of the world various non-venomous species of snake (and even lizards too) are

2 | MEDITERRANEAN MYSTERY SNAKES

St Paul casting viper into fire, 16th-Century woodcut

erroneously deemed to be exceedingly venomous by their human neighbours.

Equally ambiguous is St Luke's description of St Paul's serpentine aggressor as fastening onto and then hanging from his hand. Might this mean that the snake did not actually bite St Paul's hand, but merely coiled around it, and that St Luke and the other observers only assumed that it had bitten him, when in fact it had not done so?

A Maltese specimen of the European cat snake
Telescopus fallax (Jeffrey Skiberras, CC BY-SA 3.0)

Montpellier snake *Malpolon monspessulanus*
(Bernard Dupont, CC BY-SA 2.0)

Certainly there is no statement anywhere in the verses dealing with this incident in the Acts of the Apostles which claims that St Paul was miraculously cured of snakebite—only an assumption by St Luke and the others that he had been bitten. Of course, St Luke's training as a physician may have provided the experience to recognize characteristics of a snakebite.

An entirely different explanation that some investigators have put forward is that the island shipwrecked upon by St Paul was not Malta at all but was in fact the Croatian island of Mljet, which had the Latin name of Melita, and might therefore have been confused with the name Malta. Moreover, unlike Malta, Melita/Mljet was known to be home to bona fide vipers (now likely eradicated by the introduction of the little Indian mongoose). This intriguing suggestion stems predominantly from a detailed study of St Paul's shipwrecking that was published in Latin by Ignjat Đurđević (1675–1737), a nowadays little-known Ragusan poet and scholar.

THE COLOVIA—A MEDITERRANEAN MEGA-SNAKE?

In various of his writings, veteran Belgian cryptozoologist Dr Bernard Heuvelmans referred to the alleged presence in the Mediterranean provinces within France, Spain, northern Italy, and Greece of an unidentified snake claimed by observers to be 9-12 ft long (and occasionally ever longer).

Other mystery beast investigators have also reported this serpentine enigma, which is often said to be dark green in colour, and in Italy is referred to as the colovia. One such snake was actually responsible for a traffic accident when it unexpectedly crossed a busy road near Chinchilla de Monte Aragón, in Spain's Albicete Province, on 22 July 1969. Back in December 1933, a colovia was tracked down and killed in a marsh close to the Sicilian city of Syracuse, but its carcase was not preserved.

If we assume that the colovia's dimensions may well have been somewhat exaggerated or over-estimated by eyewitnesses, a plausible identity for it is the Montpellier snake *Malpolon monspessulanus*. Named after a city in southern France, this mildly-venomous rear-fanged colubrid is common through much of the Mediterranean basin. It is quite variable in colour, from dark grey to olive green, and can grow up to 8.5 ft long, possibly longer in exceptional specimens. Its presence has not been confirmed in Sicily nor anywhere in mainland Greece (its eastern subspecies, *M. m. insignitus*, deemed a separate species by some workers, occurs on a number of Greek islands, as well as on Cyprus), but these areas are certainly compatible with its survival.

So perhaps reports from there of unidentified colovia-type mystery snakes indicate that the Montpellier snake's distribution range within Europe's Mediterranean lands is even greater than presently recognised.

Having said that, a very different identity for the colovia has been suggested to me by a Sicilian naturalist with the Google/Blogger username Matteo, who posted the following comment, dated 17 November 2020, on my *ShukerNature* blog:

> For what concerns Colovia (even though in Sicily the name changes in every village, in mine it's called Culofia for example) the most likely explanation [to] me is actually the barred grass snake, *Natrix helvetica sicula*.
>
> Here in fact old females of this subspecies become usually almost black and, in fact, despite there are probably no official records of that, in the past they were able to grow much bigger than now because of less antropic selection (being bigger makes you more vulnerable to killings made by a lot of people here unfortunately).
>
> I've heard a lot of first hand accounts in the past and they all said that the size of the snake called "Colovia" exceeded 6.5 ft, the most notable account was from a zoology professor who measured one of this giant Barred grass snake [at] 6.725 ft during the [19]80's.
>
> Nowadays when inquired about "Colovia" every naturalist in Sicily answer[s] you that it is just an old big Barred grass snake.

Albeit rare, black grass snakes are by no means unknown, with others often being very dark, especially in colder climes, where such colouration is beneficial to conserving heat.

As for its length: barred grass snakes often attain a total length of at least 3 ft, sometimes more, and, as noted by Matteo, it is possible that in earlier days some extra-large specimens existed, but were killed due to their enhanced visibility and mistakenly perceived risk of being dangerous. So at least on Sicily, the colovia may indeed be based upon sightings of rare, exceptionally lengthy barred grass snakes.

An almost entirely black barred grass snake *Natrix helvetica*, only its characteristic ring-like collar marking remaining its typical yellow shade (© Markus Bühler)

THE VIRGIN MARY SNAKES OF CEPHALONIA

Cephalonia is the largest of western Greece's seven principal Ionian islands, lying in the Ionian Sea—which is in turn an elongated embayment of the Mediterranean Sea. As documented in my book *Mysteries of Planet Earth* (1999), every year on 16 August—known here as the Feast of the Assumption of Our Lady (the Virgin Mary)—the small southeastern village of Markopoulo hosts a Marian celebration, but its most famous, and mystifying, attendants are not of the human variety. Virtually every year for more than two centuries, during the fortnight leading up to this festival considerable numbers of snakes mysteriously appear at the foot of the Old Bell

Steeple by Markopoulo's Church of Our Lady, and just as mysteriously vanish again when the festival ends.

Their unusual behaviour has earned these serpents the local names of 'Virgin Mary snakes' and 'Our Lady's snakes'. This religious association is heightened by the small black cruciform mark that they allegedly bear on their heads and also at the forked tip of their tongues. They all appear to belong to the same single species, but which one this is does not seem to have been formally ascertained by herpetologists. However, they have attracted the attention and interest of several correspondents of mine, as now revealed.

According to one of them, Cephalonia chronicler Victor J. Kean, these snakes are non-venomous, are said to have "skin like silk", and are popularly believed by the villagers to possess thaumaturgic powers. One plausible candidate is the four-striped snake *Elaphe quatuorlineata*, a non-venomous constricting species of colubrid that occurs on Cephalonia, and whose head can bear a variety of dark markings, especially in its bolder-marked juvenile form. Moreover,

Four-striped snake *Elaphe quatuorlineata*
(Carlo Caroni, CC BY-SA 2.5)

herpetologist Dr Klaus-Dieter Schulz has pointed out that this species is known to be associated with Christian traditions elsewhere in southern Europe, including the annual snake procession at Cucullo, Italy, in honour of St Dominic.

When he paid a visit to Markopoulo on 16 August one year during the mid-1990s, Alistair Underwood from Preston, in Lancashire, England, observed the Virgin Mary snakes congregating outside the Church of Our Lady, where they were freely handled by the local villagers, who even draped them fearlessly around their necks. The villagers also allowed them to enter the church, and to make their way towards a large silver icon of the Virgin Mary. Some websites that I have seen in which this ceremony is described claim that the species in question is the European cat snake, already discussed in the present chapter as a contender for the identity of St Paul's viper. This colubrid is indeed native to Cephalonia and several other Greek islands too, and as previously mentioned its rear-fanged nature means that although it is venomous, its venom is rarely injected in defensive biting, so it is not deemed to be a threat to humans.

According to Cephalonian researcher Spyros Tassis Bekatoros, the only years in which the Virgin Mary snakes have not made an appearance at Markopoulo's Marian festival are those spanning the German occupation of Cephalonia in World War II (during which period the occupying forces may have banned the Marian festival after learning about its ophidian participants), and the year 1953, when much of the island was devastated by an earthquake. This latter information may hold clues regarding the link between these snakes and the festival.

Snakes respond very readily to groundborne vibrations. Consequently, Alistair Underwood suggested that the increased human activity with its associated groundborne vibrations occurring during the Marian festival and its preceding preparations may explain the coincident appearance of the Virgin Mary snakes during those periods. If so, then the exceptional terrestrial reverberations that occurred during the 1953 earthquake would have greatly disturbed the snakes, disrupting their normal behaviour and obscuring the lesser vibrational stimuli emanating from human activity at the Marian festival that year.

THE HORNED TAGUERGA OF TUNISIA

In *Exploration Scientifique de la Tunisie, Vol. 1* (1884), French archaeologist and diplomat Charles Tissot reported the alleged occurrence of a very sizeable Tunisian mystery snake known as the taguerga, which supposedly bears a pair of short but sharp horns on its head. Vehemently believed by the locals to be extremely venomous, this greatly-feared reptile is said to be as thick as a man's thigh, and to attain a total length of 7-12 ft. It reputedly frequents the mountains of southern Tunisia's Sahara region.

The locals consider taguergas to be specimens of the common horned viper *Cerastes cerastes* (a species that is indeed native to Tunisia) but which have attained an exceptionally venerable age and have continued growing throughout this abnormally-extended period of time, thus explaining their great size, as horned vipers do not normally exceed 3 ft long. Conversely, Dr Bernard Heuvelmans speculated that it may be a puff adder *Bitis arietans*, which sometimes bears horn-like scales upon its head. However, this species only rarely exceeds 5 ft long, and is not known to occur in Tunisia, although it is recorded from Morocco.

Horned viper *Cerastes cerastes* (Holger Krisp, CC BY 3.0)

3
THE HORN SNAKE AND THE HOOP SNAKE—NORTH AMERICA'S MOST (IN)FAMOUS PSEUDO-SERPENTS

I must not forget, in these random sketches, my old friend and neighbour, Uncle Davy Lane. . . . Nothing could move him out of a slow, horse-mill gait but snakes, of which "creeturs he was monstrous 'fraid." The reader shall soon have abundant evidence of the truth of this admission in his numerous and rapid flights from "sarpunts." . . . He became quite a proverb in the line of big story-telling. True, he had many obstinate competitors, but he distanced them all farther than he did the numerous snakes that "run arter him." . . .

"But at last I ventured to go into the face uv the Round Peak one day a-huntin.' I were skinnin' my eyes fur old bucks, with my head up, not thinkin' about sarpunts, when, by Zucks! I cum right plum upon one uv the curiousest snakes I uver seen in all my borned days.

"Fur a spell I were spellbound in three foot uv it. There it lay on the side uv a steep presserpis, at full length, ten foot long, its tail strait out, right up the presserpis, head big as a sasser, right toards me, eyes red as forked lightnin', lickin' out his forked tongue, and I could no more move than the Ball Rock on Fisher's Peak. But when I seen the stinger in his tail, six inches long and sharp as a needle, stickin' out like a cock's spur, I thought I'd a drapped in my tracks. I'd ruther a had uvry coachwhip [snake] on Round Hill arter me en full chase than to a bin in that drefful siteation.

"Thar I stood, petterfied with relarm—couldn't budge a peg—couldn't even take old Bucksmasher off uv my shoulder to shoot the infarnul thing. Nyther uv us moved nor bolted 'ur eyes fur fifteen minits.

"At last, as good luck would have it, a rabbit run close by, and the snake turned its eyes to look what it were, and that broke the charm, and I jumped forty foot down the mounting, and dashed behind a big white oak five foot in diamatur. The snake he cotched the eend uv his tail in his mouth, he did, and come rollin' down the mounting arter me just like a hoop, and jist as I landed behind the tree he struck t'other side with his stinger, and stuv it up, clean to his tail, smack in the tree. He were fast.

"Of all the hissin' and blowin' that uver you hearn sense you seen daylight, it tuck the lead. Ef there'd a bin forty-nine forges all a-blowin' at once, it couldn't a beat it. He rared and charged, lapped round the tree, spread his mouf and grinned at me orful, puked and spit quarts an' quarts of green pisen at me, an' made the ar stink with his nasty breath.

"I seen thar were no time to lose; I cotched up old Bucksmasher from whar I'd dashed him down, and tried to shoot the tarnil thing; but he kep' sich a movin' about and sich a splutteration that I couldn't git a bead at his head, for I know'd it warn't wuth while to shoot him any whar else. So I kep' my distunce tell he wore hisself out, then I put a ball right between his eyes, and he gin up the ghost.

"Soon as he were dead I happened to look up inter the tree, and what do you think? Why, sir, it were dead as a herrin'; all the leaves was wilted like a fire had gone through its branches.

"I left the old feller with his stinger in the tree, thinkin' it were the best place fur him, and moseyed home, 'tarmined not to go out again soon. . . ."

H.E. Taliaferro ('Skitt')—'Uncle Davy Lane'

Over the years, the annals of zoology have received and dutifully logged various reports of some truly remarkable pseudo-serpents, i.e. false snakes once deemed to be genuine species but subsequently exposed as imaginative folktales, deceiving hoaxes, or monstrous misidentifications. One of the most intriguing, and (in)famous, examples is the North American horn snake—not least because it is actually two pseudo-serpents in one!

3 | HORN SNAKE AND HOOP SNAKE

The earliest notable account of the horn snake appeared in American explorer John Lawson's important work *A New Voyage to Carolina* (1709; retitled *The History of Carolina* in later editions), whose description succinctly includes all of the principal characteristics of this singular, highly controversial reptile:

> Of the Horn Snake, I never saw but two that I remember. They are like the Rattlesnake in Colour, but rather lighter. They hiss exactly like a Goose when anything approaches them. They strike at their Enemy with their Tail, and kill whatsoever they wound with it, which is armed at the End with a Horny Substance like a Cock's Spur. This is their Weapon. I have heard it credibly reported by those who said they were Eye-Witnesses, that a small Locust Tree, about the Thickness of a Man's Arm, being struck by one of these Snakes at Ten o'clock in the Morning, then verdant and flourishing, at Four in the Afternoon was dead, and the Leaves dead and withered. Doubtless, be it how it will, they are very venomous. I think the Indians do not pretend to cure their wound.

In the 1722 self-revised edition of his 1705 tome *History and Present State of Virginia*, Virginia historian and government official Colonel Robert Beverley emphasised the nature of the horn snake's stinging tail as a formidable weapon:

> There is likewise a Horn Snake, so called from a Sharp Horn it carries in its Tail, with which it assaults anything that offends it, with that Force that, as it is said, it will strike its Tail into the Butt End of a Musket, from whence it is not able to disengage itself.

The first naturalist to document the horn snake in detail was Mark Catesby, in the first volume of his major work *The Natural History of Carolina, Florida and the Bahama Islands* (1731), summarising the descriptions provided previously by Lawson and Beverley, but discounting its tail's deadly nature as outrageous fiction and identifying its species as a 'water viper', to which he gave the formal name *Vipera aquatica*. According to Catesby, the horn snake's tail-sting or spine was merely a blunt, horny, and completely innocuous structure about half an inch long.

Curiously, however, the species that he dubbed *Vipera aquatica* and labelled as the horn snake is traditionally believed to have been the water moccasin *Agkistrodon piscivorus*—the world's only species of semi-aquatic viper. Yet although it does possess a short, thick, blunt-ended tail, the latter does not bear a spine at its tip. Consequently, some modern-day herpetologists dispute that Catesby's so-called 'water viper' (and thence his horn snake) was indeed the water moccasin.

Water moccasin *Agkistrodon piscivorus*, threat display (PD/Pixabay)

Notwithstanding Catesby's scepticism regarding the venomous nature of the horn snake's tail spine, this feature was steadfastly reiterated in subsequent accounts elsewhere (so too was the claim that this species was reddish or at least partly reddish in colour). And to complicate matters still further, a second, even more fantastic, zoologically-implausible characteristic was soon attributed to this already much-muddled mystery snake—the supposed ability to turn itself into a vertical hoop by grasping its tail in its jaws just like the mythical ouroboros, thereby enabling it to roll along

3 | HORN SNAKE AND HOOP SNAKE

the ground at great speed like a living tyre. When carrying out this bizarre mode of locomotion, the horn snake thus became known as the hoop snake.

An early hoop snake account was penned by American traveller J.F.D. Smyth in 1784, following a stay in western North Carolina, and was published in Volume 1 of his multi-tome travelogue *Tour in the United States of America*. After describing the by now familiar morphological characteristics of the horn snake, Smyth added the following very remarkable behavioural information:

> As other serpents crawl upon their bellies, so can this; but he has another method of moving peculiar to his own species, which he always adopts when he is in eager pursuit of his prey; he throws himself into a circle, running rapidly around, advancing like a hoop, with his tail arising and pointed forward in the circle, by which he is always in the ready position of striking.

Ouroboros drawing from a late medieval Byzantine Greek alchemical manuscript

It is observed that they only make use of this method in attacking; for when they fly from their enemy they go upon their bellies, like other serpents.

From the above circumstance, peculiar to themselves, they have also derived the appellation of hoop snakes.

The next couple of centuries saw many published reports of hoop-rolling horn snakes—hailing from a wide geographical spread, including the Minnesota-Wisconsin border, North Carolina, and British Columbia in Canada—despite their self-evident improbability. A typical example, which concisely contains all of the intrinsic horn/hoop snake motifs, is the following account, published on 8 November 1884 by an Australian newspaper entitled the *Maitland Mercury and Hunter River General Advertiser* but documenting an alleged incident that took place in Virginia, USA:

> One day last week a little girl, whose name slipped the correspondent's usually retentive memory, was chased by a monster hoop snake nearly a mile. Just as it seemed that it was about to strike her, she dodged behind a large apple tree. The rapidly whirling snake turned to follow and struck the tree with such force as to drive the horn-spike into the hard wood over two inches. The child was so frightened that she sank down, her heart thumping as though it would burst out of her body.
>
> One of her brothers, who had seen her flying down the hill, went to see what was the matter. When he reached the tree it was quaking like an aspen and its leaves and fruit falling to the ground in a perfect shower, the prostrate girl being almost buried beneath them. As soon as he got her restored to consciousness he took a fence rail and killed the venomous reptile, which was eleven feet two and a half inches in length and eight inches in circumference. The horn point on the tail was six and a half inches long, and so deeply imbedded in the hard wood that it could not extricate itself. This all happened near South Mountain, Va [Virginia].

With the girl's name conveniently forgotten, the correspondent responsible for the account not named, and the eminently unlikely nature of the entire incident, the most reasonable assumption is that this incident, like so many others of its kind involving extraordinary, unbelievable beasts, was a journalistic invention. Yet even today, supposedly serious reports of hoop-rolling horn snakes are still being documented, thus sitting uncomfortably alongside unequivocally tongue-in-cheek, light-hearted versions, cartoons, and other jokey representations of this classic pseudo-serpent.

Hoop snake (© Richard Svensson)

Moreover, it is nothing if not telling that although celebrated American snake expert Raymond Ditmars (1876-1942) placed 10,000 dollars in trust at a New York bank to be awarded to the first person who provided him with conclusive evidence for the reality of the hoop snake, this very substantial prize was never claimed.

But are reports of horn and hoop snakes absolutely fictional, or could there be at least a kernel of truth at the heart of such ostensibly unfeasible tales? Quite apart from the fact that there are many fully-attested sightings of snakes grasping their tails in their mouths (albeit while lying on the ground, and therefore yielding horizontal circles rather than the hoop snake's vertical ones), there are certain fully-recognised species of North American snake that do bear a spiny structure at the tip of their tail. So it may be that some of these latter species have helped inspire and shape the legend of the horn snake.

One of the leading candidates for this role is the mud snake *Farancia abacura*, a semi-aquatic, non-venomous species of colubrid native to the southeastern USA. Up to 6 ft long, black dorsally, black and orange ventrally (with the orange sections extending upwards laterally, thereby corresponding with certain horn snake accounts referring to reddish-orange sides), this distinctive snake has only a short tail, but it bears a noticeable spine at its tip, which in reality is a greatly-enlarged terminal scale of hard, horny constituency and quite sharp at its tip. Of course, the spine is not venomous, but this species shares a sufficient number of other characteristics with the legendary horn snake—both the tail spine and the shortness of the tail itself, a tendency to prod prey with its tail spine, plus orange flanks, and a water-frequenting preference—for there to be little doubt that it has actively influenced traditional, non-scientific belief in sting-tailed horn snakes.

Certainly, eminent American herpetologist Dr Karl P. Schmidt (1890-1957) favoured this identity for the latter pseudo-serpent when documenting the horn/hoop snake saga in an article published

Mud snake *Farancia abacura* (John Sullivan, CC BY-SA 3.0)

in the January/February 1925 issue of the American periodical *Natural History*. This theory has also been championed much more recently, by another American herpetologist, Dr J.D. Wilson, in a mud snake article published by the Savannah River Ecology Laboratory in 2006, and not only for the horn snake specifically but also for its locomotory hoop snake alter ego. A closely-related species, the rainbow snake *F. erytrogramma*, which again is semi-aquatic, non-venomous, native to the southeastern USA, and very similar to the mud snake by virtue of its body colouration, short tail, and readily-visible tail spine, is actually referred to colloquially as the hoop snake across much of its geographical range.

Yet another North American non-venomous colubrid that has been implicated with the hoop snake legend is the coachwhip *Masticophis flagellum*, a snake endemic to the southern USA and also northern Mexico. Up to 6.5 ft long, this species is sometimes reddish-pink in colour, recalling once again descriptions of the horn snake. Moreover, although it does not possess a tail spine, it is a fast-moving, very agile species, and Schmidt, among others, has suggested that the hoop snake component of the horn snake myth may have originated from sightings of species like this one (as well as fellow non-venomous North American colubrid the eastern racer *Coluber constrictor*—and in particular its most distinctive subspecies, the blue racer *C. c. foxii*, gliding along at great speed and in an undulating manner over the tops of bushes without descending to the ground, thus recalling the hoop snake's supposed rolling mode of progression.

Interestingly, horn and hoop snake traditions are not exclusive to North America. Comparable tales have been recorded from Australia too. This island continent is home to the highly venomous death adders—a genus (*Acanthophis*) of viper-impersonating elapids whose several species are all famed for their very conspicuous tail spine.

Central and West Africa are also sources of sting-tailed horn/hoop snake reports, which in this case appear to have been inspired by harmless blind burrowing snakes of the genus *Typhlops*, which possess very prominent tail spines. Moreover, Schmidt suggested that slaves brought to North America from these regions of Africa may have contributed to the New World horn snake folklore by recalling stories of African burrowing snakes that subsequently became transferred to America's own equivalent species (though not

Eastern coachwhip *Masticophis flagellum flagellum*
(Peter Paplanus, CC BY 2.0)

Eastern racer *Coluber constrictor*
(Peter Paplanus, CC BY 2.0)

3 | HORN SNAKE AND HOOP SNAKE

of the genus *Typhlops*, as this is confined to Central and South America in the New World).

Yet regardless of the varied scientific explanations documented and discussed that discount the horn and hoop snake as being wholly fictitious, belief in the reality and lethal nature of these pseudo-serpents is still deeply ingrained among great swathes of the general public across North America and elsewhere. So much so, in fact, that it seems likely that their origins will forever remain controversial, and with any investigations of scientifically-untrained eyewitness reports destined merely to go round and round in circles—just like the hoop snake itself!

4
THE CURIOUS CASE OF THE CROWING CRESTED COBRA

> A beast over which controversy rages at this moment is the 'crowing crested cobra', which, the natives say, is a snake, like a cobra, with a crest on its head and a loud, distinct cry like the crow of a cock.
>
> Captain William Hichens—*Discovery* (December 1937)

Judging from Hichens's description, the above mystery beast must bear a close resemblance to the popular conception of a cockatrice—that mythical, cockscomb-crested, crowing serpent derived from an egg laid by a cockerel and hatched by a toad. Yet whereas the cockatrice is fictional, a fabulous beast of Western legend, the existence of the crowing crested cobra is vehemently affirmed not only by native tribes spanning much of East and Central Africa, but also by a number of the Dark Continent's Western explorers, travellers, and settlers—notwithstanding the fact that by all the traditional tenets of herpetology, such a creature is a zoological impossibility.

DISTRIBUTION, DESCRIPTION, AND LIFESTYLE

Possibly the first Western account of this mysterious reptile was a short description included in Horace Waller's *The Last Journals of*

David Livingstone, Vol. II (1874), but many others have appeared since then. One of the most detailed is that of Dr J. Shircore, writing in 1944 from Karonga, Nyasaland (now Malawi), in the periodical *African Affairs,* which brings together much of what has been reported on this subject.

The alleged distribution of the crowing crested cobra is quite immense, covering some 800,000 square miles, from Natal northwards to Victoria Nyanza, and westwards to Lake Tanganyika and Zambia, and the Indian Ocean. Over this huge territory, it has acquired many names by the various tribes present. These names include: bubu (as noted by Livingstone) at Shupanga on the Lower Zambezi, inkhomi ('the killer') in Chi-ngoni and Chi-nkhonde (Bantu languages of southern Africa), hongo in Chi-ngindo (of Tanzania), kovoko in Ki-nyamwezi (of Tanzania and southeast Africa), ngoshe in Chi-wemba (of Malawi), songo in Chi-yao (of Malawi), and mbobo by Zimbabwe natives. Also, in his checklist of apparently unknown animals (*Cryptozoology,* 1986), Dr Bernard Heuvelmans noted that it was referred to as the n'gok-wiki by the Baya of the Central African Republic. And oddly, as reported by Henri Lhote and Helfried Weyer in their book *Sahara* (1980), there are even stories that this vast desert houses pythons with hairy necks!

More recently, during the CFZ's 'The J.T. Downes Memorial Gambia Expedition 2006', the expedition team learned that the ninki-nanka, a reptilian Gambian mystery beast hitherto thought to be dragonesque in form, was actually likened by the locals to a huge crested snake.

The names may be different, but its description is fairly constant. Reputed to measure up to 20 ft (thus exceeding even the dreaded king cobra or hamadryad *Ophiophagus hannah* of Asia, the world's longest *known* species of venomous snake), the crowing crested cobra is said to be a very formidable and extremely ferocious, vicious species. It is usually buff-brown or greyish-black but with a scarlet face, and of arboreal inclination, despite its great size. Its 'cobra' appellation is something of a misnomer, as it does not possess a hood.

Instead, and distinguishing it instantly from all known snakes, it allegedly bears a prominent bright-red crest, resembling a cockscomb but projecting forwards rather than backwards. Both sexes have this crest, but the male supposedly sports a conspicuous pair of red facial wattles too, enhancing its similarity to a cockerel. The

4 | THE CROWING CRESTED COBRA

greatest correspondence between the latter fowl and this extraordinary snake, however, arises from the male's astonishing ability (according to eyewitness accounts) to crow loudly, just like a farmyard rooster! And to complete this remarkable parallel, the female apparently emits a hen-like clucking sound. In addition, both sexes can produce a distinctive warning note, best represented as 'chu-chu-chu-chu', repeated rapidly several times.

My reconstruction of the male crowing crested cobra, as based upon eyewitness accounts (© Dr Karl Shuker)

Just as curious as its appearance is its diet, for according to Shircore this huge snake subsists upon an almost exclusive diet of maggots, obtained from the dead bodies of other animals. Moreover, it reputedly kills animals for the express purpose of consuming the maggots that will emerge from eggs laid by flies on the rotting carcasses—a trait, incidentally, also noted for certain smaller snakes, and even some rodents and cuckoos. Nevertheless, in view of its enormous size, it is highly unlikely that the crowing crested cobra could thrive solely upon maggots, and in his own account of this extraordinary creature in *Les Derniers Dragons d'Afrique* (1978), Heuvelmans noted that according to veterinarian Dr Dennis A. Walker, specimens sighted in Southern Rhodesia (now Zimbabwe) prey upon hyraxes, those diminutive rodent-like hoofed mammals related to elephants. Walker also mentioned that in addition to their arboreal tendencies, these snakes could be found among kopjes (hillocks) and large rocks, which is where hyraxes often occur.

And if the huge red-crested serpent reported from the Congo region by animal collector Charles Cordier (*Zoo,* April 1973) is one and the same as the crowing crested cobra described from elsewhere, this mystery snake may also have aquatic inclinations, because the Congolese version can be found stretched out on trees alongside riverbanks.

The exceptional appearance of this huge but scientifically unrecognised serpent may be more than enough in itself to terrify anyone encountering it unexpectedly, but the principal reason for the absolute horror that it incites among the native tribes is due to the devastating combination of its unnerving willingness to attack people at the slightest provocation, and its deadly venom—so potent that a bite is supposedly followed almost instantaneously by death. According to Shircore, its usual mode of attack is to remain concealed upon branches overhanging a path, and then to lunge downwards at the head or face of any unwary person walking by underneath. Indeed, its Chi-yao name, songo, translates as 'that which strikes downwards and pricks the head'. Some natives have sought to safeguard themselves against its lethal onslaughts by carrying pots of boiling water on their heads when journeying through forested areas said to be inhabited by this highly dangerous creature; if the snake should then strike, it would burn or kill itself.

Interestingly, in his *Memories of a Game-Ranger* (1948), Harry Wolhuter recalled that some southern African natives tell of a similar mystery snake, crested and vocal, called the muhlambela, and measuring almost 12 ft long. It too strikes at the heads of the unwary. However, its voice is a deer-like bleat rather than a cock-crow, and its crest is composed of feathers (although this bizarre feature may in reality have a surprisingly prosaic explanation, as will be explained a little later here).

SOME IDENTITIES AND SOME RELICS

All of the above seems so fantastic, so nightmarish, that it should come as no surprise to learn that many zoologists are very sceptical as to whether such a macabre, phantasmagorical serpent as the crowing crested cobra could truly exist, still awaiting formal discovery and description by science. Surely it must be merely a particularly graphic example of primitive superstition and imagination, with no basis in corporeal reality? This issue has inspired heated debate, but has yet to be resolved.

Former game warden Lieutenant-Colonel Charles R.S. Pitman believed the crowing crested cobra to be a non-existent composite entity, 'created' from the erroneous lumping together of reports appertaining to various totally different snakes. In his *Report on a Faunal Survey of Northern Rhodesia* (1934), Pitman stated that the Gaboon viper *Bitis gabonica* and the rhinoceros viper *B. nasicornis* (two highly venomous horned vipers inhabiting Zambia, formerly Northern Rhodesia) have strikingly coloured heads, in keeping with the brightly hued face attributed to the crowing crested cobra. Furthermore, he noted that in Kawambwa the Gaboon viper is oddly claimed to be the 'crested snake which crows' (even though it isn't and doesn't).

Pitman also noted that the natives inhabiting parts of the Barotse Valley allege that the male black mamba *Dendroaspis polylepis,* another deadly species, has a crest and is capable of crowing. Although the latter ability has yet to be proven, there is some truth in their allegations regarding a crest.

Gaboon viper *Bitis gabonica* (Marius Burger, CC-0)

In *African Wild Life* (December 1961), Umtali Museum worker and noted herpetologist Donald C. Broadley recorded that an old mamba sometimes experiences difficulty in shedding the skin on its head, pieces sticking to its nape instead of peeling off; after successive unsatisfactory sloughings, a distinct ruff or crest of unshed skin is thus acquired. Several 'crested' snakes caught for identification have proven to be black mambas adorned in this way—including a monstrous 14.5-ft specimen described by the natives as bearing feathers on its head (explaining the muhlambela?), shot by J.A.W. Bennetts in Natal (*African Wild Life,* 1956).

Incidentally, in a much more recent publication, *Snakes of Zambia* (2003), co-authored by Broadley, the notion of crested mystery snakes being black mambas with incompletely sloughed neck skin is reiterated, followed by a most interesting statement that according to an unpublished claim by eminent African ornithologist C.W. Benson: "The call usually attributed to this mythical snake is that of a bird, the Pigmy Rail (*Sarothrura elegans*)".

Also, in his *Last Journals,* Livingstone suggested that the bubu was the black mamba. And South African herpetologist F.W. [Frederick William] Fitzsimons noted in his book *Snakes* (1932)

Black mamba *Dendroaspis polylepis*
(Nick Evans, CC BY-SA 4.0)

that black mambas in trees do lunge down at the heads of people below.

In his book *The Adventures of an Elephant Hunter* (1912), Scottish-born soldier, ivory-seeker, and professional elephant hunter James 'Jim' Sutherland included the following details regarding what he referred to as the songwe:

> The natives all say that the nakahungu [black mamba] is the largest poisonous snake in Africa with the exception of the dreaded songwe.
>
> Among all the tribes of Eastern and Central Africa with whom I have come in contact, I have heard amazing stories of a snake called the songwe which, the natives most positively assert, has a red comb like a cock's on its head and crows in the same manner as that bird. They allege that the songwe deliberately waits on frequented paths for human beings and kills them, and some of my men stoutly affirm that they have been pursued by this reptile, though I, myself, have never encountered it, in spite of the fact that I have been in all kinds of country where snakes abound. I have even offered a reward to any native bringing me this redoubtable serpent, either dead or alive, but this reward has never been claimed. I am, therefore, inclined to think, though I will not positively state, that the songwe lives only in their imaginations, and Simba, my tracker, who is a man of very skeptical and rational mind, says he believes it to be a fabulous snake, or probably the above-mentioned nakahungu, enlarged upon by those who have been scared by it.

Recalling Sutherland's songwe account in his own book, *The African Adventurers* (1992), fellow hunter/author Peter Hathaway Capstick expanded upon the mamba theory as the most likely explanation for African crowing crested mystery snakes:

> Sutherland speaks about the *songwe*, the semi-mythical snake popular in Mozambique as well as in today's Zambia. . . . Personally, I think that the

songwe is real, a part of African legend but a part of reality also.

Certainly, the idea of a cock's comb and the cry of a rooster is invention, but I have seen two huge black mambas, both of which I killed, that had a "frill" of sloughed skin around their necks, which, because of the waist-shape of the head leading into the body, did not come free with the last shedding of skin. I believe that this was the origin of the *songwe*. These mambas were very thick for mambas and certainly long. Maybe they weren't as long as a black mamba is supposed to get (one was nine feet and the other a bit over ten feet), but they were obviously very old snakes and most cantankerous. The backlighted view of these snakes would have made them appear as if they had a ruffed collar; the fabrication of a comb and a cock's crow would almost naturally follow.

So could it be that the crowing crested cobra is nothing more than a confusion or conceptual potpourri of the most venomous formally recognized snakes encountered by tribes in East and Central Africa? That is, a wholly symbolic representation of all that they fear most in serpentine form, rather than a valid, distinct, flesh-and-blood species in its own right?

Without any complete or partial remains of crowing crested cobras, this hypothesis is quite tenable—however, some sundry remains of this extraordinary creature do appear to have been obtained. At the time of his report, Shircore owned what he believed to be the bony skeleton of the fleshy cockscomb, and a portion of the neck (containing several vertebrae), from one of these snakes. Describing the cockscomb:

> Its skeleton consists of a thin lanceolate plate of bone (1.5 ins long by 0.5 in wide, at its broadest part) with a markedly rounded smooth ridge, 0.5 in wide, slightly overhanging both sides of the upper border, with a distinct voluted curve to the left. The lower border is sharp-edged and faintly ridged. The lateral surfaces are concave, throughout the long diameter. The whole fragment is eminently constructed for

4 | THE CROWING CRESTED COBRA

the insertion and attachment of muscles—much the same as the structure of the breast-bone of a bird. Some skin, part of which, spread smoothly above the base of the plate, on one side, is red in colour: and attached to the lower angle is a dark wrinkled bit, which appears to be a remnant of the head-skin—all of which should be valuable for purposes of identification. A small portion of the bone, tapering towards both ends, 0.5 in long by 0.5 in wide, is missing from the lower anterior border, including the tip—it was broken off for use as medicine by the witch-doctor, from whom the specimens were obtained.

This structure is clearly something more than an artifact of unshed skin, and bearing in mind that its description is from the pen of a medical doctor, trained in meticulous scientific observation, we can surely have no doubt regarding its accuracy. As to the identity of the species from which these remains originated, no zoologist has so far reconciled them with any species currently known to science.

Depiction of possible appearance of a crowing crested cobra's head (© Markus Bühler)

Shircore's report took the form of two notes, the second written some time later than the first, after which both were submitted to *African Affairs* and published as one. The above description appeared in the first note, but in the second he recorded that he had since obtained two further preserved specimens. One, from a relatively small crowing crested cobra, consisted of five lumbar vertebra, which were 0.28 in long and 0.20 in wide, with the concave, articulating face 0.08 in from top to bottom and 0.12 in across; two ribs 1.02 in along the curve; a 0.40 x 0.32-in piece of skin; and the laterally flattened, granular-textured skin-tip of its crest, measuring 0.24 in long and 0.12 in wide at its base. The second specimen was a single dorsal vertebra, said to have been obtained from the remains of a huge crowing crested cobra that had killed a man; the vertebra's articulating surfaces measured an impressive 0.32 x 0.36 in. Sadly, these potentially significant relics' current whereabouts are apparently unknown.

Speaking of procured specimens of crested snakes: the May 1907 issue of a former British monthly journal of natural history entitled *The Zoologist* contained an article by Charles M.D. Stewart concerning a crested vocalizing mystery snake called the ndhlondhlo. According to Stewart, it used to be frequently reported by native people inhabiting Natal and Zululand (in what is nowadays South Africa) but no longer was, causing Stewart to fear that it had become extinct. The ndhlondhlo was said to be extremely sizeable, exceedingly venomous, and "was reputed to have upon its head a crest resembling a feather [recalling the muhlambela documented earlier in this present chapter], and to whistle shrilly when excited". When Europeans hearing such reports opined that it was simply a very old black mamba, the locals vehemently denied this, stating that it was definitely a distinct species in its own right.

Anxious to learn more about the ndhlondhlo, Stewart wrote to C.R. Saunders, who at that time was Civil Commissioner in Zululand. In his reply, Saunders not only confirmed the widespread native belief that the ndhlondhlo was real and distinct from all other snake species but also revealed that in c.1874, near the Tongaat River in Natal, he himself had shot dead an unusual snake that was claimed by locals to be a bona fide ndhlondhlo. Although it superficially resembled a black mamba, it was no less than 16 ft long, and was much lighter in colour than numerous black mambas seen by him, "being of a dark slate-colour, particularly about the head, which was almost a pale bluish colour". Most noticeable of all, however, was the hood or crest-like structure upon its head:

> On examining its head there were some long scales—three, I think—which, when lifted up, formed a sort of hood. These scales were from half an inch to an inch long.

Sadly, this intriguing specimen seems not to have been retained once it had been examined and measured by Saunders and some elderly natives.

When Stewart questioned Mataffayen, his venerable native wagon-driver, on the subject of the ndhlondhlo, Mataffayen, who claimed to have seen ndhlondhlos dead and alive, stated categorically that the head feathers reputedly borne by this mystery snake were not actual feathers, but simply resembled feathers. This lends weight to Saunders's description of the three long scales present upon the head of the snake that he had killed.

Near the end of his article in *The Zoologist,* Stewart recalled being told by Dr R.J. Colenso, son of the then Bishop of Natal, that as a boy he had seen a large, dark-coloured snake moving through some 3-ft-tall grass but with its head held well above the grass, revealing that it was crested:

> [Colenso] distinctly observed a crest resembling a feather, which sloped back from the head, somewhat as the crest of a Cockatoo does . . . [and] appeared to spring from the after-part of the occiput [back of the head].

According to Colenso, the snake did not appear to be irritated but perfectly calm as it made its way through the grass, thus indicating that the crest "was not a mere elevation of neck-scales in a moment of anger, but that it was a true crest".

Judging from all of this detail, whatever the ndhlondhlo is, or was, its crest seemed far too orderly in structure to be merely a random aggregation of sloughed skin.

Another very noteworthy report is that of John Knott (*African Wild Life,* September 1962). Driving home from Binga, in the Kariba area of Southern Rhodesia, during the end of May 1959, Knott accidentally ran over a large, jet-black snake measuring 6.5-7 ft long. The snake was mortally wounded, so that, although still alive, it was incapable of escape or attack when Knott stepped out of his Land Rover to investigate. He was very surprised to discover that the snake bore a distinct crest on its head, perfectly symmetrical and capable of being erected by way of five internal prop-like structures.

This description recalls a very peculiar Australian reptile known as the frilled lizard *Chlamydosaurus kingii*. The first sighting of this species by a Westerner was made on 8 October 1820 by Allan Cunningham at Careening Bay, Port Nelson, in Western Australia. As he recounted in P.P. King's *Narrative of a Survey of the Intertropical and Western Coasts of Australia Between the Years 1818 and 1822* (1827):

> I secured a lizard of extraordinary appearance, which had perched itself upon the stem of a small decayed tree. It had a curious crenated membrane like a ruff or tippet around its neck, which it spreads five inches in the form of an open umbrella.

Vintage engraving of a frilled lizard in threatening posture with frill expanded, as featuring on the front cover of my book *Extraordinary Animals Worldwide* (© Dr Karl Shuker)

4 | THE CROWING CRESTED COBRA

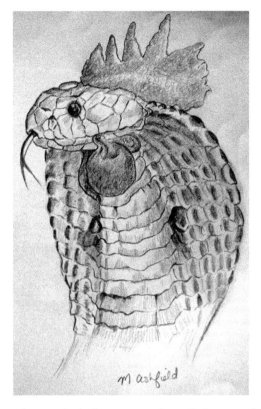

Another artistic interpretation of the crowing crested cobra's possible morphology
(© Maureen Ashfield, courtesy of Carl Marshall)

This lizard is totally harmless, eluding predators by sprinting away bipedally like a miniature dinosaur. If cornered, however, it expands its bizarre frill as a shock tactic. Interestingly, this frill is erected by means of bony structures extending into it from the lizard's mouth, thereby expanding whenever the mouth is opened wide. A comparable structural arrangement, operated by muscles attached to the prop-like components observed by Knott, could mobilize the crest of the crowing crested cobra.

So deadly a beast as this snake obviously does not inspire willingness on the part of local people to catch specimens for scientific study—a plausible enough reason for the scarcity of remains. However, there is another important reason for that. According to Shircore, this species is very closely associated with snake-worship by certain tribes (especially those referring to it as the inkhomi). Its skin and crest are prized by its worshippers, and other parts of its body are essential ingredients for many charms and medical potions utilized in tribal witchcraft and witch-doctor activity.

Consequently, whenever such a snake is killed, its remains rarely if ever fall readily into the hands of anyone outside these tribes. Of course, if some ardent anthropologist were to serve an apprenticeship in such a cult, he may then be given access to remains of this snake—but whether, under these conditions, he would ever be granted the opportunity to apply any scientific analysis to them is another matter entirely.

Judging from the above accounts, the crowing crested cobra would indeed seem to be real and distinct, at least on morphological grounds. Moreover, one further and extremely intriguing aspect of this already fascinating case is the existence of some remarkable parallels to it in various widely disparate corners of the world.

CARIBBEAN COUNTERPARTS

In his book *The Romance of Natural History, Second Series* (1867), English naturalist Philip H. Gosse reported that a peculiar snake, wholly unknown to science, apparently existed on certain of the islands in the West Indies chain. Except for its much shorter length, this snake bears an uncanny resemblance to Africa's crowing crested cobra. In 1845-46, Gosse visited Jamaica, and while there:

> I heard accounts of a wonderful animal occasionally seen in the eastern districts of the island, which was reported as a Snake with a cock's comb and wattles, and which crowed like a cock.

Sounds familiar, doesn't it?

Yet surprisingly, in complete contrast to the attention attracted by Africa's crowing crested cobra, the Caribbean's counterpart seemed afterwards to sink into obscurity. In a bid to rectify that sad situation, this chapter will provide all of the eyewitness accounts cited by Gosse in his book.

He received his first from a medical man of repute, who informed Gosse that:

4 | THE CROWING CRESTED COBRA

> ... he had seen, in 1829, a serpent of about four feet in length, but of unwonted thickness, dull ochry in colour with well-defined dark spots, having on its head a sort of pyramidal helmet, somewhat lobed at the summit, of a pale red hue. The animal, however, was dead, and decomposition was already setting in. He informed me that the negroes of the district were well acquainted with it; and that they represented it as making a noise, not unlike the crowing of a cock, and as being addicted to preying on poultry.

This remarkable reptile has also been recorded from the island of Hispaniola (Santo Domingo), where one of Gosse's friends, Richard Hill, learned of it. According to Gosse, when visiting one of his Spanish acquaintances in Haiti (occupying Hispaniola's western portion), Hill had been informed by him that he had seen one of these snakes in that country's far eastern section:

> My friend's Spanish informant had seen the serpent with mandibles like a bird, with a cock's crest, with

Philip H. Gosse

scarlet lobes or wattles; and he described its habits,—perhaps rather from common fame than from personal observation,—as a frequenter of hen-roosts, into which it would thrust its head, and deceive the young chickens by its imitative physiognomy, and by its attempts to crow, like their own Chanticleer. 'Il canta como un Gallo,' was the report in Hayti, just as in Jamaica.

Before Gosse's return to Europe, a Jamaican resident, Jasper Cargill, offered a sovereign for a specimen of this snake that he could present to Gosse. Unfortunately, Cargill was not successful in obtaining one, but Hill was later able to send Gosse details of two encounters with this snake in relation to Cargill, though no specimen was preserved on either occasion. The first had involved Cargill himself, some years before Gosse's visit to Jamaica:

> . . . when visiting Skibo, in St. George's, an estate of his father's, in descending the mountain-road, his attention was drawn to a snake of a dark hue, that erected itself from amid some fragments of limestone-rock that lay about. It was about *four feet long,* and unusually *thick-bodied.* His surprise was greatly increased on perceiving that it was *crested,* and that from the side of the cheeks depended some *red-coloured flaps,* like gills or wattles. After gazing at him intently some time, with its head well erect, it drew itself in, and disappeared among the fragmentary rocks.

Cargill's second account concerned an incident involving his son, which took place on or around 30 March 1850. According to Hill:

> . . . some youngsters of the town came running to tell me of a curious snake, unlike any snake they had ever seen before, which young Cargill had shot, when out for a day's sport among the woodlands of a neighbouring penn. They described it as in all respects a serpent, but with a very curious shaped head, and with wattles on each side of its jaws. After taking it

in hand and looking at it, they placed it in a hollow tree, intending to return for it when they should be coming home, but they had strolled from the place so far that it was inconvenient to retrace their steps when wearied with rambling.

As it happened, one of the youths did return the following morning, but although he was sure that he had found the correct tree, there was no sign of the snake's body, leading him to conjecture that it had been taken by rats during the night. When this incident was recounted to Mr Hill, his godson Ulick Ramsay came to him to inform him that he too had spied such a snake only a short time earlier:

> . . . not long previously, he had seen in the hand of the barrack-master-serjeant at the barracks in Spanish Town, a curious snake, which he, too, had shot among the rocks of a little line of eminences near the railway, about two miles out, called Craigallechie. It was a serpent with a curious shaped head, and projections on each side, which he likened to the fins of an eel, but said that they were close up to the jaws.

That was the last report cited by Gosse. What are we to make of these Greater Antillean anomalies? Certainly they all seem to refer to the same species, but, just as certainly, one that is not recognized by science. Of course, it would be tempting to postulate that these West Indian reports are nothing more than derivations of the African crowing crested cobra beliefs, resettled in these islands along with all of the other folklore and superstitions conveyed here by the countless African natives who were mercilessly transported from their homes as slaves during those terrible years of the slave trade.

However, this cannot be the explanation, because such snakes have also been reported by Western observers, some of high standing (remember the well-respected medical man on Jamaica?). In fact, there is no greater reason for disbelieving the reports of West Indian crowing crested serpents than for disbelieving those of their African counterparts.

A SAMOAN SURPRISE

In the May 2007 edition of his online *BioFortean Review* journal, American cryptozoologist Chad Arment revealed an additional, unexpected example of a crowing snake—reported from the Samoan island of Savai'i. Chad noted that at least two authors have referred to the existence here of such a serpent. One of these was Albert Barnes Steinberger. In his *Report on Samoa* (1874), he stated:

> I saw the first reptiles in the islands at the village of Asou, in Savaii, and there learned of the 'crowing snake,' (*Vivimi gata*.) It is the subject of native songs. The testimony of both whites and natives points directly to the fact that they have a snake which crows like a cock. I did not see or hear one. The apparent physical impossibility of such an anomaly made me skeptical, but the unequivocal testimony of the missionaries to the existence of such a reptile seems too strong to be rejected.

Author #2 was Consul-General James H. Mulligan, who, in his *Consul Reports* for May 1896, commented as follows regarding this curious reptile:

> There are persons whom I should regard as reliable, who stoutly maintain the existence in these islands of a very large serpent, which gives out a noise somewhat like the crowing of a cock—a serpent which I have heard spoken of as a crowing snake. Other persons of long residence speak of it as a myth. A party of labourers at work in a clearing near this town, not long since, were scattered by the appearance of a large serpent, which swung itself from the branch of one tree to that of another. The men united in the assertion that it made a crowing sound, was of enormous size, and moved with great rapidity. I vouch for none of these assertions, but give them for what they are worth; but the existence of the crowing snake is by some held to as firmly in Samoa as it is by others abroad believed to belong in these islands.

4 | THE CROWING CRESTED COBRA

Apart from the apparent absence of a cockscomb and wattles (none is mentioned in these reports), this very vocal Samoan mystery snake is certainly more than a little reminiscent of the crowing serpents documented above in this chapter.

There is also a traditional legend of a crowing snake in the independent Pacific island state of Palau.

CROWING SNAKES IN THE PHILIPPINES

No less than three wholly independent sources have provided me with information indicating the apparent presence of crowing snakes in the Philippines too.

Accessing the website Cryptozoology.com in December 2008, I was very interested to learn there that such a creature, known locally as the banakon, and familiar to a number of tribes (in particular the Matigsalug), reputedly inhabits the Philippine island of Mindanao's rice paddy fields. According to native accounts, the banakon is very large, venomous, aggressive, and highly territorial. They describe it as black or very dark in colour, with a diamond-shaped mark on its mullet-shaped head ('banakon' apparently translates as 'mullet-head'), plus two small horn-like head projections, and the distinctly un-snake-like ability to crow, albeit with a deep pitch.

Conversely, some descriptions of the banakon are wholly different from the version given above, stating instead that it is of variable size, silver in colour with iridescent scales, and, most remarkable of all, a pair of short legs near its head. This last-mentioned feature readily recalls Mexico's legged amphisbaenians (worm lizards) known as ajolotes, and also certain species of skink lizard. Could there be two entirely different but equally cryptic reptiles involved here, one a large snake, the other some form of amphisbaenian or true lizard? Or perhaps one or both are merely fantasy creatures of local legend.

On 10 June 2014, I received further information concerning what appears to be the same Filipino crowing cryptid, although the name applied to it on this occasion was the trabunko. Philippines-based *Facebook* correspondent Omi Draper informed me that he once interviewed a farmer here who saw one many years ago. He informed Omi that it gives voice to a loud rooster-like cry when about to die. Moreover, Omi learnt from a local friend that in one area these snakes used to be actively hunted, captured alive, then sold to Chinese buyers who believed them to be servants of certain Chinese deities. Omi traced a Chinese temple that had allegedly bought one such snake, but he had no luck in seeing it. Quaint folklore, or curious fact?

And on 8 March 2016, I received the following very interesting email from Philippines inhabitant Marc Clam:

> My name is Marc from Philippines, just moved in Cavite from Batangas Province for my new job in a Manufacturing Company.
>
> Today, during our lunch break my friends and I were talking about bird hunting places here in the Philippines, and one friend from Ternate, Cavite told us that in their place somewhere near Mount Palay is a nice place for hunting for deer and wild boars back then but not anymore until it was declared as national park reservation. He also added that people living nearby have lots of stories about the snake that crows like a rooster and he added that some have seen and described [it] as a combed-crown head snake.

Ajolote *Bipes biporus* (Marlin Harms, CC BY 2.0)

4 | THE CROWING CRESTED COBRA

Of course, the rest of us didn't believe such folklore, but another friend also came by and heard us talking about it, and told us that at his grandpa's farm, he actually heard the crowing amidst in a bamboo tree at the roadside, but they were warned by his grandpa, not to come near cause it is just a snake mimicking the sound of a chicken.

Now, curious as a cat, I went back to my office and searched it at Google and I came across your blogs, but I still couldn't find any actual photo of what it looks like, and I am thinking about having a little adventure of busting a myth.

Clearly, reports of crowing snakes are by no means unprecedented in this island country.

INDIGENOUS IN INDIA?

On 9 July 2020, I received the following brief but interesting post from Changchang A. Sangma responding to my *ShukerNature* blog's coverage of the crowing crested cobra:

Here in Baghmara (Meghalaya, India), my neighbours claimed to have seen one near their home. That serpent matches the exact description.

To date, this is the only Indian report of an ostensibly crowing crested snake that I am aware of, so if anyone reading this chapter knows of any additional ones, I'd be very pleased to receive details.

A COCKEREL-CRESTED SERPENT COVETED BY TRADESCANT?

John Tradescant the Elder (c.1570s-1638) was a famous English naturalist, professional gardener, and traveller. However, he also became well known for his immense personal collection of curiosities and natural history specimens (some of which survive to this day within the Ashmolean Museum at the University of Oxford,

England), which was popularly dubbed The Ark, and was contained in a large house at Lambeth, London. Moreover, The Ark's contents were actively added to by Tradescant's son, John Tradescant the Younger (1608-1662).

Of potential relevance to the subject of this present chapter is a letter that the elder Tradescant wrote to the then secretary of the English navy, in which he listed various items that he would very much like to obtain. These included:

> All sorts of Serpents and Snakes Skines [sic] & Especially of that sort that hathe a Combe on his head Lyke a Cock.

What are we to make of this request? Back in Tradescant's time, bestiaries still promulgated the supposed reality of all sorts of fabulous beasts, such as unicorns, satyrs, mermaids, and a diversity of dragons. So it is most likely that he was thinking of the mythical cockatrice. Conversely, in view of his own extensive travels, it is not impossible that he had heard rumours of Africa's alleged crowing crested cobra (or perhaps of one from some other exotic locality?). All that we can say for sure is that no such specimen is present among those from The Ark that still exist today.

WHEN MADNESS, MURDER, AND MONSTERS TAKE FLIGHT?

Ending this investigation of crowing crested conundra is a decidedly enigmatic case hailing from Russia.

North of St Petersburg, Russia, in the Vepskaya Heights is a small but much-dreaded, dense area of forested marshland, infamous for the discovery here of 16 naked human corpses since 1993, whose cause of death remains unknown. They showed no signs of violence, but they seemed to have gone mad before dying, as they had stripped all their clothes off, had eaten dirt, thrown away edible foodstuffs that they had been gathering in the forests, and replaced it in their baskets with their own clothes.

Several possible explanations have been aired by baffled investigators, including a serial killer, some strange form of fever, or the effects of ingesting toxic mushrooms or some other comparably deadly items while collecting their berries, fungi, etc. Perhaps the most intriguing suggestion of all, however, is that the dead people are the victims of a controversial, still-unidentified species of snake said to inhabit the bogs in this area.

According to local testimony collected since the 1980s, such snakes are readily distinguished by a fleshy growth on their head in male specimens that resembles a rooster's cockscomb. In addition, they have a lethally venomous bite, are often found in the trees here, and can leap great distances from tree to tree, so that they are nicknamed the flying monsters. Only one known type of snake can glide in this manner—the so-called flying snakes (genus *Chrysopelea*, containing five species) of southeast Asia. One unsolved mystery, the explanation for the dead bodies, has thus become two, with a creature of cryptozoology cited as that selfsame explanation.

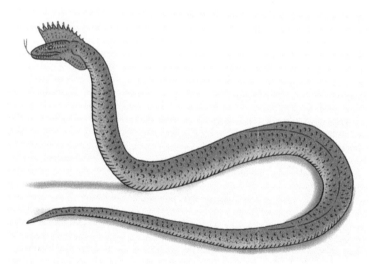

Is this what the crowing crested cobra looks like?
(© Tim Morris)

FOR CROWING OUTLOUD—AN ANSWER?

As for Africa's crowing crested cobra and its various equivalents elsewhere, what about their strangest characteristic of all, their alleged ability to crow? Is that genuine, or is it unadulterated fantasy?

It may come as a major surprise to learn that several *known* species of snake are also said to emit some very unsnake-like sounds, including bell-like notes, bird-like chirps, and even loud cat-like yowls—the last-mentioned of which was formally confirmed during the early 1980s when a major cave system in southeastern Asia was explored. So, what was heard—and found—there? For that and much more too on the very unorthodox subject of vocalising snakes, Chapter 16 awaits your attention!

5
THE SCARLET VIPER—NO LONGER A MYSTERY OF NATURAL HISTORY

> The small red viper is a reptile far better known to those whose occupations take them to the haunts of snakes than to scientific naturalists. Indeed by the latter its existence is generally ignored. Many works on natural history make no allusion to it. . . . It is a reptile that has had but little attention paid to it, probably on account of its great rarity and its very local distribution.
>
> Gerald R. Leighton—*The Life-History of British Serpents and Their Local Distribution in the British Isles*

It is well known that the adder or European common viper *Vipera berus* occasionally produces albinistic (all-white, pink-eyed) and melanistic (all-black) individuals, due to the expression of certain mutant gene alleles. I was fortunate enough to see a bona fide black adder myself (and not of the Rowan Atkinson variety either!) when visiting Woody Bay in North Devon, England, back in 1993. Of course, these are not separate species, merely genetically-induced colour varieties (morphs) of the common adder.

As recently as the early 1900s, however, many natural history tomes were still soberly stating that Britain was also home to a much more remarkable, additional viperine form, one so distinct in

My briefly-glimpsed black adder at Woody Bay (© Dr Karl Shuker)

Variation within *Vipera berus* (Tigerente, CC BY-SA 3.0)

5 | THE SCARLET VIPER

fact that it was classed as a separate species in its own right—*Vipera rubra*, the scarlet or small red viper.

As its names suggest, this eye-catching serpent was bright red in background colour, with a brown rather than a black dorsal zigzag stripe, and was claimed to be somewhat smaller than the normal adder. It was also said to have once been widely distributed across England (as well as certain parts of Scotland), but never common anywhere, except perhaps in southern Dorset—particularly around Corfe Castle, and also Lulworth Cove according to a short *Pet Reptiles* article from 2001 by CFZ founder Jonathan Downes.

In those latter areas, the scarlet viper was apparently a familiar sight, which makes it all the more surprising that nowadays it is ostensibly long-vanished, and not only from such localities either, but from the British natural history literature too, almost as if this enigmatic snake had never existed. Why should that be? Whatever has happened to it?

Let me begin my investigation by presenting what was for a very long time the most comprehensive documentation ever published of this serpentine species, a veritable study in scarlet, in fact (until superseded by my own coverage here), and within which it was assigned its now-obsolete taxonomic binomial name.

Chapter 15 in herpetologist Dr Gerald R. Leighton's book *The Life-History of British Serpents and Their Local Distribution in the British Isles* (1901) was entitled 'The Small Red Viper', and was devoted entirely to it. As even this account was only very short (especially for an entire chapter), however, and yet is also of major significance to the subject of this mysterious snake form but is nowadays scarcely known or readily accessible, I am reproducing it in full herewith:

> The small red viper is a reptile far better known to those whose occupations take them to the haunts of snakes than to scientific naturalists. Indeed by the latter its existence is generally ignored. Many works on natural history make no allusion to it, and where it is mentioned it is referred to as a variety of the common adder, or as merely the young of that species. Any departure from those views, if noticed at all, is sure to be severely criticised, if not resented as presumptuous. If, however, an observer is to be true

to himself, he must record his observations, and is entitled to deduce conclusions therefrom irrespective of results. Careful study of British adders has driven me to regard the small red viper as a valid species, quite as distinct from the ordinary adder as a swallow is from a martin or a stoat from a weasel. It is a reptile that has had but little attention paid to it, probably on account of its great rarity and its very local distribution, and also, no doubt, because it is very much more difficult to capture than the ordinary adder.

The small red viper resembles the common adder in the arrangement of its head-plates and in the number of belly-shields, and is therefore put in the same species. It differs from the adder in most other respects; but the differences, by an arbitrary arrangement, are not regarded as essential. These differences are, however, constant, which to my mind is an all-important point. It has been said that the small red viper is held to be either a variety of the adder or the young of the adder. The latter view is the important one from the point of view of its validity as a species. This opinion presumably is based upon the fact that certain ordinary adders exhibit a red colour. It is assumed that these adders, if they could have been examined when young, would have appeared to be small red vipers. But it so happens that this red colour in ordinary adders is characteristic of one sex only, and that the female. Thus in Mr Boulenger's most valuable paper on the "Variations of the Viper in Great Britain" [*Zoologist*, March 1892, by Belgian-born British Museum zoologist George A. Boulenger] the following occurs: "Brown and brick-red specimens, with the markings of a more or less dark-brown, *are females*." This is absolutely true, the colours mentioned never being found in the ordinary male adder. The question therefore arises, Are all these so-called small red vipers simply young *female* adders? This could only be settled by obtaining specimens of this colour of both sexes. I had long

5 | THE SCARLET VIPER

believed in the distinctness of the small red viper from the adder, from its constancy in size and colour, but had never taken a male specimen until the 26th April 1901. I was at that time investigating the Ophidia of Central Dorset, and on the day mentioned took a specimen locally known as the little viper. It was the usual red colour, but a glance at the tail at once showed it to be a male. I demonstrated the male organs to the Rev. F. W. Brandreth, to whom I am indebted for the opportunity of examining that most snaky neighbourhood. The length of the specimen was 12½ inches. This viper is well known in that locality, though of much less frequent occurrence than the ordinary adder, which is abundant. The male adder there is pale-grey with very black markings and bluish-black belly, not in the least like the small red viper.

Moreover, if the red viper were a young female adder, a large number of specimens ought to show the gradations of the one passing into the other. This is not seen in any of the hundreds of female adders I have examined.

Distribution.—On account of its infrequent occurrence, and the absence of authentic county records, it is a matter of some considerable difficulty to determine its exact distribution. F. G. Aflalo [*Natural History (Vertebrates) of the British Islands*, p. 304.] mentions that it is found in Herts, Somerset, and Devon, also in parts of Scotland, and these three counties are usually the ones mentioned in this connection. He also refers to the capture of "a small red kind" in Fairlight Glen, near Hastings, in further reference to which he writes to me:—

"I wish I could give you the accurate information you seek touching those Fairlight red adders, which I distinctly remember killing on two or three occasions, some twenty years ago. But I did not in those days—it must have been during the period 1881-1883, during which I lived at Hastings—see any particular interest in a snake beyond its power of dying picturesquely, and all I can recall is the *decided reddish* hue of some of the adders {*not all, mind*) that we found thereabouts, and the belief among the villagers in the neighbourhood of Fairlight and Ecclesbourne that these red adders were more dangerous than those of normal colour. More than this memory does not spare me."

The Rev. H. A. Macpherson, in his 'Fauna of Lakeland,' records the occurrence of a specimen thus:—

"Most of the Lakeland vipers are grey or brown in ground colour, regardless of their sex. The only instance at present known to me of the capture of a 'red' individual within our limits relates to a viper which Joseph Boadle presented to the Whitehaven Museum. 'Instead of being grey and black, it is a dull ferruginous red, and the zigzag markings are a dark mahogany colour.' This animal had been caught near Rig House, Dean, West Cumberland" (recorded in the 'Whitehaven Times,' December 3, 1874). [Here, Leighton appended the following footnote: From this description the specimen might have been a female adder, the size not being given, nor the sex.]

But as a matter of fact, the distribution of the small red viper is much wider in England than has hitherto been recognised, and not the least interesting of the results of my effort to obtain a complete account of the *county* distribution of our serpents has been the discovery that this species is to be found in at least fifteen English counties, five of which have already been mentioned. I have myself observed it twice in Herefordshire, both times in the same locality—namely, on Garway Hill, once in 1898 and once in 1900. I have also taken one specimen in Monmouthshire, on August 1, 1900; this latter specimen measured 9¾ inches, and was captured on the summit of the Graig Hill. I showed it at the annual meeting of the Woolhope Field Naturalists' Club in 1900. I have also taken one—a male—in Central Dorset (Buckland Newton) as mentioned. A reference to the county reports in this book will show that it also occurs in the following additional counties: Berkshire, Oxfordshire, Lincolnshire, West Sussex, Northumberland, Durham, Dorset, Devon. In most cases, however, it is an unusual occurrence, and though its distribution is a fairly wide one, its numbers seem to be small. No doubt a further investigation will establish its occurrence in some other counties.

Description.—The name small red viper is sufficiently descriptive, as the serpent is both small, red, and a viper. It can be at once distinguished by its red, coppery, or ferruginous colour, which is the only colour it shows, the markings being a darker shade of the same colour. The zigzag back-line and the V-shaped head-mark are both present in the same positions as in the adder, but the extra side-line of black or brown patches seen in the latter have been absent in the specimens of small red vipers I have examined. There is not the amount of colour variation we saw in the adder, the only variation being in shade, from bright copper colour to a darker mahogany shade. The tail is very sharply marked off from the body in females, and ends in a very fine point.

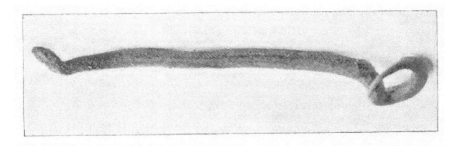

Scarlet viper collected by Gerald Leighton in Monmouthshire

Size.—If the colour of this species is distinctive, the size is no less so. As in the adder, the average length varies somewhat in different localities, but *the largest small red viper* is hardly the length of the smallest adult adder. The adult adder averages from 18 to 25 inches; the small red viper averages from 10 to 15 inches in length. The most common measurement is about 12 inches. This is of some practical importance, as only last year my attention was drawn to a statement in some newspaper correspondence, where a writer informed his readers that they need never be afraid of the larger snakes in this country, as our sole venomous serpent was only about 10 inches long. It turned out that his experience had been gained in a part of Devonshire where the small red viper occurred, and this was the only kind he was familiar with. I mention this because it is a proof of my contention for the validity of the species.

Venomous, &c.—In places where the small red viper is found it is regarded as being particularly venomous, and more to be feared than the ordinary adder. Whether this is really so or not I cannot say, but there is no doubt that it is more pugnacious and less timid. On being disturbed it does not seem to make every effort to glide quietly away, as does the adder, but, curling its tail in a circle on the ground, erects its head and hisses vigorously.

Much requires to be learnt regarding its food and reproduction, the great difficulty being to secure enough specimens to form reliable data.

The illustration of the small red viper [included here in this present chapter] is from the one I captured in Monmouthshire.

Specific name.—If naturalists could see their way to use some specific name, such as *Vipera rubra*, when referring to this viper, it would greatly conduce to accuracy and clearness, and would avoid the confusion which at present exists.

5 | THE SCARLET VIPER

The Aflalo reference cited by Leighton in his above-quoted coverage of the scarlet viper was *A Sketch of the Natural History (Vertebrates) of the British Isles* (1898). Written by Frederick G. Aflalo, it included the following brief recollection regarding such snakes:

> In 1881 I remember catching in Fairlight Glen, near Hastings, a small red kind [of adder/viper], which was locally described as particularly venomous. Dr Stradling tells me that the red phase, there regarded as a valid species, is also credited in Herts, Somerset, Devon, and parts of Scotland, with special virulence.

In 1833, the *Magazine of Natural History* had published a short paper by English naturalist and taxonomist Hugh E. Strickland on the scarlet viper (or red viper as he called it), in which he argued in favour of its status as a valid species, based upon morphological differences.

Hugh E. Strickland

His paper also contained the fascinating information that long before Leighton had suggested *Vipera rubra* as a formal taxonomic name for this snake, no less than an authority than Linnaeus himself had already named it (and as a species in its own right), dubbing it *Coluber chersea* (and the common adder *Coluber berus*). Strickland additionally noted:

> It was first noticed as a British species by Mr. Rackett, in the *Linnaean Transactions*, vol. xii., where he states that it occurred in Cranbourne Chase in Dorsetshire; and Mr. Sheppard, in the same work, has recorded his discovery of it in various parts of Suffolk. Since that time, however, Dr. Leach, in the *Zoological Miscellany* [vol. 3], has regarded this as a variety of the common viper; and Dr. Fleming has done the same in his excellent work on *British Animals*. I conclude, however, that neither of those authors can have seen the animal, as its characters are such as to remove all doubt of its being a distinct species. Two specimens were caught near Evesham in the summer of 1831, of which one was presented to the Zoological Society, and the other is now in my collection. . . . Linnaeus has correctly described this species in the *Swedish Transactions*, where he gives 9½ in. as the length. . . . I may here add the authority of Cuvier in favour of this species being distinct. (See *Le Règne Animal*, vol. ii. p. 92.)

I have also been able to find a couple of short accounts regarding alleged scarlet vipers within the *Dorset Natural History and Archaeological Society Proceedings*, both of them contributed by Eustace R. Bankes from Norden, Corfe Castle, Dorset.

The first one appeared in vol. 27 (published in 1906), and reads as follows:

> SMALL RED VIPER.—A beautiful specimen of this small and very local species (*Vipera rubra*, Leighton), was captured at Corfe Castle by my brother, Mr. Arthur E. Bankes, on May 18, 1905. So far as I can ascertain, this interesting viper had not been previously

5 | THE SCARLET VIPER

Vintage photograph depicting the ruins of Corfe Castle and the same-named village surrounding it

met with in the Isle of Purbeck, though it has occasionally been observed elsewhere in Dorset.

The second account appeared in vol. 29 (1908), concerned an incident featuring Bankes's wife, and reads as follows:

> SMALL RED VIPER (*Vipera rubra*, Leighton).— On June 10, 1907, Mrs. Eustace R. Bankes killed at Norden, Corfe Castle, a remarkably small pale reddish viper. Believing it to be the true small red viper (*Vipera rubra*, Leighton), I forwarded it to Professor Gerald R. Leighton, M.D., who informed me that it was undoubtedly a male example of this species. Of this interesting and scarce reptile, the only other Purbeck specimen that I have ever seen occurred at Corfe Castle, on May 18, 1905. (Proceedings XXVII., 262).

Various additional, comparable accounts of encountering or killing scarlet vipers in various locations across England appeared in local natural history periodicals for a time, but interest in this serpent form (not to mention specimens of it, apparently) soon declined, and it has rated virtually no attention since. Indeed, I am aware of only a single (and very brief) modern-day mention of it—within his book *Reptiles and Amphibians in Britain* (1983), part of the 'Collins New Naturalist Series', Deryk Frazer stated:

> The 'little red adder' of early herpetologists is a colour phase found in some juvenile females, which eventually become less distinctively coloured.

So what are we to make of the scarlet (aka small/little red) viper? A valid if all-but-vanished species as averred by Leighton and Strickland among others, or merely a distinctive colour morph of *V. berus* as nowadays believed by those few who are even aware of its history?

I am firmly within the latter camp. Every aspect of its morphology and widely-scattered but everywhere-localised distribution in Britain is consistent with the morph identity. In any case, it is not as if a scarlet viper would be such an unlikely, improbable herpetological entity. Occurring in a vast range of different animal species, there is a genetically-inherited condition analogous to albinism and melanism that is known as erythrism, and individuals exhibiting it are abnormally red in colour. Erythristic iguanas, for instance, are bright orange-red instead of their normal green shade.

Consequently, an erythristic common adder would make a very plausible scarlet viper. Indeed, I have discovered that red phase individuals have been recorded from certain other viper species too, including the Central African bush viper *Atheris squamigera*.

Furthermore, body size is often linked to the mutant gene alleles causing these colour morphs. Melanistic leopards and jaguars, for instance, tend to be larger than their normal-coloured spotted counterparts. So the scarlet viper's smaller size could simply be another facet of the mutant erythristic gene allele's phenotypic expression (rather than being an age-related aspect as conjectured above by Frazer). Multi-potent alleles are referred to as pleiotropic, effecting changes to more than one facet of an individual's outward appearance (or even its physiology in some instances).

Whereas the background colouration of normal female adders is typically brown, in normal male adders it is typically grey. So, as I have yet to uncover any accounts of male scarlet vipers (other than those claimed by Leighton, but who did not appear to receive any independent scientific corroboration of his claims) or even pairs of such snakes, let alone any scarlet viper populations, this very distinctively-hued serpent's occurrence may well have been due to a mutant erythrism-inducing gene allele that was sex-linked—as with the mutant allele responsible for tortoiseshell cats, for instance, which are almost always female. Equally, however, and again as with tortoiseshell cats, a freak male erythristic adder specimen may occur very occasionally, which could explain Leighton's supposed male scarlet viper that he captured.

In any case, it is not even as if there is no precedent for the occurrence of a distinctive colour variety limited to female adders. One such variety, very different from the scarlet viper yet equally eye-catching, was noted by the afore-mentioned zoologist George A. Boulenger in his Leighton-cited *Zoologist* article from March 1892 on adder variation:

> A very pretty colour-variety, which affects only females, is olive with brick-red band and spots.

Moreover, colour morphs tend to arise spontaneously across the full extent of the distribution range of the species to which they belong, yet are often of only very localised occurrence within any one region of that full distribution range (the latter anomaly being caused by genetic drift). Needless to say, this unusual pattern of distribution corresponds precisely with that of the scarlet viper. And because of this colour variety's rarity both generally and locally, it is very likely that the sex-linked mutant allele causing its erythristic state is recessive, i.e. expressed only by individuals possessing two copies of this allele.

Finally, numerous cultures down through time and right across the globe have nurtured mistaken folk-beliefs claiming that various reptile forms seen more rarely or appearing stranger in appearance than commonly-spied, typical versions are more dangerous, or, specifically, more venomous. Indeed, there are even many cases on record of entirely harmless, wholly non-venomous reptiles being vehemently yet erroneously deemed to be lethally toxic. Consequently, local claims that the scarlet viper is more venomous than adders of normal colouration are by no means unprecedented, but unless they are ever scientifically confirmed they cannot be automatically considered factual.

In short, the so-called scarlet or small red viper of Leighton and certain other herpetological chroniclers from the late 1800s/early 1900s was not a separate species at all. Instead, it was simply based upon sightings of erythristic female common adders whose aberrant colouration is due to the expression of a specific mutant gene allele that is probably recessive and apparently sex-linked.

On 3 September 2013, I uploaded a very much shorter version of the above account onto my *ShukerNature* blog (at that time, I hadn't discovered Leighton's book or any of the other early reports reproduced here), in the hope that it may elicit some additional, contemporary information concerning scarlet vipers. And, sure enough, it did.

Later that very same day, my blog received a response from a reader with the user-name Ingo, who informed me:

> Reddish *Vipera berus* are not unknown. I do know no specimens from the locations you name, but you may find some pics of specimens with quite some red here:
>
> http://www.flickr.com/photos/anthonytinti/8503738237/
>
> http://www.hylawerkgroep.be/jeroen/index.php?id=58
>
> Here you find an almost patternless very red female:
>
> http://www.viperas.de/images/herpetofauna/dtarten/schlangen/kreuzotter/berus-daniel.jpg

The first of the three above links provided by Ingo was to a *V. berus* photograph posted on *Flickr* by a user called Antho-NY, who had snapped it on 24 February 2013. No location details were given. Interestingly, although its dorsal zigzag was indeed brown rather than black, this specimen's background colour was actually bright gold rather than red. Needless to say, however, a golden viper is no less noteworthy than a scarlet one!

The second of Ingo's links was to an illustrated report of a short herpetological field trip to Belgium and France during 8-13 June 2011 by Jeroen Speybroeck and some friends. Among the photos snapped by Jeroen during their trip and included in this online report was one of an adder, but it was merely brown rather than the red colouration that I'd been expecting. Thus it would simply appear to be a normal brown female *V. berus* specimen, and therefore not relevant to the subject of scarlet vipers.

The third of Ingo's links, conversely, was to a close-up photo of a truly extraordinary *V. berus* specimen—as snapped by someone referred to as Daniel, and featured on Andrei Schmid's *Viperas* website based in Germany. Brick-red in background colour, with a dorsal zigzag pattern of comparable shade and therefore only discernible by virtue of its darker edging, this spectacular serpent was unequivocally a scarlet viper!

Also on 3 September 2013, I received the following comment and link relating to scarlet vipers from Danish zoologist and cryptozoological researcher Lars Thomas of Copenhagen University's Zoology Museum:

> They are not exactly common in Denmark, but you do see them now and then—
> http://www.naturplan.dk/foto/preview.php?id=2788

The link took me to a photograph on the Danish website *Naturplan Foto* that had been snapped in Tange Bakker, Ribe, Denmark by Lars Multha Rasmussen. It depicted a very striking bright-red specimen of *V. berus*—in short, another bona fide scarlet viper!

Moreover, on 28 October 2013, Dr Guntram Deichsel from Germany kindly emailed to me a pdf file containing a selection of superb close-up colour photographs snapped by him and various colleagues of some very eye-catching *V. berus* colour varieties encountered in Germany.

These included: a melanistic specimen, snapped by Jochen Weidelener on 12 July 2004 in Emerfeld (the German vernacular name for this all-black morph is 'hell adder'); a black but incompletely-melanistic specimen (as it sported a very conspicuous white lip), snapped by Guntram on 28 April 2000 in Bad Wurzach; two separate photos of a reddish-brown female specimen with a normal grey male, both photos snapped by Guntram on 24 May 1964 in

Normal grey male and white-lipped melanistic European adders *Vipera berus* (© Dr Guntram Deichsel, CC BY 2.5)

Bad Buchau (the German vernacular name for scarlet female vipers is 'copper adder'); another, brighter reddish-brown female specimen, snapped by Joachim Rutschke in April 2013 at Gifhorn; and a black specimen with a distinctive red head, snapped by Guntram in May 2004 at Oberstdorf; plus, most interesting of all from a geographical standpoint, what Guntram referred to as a red female specimen with a normal male, snapped by him on 3 May 2006 at the New Forest Reptiliary in Dorset, England!

And indeed, if not actually scarlet, this female adder was certainly copper-coloured, as described for some specimens of the scarlet viper featured in early English reports. Excitingly, therefore, it would seem that the scarlet viper morph still exists in England after all.

In a follow-up email of 29 December 2013, Guntram confirmed that in some red specimens, the brown dorsal zigzag pattern is virtually absent. This readily recalls the brick-red specimen photographed by Daniel.

From the unequivocal photographic and testimonial evidence provided by Ingo, Lars Thomas, and Guntram Deichsel, so-called

5 | THE SCARLET VIPER

scarlet or small red *V. berus* specimens evidently do still occur today, in both Britain and continental Europe. Equally, my original line of speculation that such snakes most probably constitute a recessive, sex-linked, genetically-induced erythristic morph of *V. berus* rather than any taxonomically-discrete form is evidently correct.

And so, I hereby proclaim another very colourful mystery (in every sense) of the herpetological kind duly solved!

6
A SELECTION OF SECRET ASIAN AND AUSTRALASIAN SNAKES

> Drawings resembling tsuchinoko on stoneware dating back to the ancient Jōmon Period (14,000 BC to 300 BC) have been discovered in Gifu and Nagano. An encyclopaedia from the Edo Period [1603-1867 AD] contains a description of the tsuchinoko under the name tatsui hebi. Accounts of the tsuchinoko can also be found in the *Kojiki*, Japan's oldest surviving book from 680 AD.
>
> Richard Freeman—*The Great Yokai Encyclopaedia*

New species of snake are discovered in the vast areas of Asia and Australasia every year, and, judging from the selection of mystifying ophidian forms documented in this chapter, there might be some particularly notable and unusual examples still awaiting formal scientific recognition and description.

JAPAN'S TOBLERONIC TZUCHINOKO

One of Japan's most famous mystery animals, long reported yet never zoologically confirmed, is a very distinctive but highly elusive snake known as the tzuchinoko (aka tsuchinoko). According to centuries of traditional lore as well as many modern-day sightings reported from various regions of field, forest, and hilly terrain on the Japanese islands of Honshu, Shikoku, and Kyushu (but apparently not on Hokkaido, the fourth main Japanese island)), this remarkable reptile is quite short in length (no more than 3-4 ft) but very thick-bodied, and is sometimes portrayed diagrammatically as slug-like. According to more detailed descriptions, however, its body is prominently ridged dorsally and very flattened ventrally, which means that it has a noticeably triangular cross-sectional shape when viewed head-on. Consequently, this peculiar serpent has been memorably likened in some reports to one of Toblerone's famously triangular chocolate bars!

Other noteworthy characteristics include a readily-delineated neck and tail, a triangular head, clearly-defined facial pits, and a pair of squat horn-like projections above its small round eyes. In colour, it is iridescent dark grey and brown above, bearing about ten large black spots, but is bright orange underneath, and has very large body scales.

From the plethora and often very disparate array of contemporary reports, one of the most revealing and herpetologically relevant accounts remains that of a Mr and Mrs Tsujimoto, who encountered a tzuchinoko in 1970, while walking in the vicinity of Tojikimi, a mountain village southeast of Osaka. Pausing for a rest, they sat down upon a tree stump close to what they thought was a broken-off branch from it—until the 'branch' moved. They then realised that it was actually a short but extremely thick-bodied, short-tailed snake, which appeared to be triangular rather than circular

Tzuchinoko, artistic reconstruction
(© Michael Dethier/International Society of Cryptozoology)

in cross-section, and bore several dull-coloured spots (which they likened to those of a boa constrictor) upon the large brown scales of its body. The snake moved away from them at appreciable speed, travelling up the path that they had been on, and had soon vanished from sight.

In May 2000, a supposed tzuchinoko was killed by a farmer and buried, but was subsequently disinterred and its remains sent for identification to Prof. Kuniyasu Satoh at Kawasaki University of Medical Welfare. However, the farmer had described the creature's face as being round and cat-like in shape, very different from the triangular, horned form traditionally described for the tzuchinoko. After examining its carcase, Prof. Satoh announced that that he had been able to reconstruct the dead snake's bone structure from its remains, and he estimated its total length at 4 ft. Its largest ventral scales were approximately 2 in across, and the morphology of its dorsal scales corresponded with those of Japan's tiger water snake *Rhabdophis tigrinus*, a venomous colubrid. Also consistent with this species was a small fang found on the dead snake's maxillae. Thus Satoh concluded that this was indeed the identity of the latter specimen (though conceding that it was a notably large one). As this species bears no resemblance to classic accounts of the tzuchinoko, I can only assume that the farmer had been mistaken when claiming the killed snake to be one.

Based upon the report of the Tsujimotos and other consistent descriptions, longstanding tzuchinoko researchers Michel Dethier and Ayako Dethier-Sakamoto have speculated that if such a snake genuinely exists, it may be a mutant form of the Japanese pit viper *Gloydius* (=*Agkistrodon*) *blomhoffii*, or possibly even a related but totally new, still-undescribed species.

CRYPTOPHIDION—VIETNAM'S SECRET SERPENT

The volume for 1992 of the International Society of Cryptozoology's journal *Cryptozoology* marked a notable first in the history of zoological discovery. Contained within its pages was a paper presenting the formal description of a hitherto unknown snake—the very first time that a new species had been officially described and named within what was then the world's only peer-reviewed scientific journal devoted to cryptozoology.

Even so, all was not quite as straightforward as it initially seemed, as I duly revealed in my book *The Encyclopaedia of New and Rediscovered Animals* (2012). Here is what I wrote.

Sole occupant of a new genus too, this species had been dubbed the Vietnamese sharp-nosed snake *Cryptophidion annamense* by snake anatomist Dr Van Wallach and vertebrate taxonomist Dr Gwilym S. Jones from Boston's Northeastern University. Its type (and only) specimen, obtained west of Da Nang, in Annam, central Vietnam, during 1968, was one of a series of zoological specimens collected by Jones and various other colleagues while serving as U.S. naval officers during the Vietnam War. These were destined for the Smithsonian Institution's National Museum of Natural History, but somehow the type of *Cryptophidion* was lost before it could be sent to the Smithsonian, and has never been seen since. All that

Cryptophidion, ventral surface
(© International Society of Cryptozoology)

remain to confirm its erstwhile existence are three photographic slides (one showing the entire specimen ventrally in a coiled-up pose, and two showing close-up lateral views of its head), deposited in the slide collection of Harvard University's Museum of Comparative Zoology (Department of Herpetology), and it was upon these that its description by Wallach and Jones was based.

Judging from the morphological details of its type specimen (probably an adult female) depicted in the slides, *Cryptophidion* seems to be a snake adapted for a fossorial (burrowing) existence. However, it possesses a number of very distinctive features that collectively render it quite unlike any other southeast Asian snake. These include a depressed snout with a laterally pointed rostrum, greatly reduced concave nasal shields (scales) separated from the rostrum, an enlarged preorbital shield instead of a loreal and preocular shield, large temporal-like postocular shields, a temporolabial shield, and a short tail. Indeed, in the opinion of Wallach and Jones *Cryptophidion* appears to be so distinct from all other serpents that they were not even entirely certain as to which taxonomic family it rightfully belongs. On account of its distinct neck, almost flat belly, fairly slim tail, and typical anterior ventral scales, however, they considered that it most probably belongs to the colubrids.

Not everyone, conversely, shares their view regarding the dramatically discrete taxonomic status of *Cryptophidion*. On the contrary: in response to the Wallach and Jones paper, herpetologists Dr Olivier Pauwels from France's National Museum of Natural History in Paris and Dr Danny Meirte from the Royal Museum for Central Africa in Tervuren, Belgium, presented a detailed morphological comparison of *Cryptophidion* with another somewhat enigmatic, rare burrowing serpent from Asia known as the sunbeam snake *Xenopeltis unicolor*, and they concluded that the two species are one and the same.

This identification was in turn discounted by vertebrate zoologist Dr James D. Lazell who acted as one of the three editorial reviewers of the Wallach and Jones paper. Lazell readily dismissed any close degree of similarity between what he considered to be an undeniably colubrine *Cryptophidion* and the neckless, thick-tailed, boa-like *Xenopeltis*. This opinion was also reiterated in a response by Wallach and Jones themselves.

Without any additional specimens of *Cryptophidion* having been procured so far to resolve the problematical issue of its identity, however, this is where the saga of Annam's anonymous snake draws to a close, at least for the present time. Does it truly constitute a major herpetological discovery, or is it merely an unfortunate artefact of misidentification? Only time, and further specimens, will tell.

Sunbeam snake *Xenopeltis unicolor* (Bernard Dupont, CC BY-SA 2.0)

MYANMAR'S BU-RIN AND THE MEKONG'S NAGA—GIANT WATER SNAKES?

In 2001, American zoologist Dr Alan Rabinowitz documented his recent explorations of Myanmar (formerly Burma) in his book *Beyond the Last Village*, and included a short but tantalising account of a very dramatic mystery snake. He learnt of it while visiting a northern Burmese village called Putao, whose inhabitants spoke of a gigantic water snake known as the bu-rin, which they claimed attained a length of 40-50 ft and was very dangerous, attacking swimmers and even small boats.

As noted by Dr Rabinowitz, this hostile reptile sounds somewhat like a larger, aquatic version of the Burmese python *Python bivittatus*, but it has never been scientifically identified—always assuming, obviously, that it really does exist, and that even if it does, its length hasn't been grossly exaggerated. Having said that, the bu-rin is not the only mysterious giant water snake reported from this region of Asia.

6 | ASIAN AND AUSTRALASIAN SNAKES

In Hindu and Buddhist mythology, a naga is an ancient serpentine deity, sometimes portrayed as a composite entity uniting the body of a huge snake with the head (and sometimes the torso too) of a human, and bearing an erectile scaly crest resembling the hood of a great cobra on its head—or heads (nagas are often portrayed as multi-headed). In cryptozoology, conversely, 'naga' is the name given to an alleged giant water snake that inhabits the Mekong River constituting the northeastern border of Thailand with Laos.

During an expedition to that area of Thailand in October 2000, British cryptozoologist Richard Freeman collected several hitherto-undocumented eyewitness accounts of this huge serpent. One of these was from Officer Suphat—chief of police in Phon Pisai village. In 1997, he and a group of 30 people had been walking along some cliffs overlooking the Mekong when, gazing down, they saw what initially seemed to be flotsam, floating on the river. Peering closer, however, they realised that it was an enormous black snake, undulating horizontally as it swam against the river's current. According to Officer Suphat's estimate, it measured no less than 230 ft!

Yet even if we factor in a *very* generous allowance for exaggeration or poor size estimation on his part, it was still extremely

A mythological Naga (PD/Pixy)

long—unless part of what seemed to be the creature was actually its wake? Alternatively, although less feasibly, this ostensibly giant serpent may in reality have been a composite—i.e. several smaller snakes swimming in a line. When Suphat recounted their sighting to a monk, however, the monk told him that it was definitely a naga.

A few years earlier, in 1992, workmen seeking to demolish an old derelict temple in Phon Pisai were repeatedly confronted by an immense thick-bodied black snake, which would partially emerge from it and rear up at them whenever they approached. The village's Buddhist abbot also saw it. Only after an offering was left for this giant serpent did it finally depart, enabling the workmen to raze the old temple and replace it with an ornate modern version that is still there today.

Yet these are just reports, which may or may not be true. However, hope of examining some much more tangible evidence for the naga's reality was raised when Richard learnt of a purported naga bone, preserved inside a silver chalice as a holy relic and retained in Phon Pisai. Disappointingly, however, when he was granted permission to view the bone and the chalice was opened, all that it contained was a readily-identifiable elephant tooth!

It is interesting to note that the ophidian deities known as nagas are often depicted in traditional Asian art as huge black snakes (multiple heads notwithstanding!), thereby closely corresponding with their cryptozoological namesakes. One famous example is a beautiful illustration from a Bhagavata Purana manuscript dating from around 1640 AD that portrays the Hindu god Krishna dancing upon the subdued body of Kaliya—a huge black-scaled naga. Could these legendary snake-bodied gods have therefore been inspired at least in part by encounters with real-life giant black snakes in Asia? Richard has speculated that the naga may be an undiscovered species of modern-day madtsoiid, most famously represented by Australia's officially extinct *Wonambi* species (see Chapter 9 for more details).

Needless to say, however, it will take more than a misidentified elephant's tooth, or even an exquisite 380-year-old work of art, to convince science that such mega-snakes genuinely exist. But Asia is famously supplied with profuse numbers of temples and all manner of sacred relics contained within them. Who knows—perhaps somewhere concealed amid these revered edifices' incense-perfumed shadows and silence are some treasured tokens from a bona fide naga or two, just waiting to be noticed one day by someone with the necessary herpetological expertise to recognise precisely what they are.

PARKER'S SNAKE—A PUZZLE FROM PAPUA NEW GUINEA

In his book *A Guide to the Snakes of Papua New Guinea* (1996), renowned British snake expert Mark O'Shea devoted an entire page to an enigmatic, still-unidentified, but seemingly highly venomous PNG snake of aquatic lifestyle that he has dubbed Parker's snake, in honour of Australian herpetologist Fred Parker, who had first brought this mysterious serpent to scientific attention in his own book *The Snakes of Western Province* (1982). Both researchers have sought it in the field, but without success, despite specifically visiting the Western Province village of Wipim where it reputedly killed three children (see below). Between them, however, they have collected some valuable information from the local people, who, unsurprisingly, greatly fear this reptile.

In his book, Parker had reported the rapid deaths of three young girls allegedly bitten by this snake while bathing in the Ouwe Creek near Wipim during 1972-73. Other reports of it from further afield have also occurred, but without any attributed deaths. Based upon eyewitness descriptions and other native testimony, Parker's snake is an extremely venomous but also very rare aquatic snake measuring no more than 6.5 ft long, yellowish-brown to brown dorsally and pale yellow to white ventrally, with smooth scales, enlarged ventrals, and a short cylindrical tail. It is said to favour small freshwater swamps and inland streams rather than larger rivers or open swampy grassland. Although it has been seen basking on dry land, it apparently prefers hiding on the muddy bottom. Death resulting from a bite by this snake is very rapid, within just a few minutes, which is much faster than from a taipan or even a sea-snake bite.

As Mark O'Shea noted in his book, he and Parker have considered a number of possible identities for this mystery serpent. These include New Guinea's mildly venomous dog-faced water snake *Cerberus rynchops* (with its toxicity presumably exaggerated by locals), the extremely venomous mulga or king brown snake *Pseudechis australis* (although this Australian elapid has yet to be formally recorded from New Guinea), the small-eyed snake *Micropechis ikaheka* (another highly venomous elapid but this time known from New Guinea), and even some form of sea-snake or taipan. Yet as Mark freely conceded, none of these wholly corresponds with the local accounts given for it. Consequently, Parker's snake currently remains an elusive but tantalizing enigma within the ophidian literature; nothing more concerning it has emerged since the publication of Mark's book in 1996, as he confirmed to me during a *Facebook* communication between us on 22 January 2022.

AN AUSSIE MYSTERY SNAKE, OR A LEGLESS LIZARD OF OZ?

Not all mysterious snakes are huge, as exemplified by the following tantalisingly vague report of a diminutive form of unidentified serpent from Australia:

> I once came across 2 little snakes in a waterhole, somewhere in the outback (can't remember where, it was about nine years ago [i.e. c.1999] and I was travelling all around Oz) but they were about 20 cm [8 in] long with a magenta head and a yellow body. I have never been able to find a picture or find out anything about them, too bad I didn't have a camera!!

This report was posted onto the *Aussie Pythons & Snakes* online forum by someone with the username Charlie on 24 January 2008, but it received no response. So as far as I'm aware, no conclusive taxonomic identification of his small yet strikingly-coloured waterhole snakes was ever forthcoming. Nor have I had greater success than Charlie in identifying them.

On 13 November 2021, I posted Charlie's intriguing report on various *Facebook* groups devoted to cryptozoology to see what response (if any) it elicited. Several identities for the snakes were duly suggested, including the Australian tree snake *Dendrelaphis punctulatus*, red-naped snake *Furina diadema*, woma python *Aspidites ramsayi*, young specimens of the black-headed python *A. melanocephalus*, and young western brown snakes *Pseudonaja nuchalis*, but none of these corresponds closely with Charlie's description of the small, very distinctively-hued snakes that he spied.

In view of their miniature size, moreover, it is conceivable that they were not snakes at all, but instead a species of legless lizard, of which there are quite a few endemic to Australia. Some of these, moreover, are deceptively serpentine in outward appearance, especially to those who may not be too familiar with snakes—but yet again I have been unable to obtain pictures of any such reptile that matches those two mystery specimens encountered by Charlie.

An anomalous Aussie mystery snake, or a legendary lizard of Oz? Could it even be that these creatures weren't reptiles at all, but perhaps some form of invertebrate—a species of annelid worm, for instance, or planarian flatworm, the latter of which includes some brightly-coloured Australian species? Any thoughts or suggestions would be greatly welcomed!

THE UNOFFICIAL SNAKES OF NEW ZEALAND

Apart from the frozen ice continent of Antarctica, there are very few snake-free places on Earth. The latter include the island of Ireland, Greenland, Iceland, Hawaii, and New Zealand. Having said that, down through the years various snake specimens have been captured in all of these localities, but they have tended to be nothing more exciting than escapee/released non-native pets or specimens that have stowed away on ships (or even on aeroplanes) arriving from overseas. However, in relation to this scenario of unofficial snakes for New Zealand, an additional, much more dramatic (albeit improbable) possibility may also exist.

Recently, I was startled to discover that there have been a fair few reports of snakes existing in several widely separate locations on both the North Island and the South Island of New Zealand. In a fascinating online article of 3 September 2020 for *The Spinoff*, investigator Charlie O'Mannin, who has sought these unofficial ophidians in both the literature and the field, carefully reviewed this extremely interesting albeit hitherto-obscure herpetological subject.

Perhaps the most persistent example concerns claims that various old West Coast gold mines contain thriving, perpetuating populations of Australian copperheads. These venomous elapid snakes belong to the genus *Austrelaps*, and there are three species. Namely, the pygmy copperhead *A. labialis* (native to South Australia), the highland or Ramsay's copperhead *A. ramsayi* (New South Wales and Victoria), and the lowland copperhead or superb snake *A. superbus* (New South Wales, Victoria, Tasmania, and South Australia).

Unrelated to their New World namesake the American copperhead *Agkistrodon contortrix*, which is a species of viper, not an elapid, Australian copperheads are medium-sized, averaging around 3.5 ft long, rarely exceeding 6 ft. They are active in cooler climates (as occur in New Zealand), and very diverse in colour, ranging from black through a variety of browns and reds to yellowish, depending upon the individual, but as a result of only being moderately-sized and quite shy, they can be quite elusive even in their native Australian homeland. They earn their common name from their head's predominant (but not always present) copper shade.

In 2014, after interviewing several veteran gold prospectors who vehemently claimed that such stories of copperheads in mines here were true, a journalist duly contacted New Zealand's Ministry of Primary Industries (MPI), who promptly conducted a thorough

Australian pygmy copperhead *Austrelaps labialis*—but do naturalised non-native (or even scientifically-undiscovered native) specimens of *Austrelaps* species also thrive in the wilds of New Zealand? (John Langsford, CC BY-SA 3.0)

search. This was because the putative presence of snakes in NZ is deemed to be a biohazard, on account of the risk that these ostensibly non-native reptiles pose to this island country's indigenous fauna. No snakes were found, but the matter was considered serious enough to warrant the commissioning of a professional herpetologist to prepare a formal report, which included the exact GPS coordinates where according to one prospector in 1990 a copperhead had actually wound itself round his arm before vanishing when shaken off.

O'Mannin obtained a copy of this report and visited the precise location, but no serpent showed itself to him. In his own article, he also includes details of much earlier reported snakes, of which the most intriguing is a metre-long (approx. 3-ft-long) individual encountered in 1875 by loggers working within the Ureweras range, which is one of the most remote regions in the whole of North Island. They swiftly killed it, but how can this specimen's existence there be explained?

Although New Zealand has been isolated from all other land masses for many millions of years, it is home to various native species of lizard and frog, so is it totally beyond the realms of possibility that snakes do exist here too? If so, the chances are that they are nothing more special, zoologically speaking, than escapee/released non-native pets, or even specimens that have stowed away on foreign ships or planes, in imported produce most likely, as noted earlier.

Moreover, prior to the anti-acclimatisation laws enacted in New Zealand during the late 1800s, which forbade the release of non-native species into its countryside, snakes were regularly, freely imported and bred here. And a NZ colleague has informed me that NZ newspapers from 1886 indicate that at least a couple of colonists had success in establishing wild colonies near the old Wellington burroughs on North Island.

Also, some snakes are good swimmers, including, tellingly, the Australian copperheads, so perhaps via a combination of swimming and rafting on floating vegetation, some specimens have made their own way here from southern mainland Australia and/or Tasmania? Indeed, Australian copperheads spend much time in the water, where they hunt and feed primarily upon tadpoles, and frogs. Such invasive forms would therefore pose a particular threat to New Zealand's quartet of unique, mostly rare species of famously archaic, 'living fossil' leiopelmatid frogs if their presence here were to be officially verified.

Least likely, but not impossible, as New Zealand's existing native herpetofauna demonstrates, is that at least one highly-elusive endemic snake species exists here, still awaiting formal scientific discovery and description. This is a very tantalising albeit tenuous prospect, and is one, therefore, that I intend to pay close attention to in the future.

7
WHEN TWO HEADS—OR MORE—
ARE *NOT* BETTER THAN ONE!

> Scientists have long theorized that the more closely related two animals are, the more altruistically they will behave toward each other—a mother and her young, for instance. A two-headed black rat snake is teaching researchers at the University of Tennessee that the theory is not so simple. The snake is called IM (rhymes with him), for "instinct" (left head) and "mind" (right head), and it has been studied for 12 years. Far from being altruistic, the two heads often fight for an hour or more for the privilege of swallowing one mouse, even though the prey is destined for the same stomach. Over the long term, each head swallows about the same weight of food, with the right head—the more mobile—wolfing down larger mice, and the left head settling for smaller but more numerous victims, according to Gordon Burghardt, a professor of psychology and zoology. Burghardt said it appears that the head that swallows the prey is less likely to act hungry afterward than the head that did not, indicating that the act of eating, not just what is in the stomach, plays a role in the hunger drive.
>
> *Washington Post* (Washington), 6 February 1989.

Cryptozoologists are accustomed to receiving healthy doses of scepticism from mainstream zoological colleagues concerning reports of mysterious, exotic-sounding creatures. Over the years, however,

I have been very startled to discover that much the same response can sometimes be elicited by teratologists (researchers studying biological freaks and monstrosities) when speaking to mainstream colleagues regarding zoological caprices and curiosities of the teratological kind.

A modern-day two-headed snake specimen
(Ventus55, CC BY-SA 3.0)

Several years ago, I happened to mention casually to some zoologist friends a then quite recent newspaper report about the finding of a two-headed (dicephalous aka bicephalic) snake. To my great surprise, no amount of persuading would convince any of them that freaks of this kind do genuinely occur from time to time (usually due to a developmental aberration in which the embryonic snake's cephalic region is duplicated). Instead, they were adamant that such sports were total fabrications invented by the media to fool gullible readers!

Needless to say, this spurred me to research the subject of ophidian dicephaly. Consequently, in order to dispel any additional scepticism that may exist concerning it, there now follows a selection of some of the most celebrated, fully-confirmed serpentine dicephali on record.

7 | TWO HEADS OR MORE

In his *Log-Book of a Fisherman and Zoologist* (1875), the noted Victorian naturalist and eccentric Frank Buckland recorded receiving an odder-than-normal two-headed grass snake *Natrix natrix*, aged at least 3-4 months old. Whereas many dicephalous snakes have similar heads, those of Buckland's grass snake differed both in size and in location. The larger of the two heads was positioned at the end of the snake's neck (i.e. the normal position). However, the smaller head emerged directly (i.e. not borne upon any neck of its own) from a lateral location some distance further down—thereby emerging from the neck of the principal head, and constituting a parasitic twin. A dicephalous snake (or other animal) exhibiting this condition—in which one head (that of the parasitic twin) is attached either to the neck or lower jaw of the other head—is said to be desmiognathous.

During the 1920s, a wild dicephalous specimen of the milk snake *Lampropeltis triangulum* was discovered living wild in the grounds of New York's Bronx Zoo. Unlike Buckland's grass snake, however, its two heads were of equal size, and each was borne upon its own 1-inch-long neck (dicephalous animals with two necks as well as two heads are described as diauchenic). Not surprisingly, this highly distinctive serpent was swiftly captured, thereafter

A two-headed milk snake *Lampropeltis triangulum*
(Jenny Kirkhart, CC BY 2.0)

acquiring permanent residence at the zoo as a special exhibit, and was the focus of considerable attention—not least from its own keeper, particularly at feeding time. This was because both of its heads ingested food, which meant that great care had to be taken in order to ensure that its single oesophagus (gullet) did not become blocked by the double stream of food passing into it simultaneously from the snake's two mouths.

Similarly, from 19 March to July 1955 the Arizona-Sonora Desert Museum was the proud owner of a juvenile dicephalous pine snake *Pituophis melanoleucus*, which lived upon lizards devoured only by the left head. In 1983, a dicephalous water snake *Nerodia sipedon* became a major attraction at Miami's Serpentarium, and was featured in numerous newspaper accounts that year. The Serpentarium's director, Bill Haast, named the two heads Hatfield and McCoy, after the notorious feuding families from West Virginia. As it happened, however, these names would have been far more apt if they had been applied to the heads of what is probably the most remarkable two-headed snake recorded from captivity.

Instead, the heads of this latter serpentine dicephalus were respectively named Dudley and Duplex, by staff at San Diego Zoo, California, where it lived for some time during the 1970s. A

A two-headed California kingsnake
Lampropeltis getulus californiae (PD/Vassil)

7 | TWO HEADS OR MORE

diauchenic example, it was a king snake *Lampropeltis getulus*—a zoological identity destined to cause major problems for any two-headed representative, due to this particular species' dietary preference. For the king snake, albeit non-venomous, is ophiophagous—it eats other snakes! Imagine, then, the psychological turmoil that must have been taking place within the twin minds of Dudley-Duplex. For here was a situation in which two mentally-independent snakes, both instinctive serpent-eaters, were, by a developmental quirk of fate, doomed to be perpetually in one another's closest of close company. Tormented by continuous temptation, it could surely be only a matter of time before the inevitable happened.

And one day it nearly did—keepers arrived only just in time to prevent Dudley from being swallowed by Duplex! On this occasion, peace was restored, and the crisis was averted, but quite evidently the memory lingered. For not long afterwards, Dudley took his revenge and actually succeeded in swallowing Duplex—only to discover too late of course that in killing Duplex he had fatally wounded himself. A short time later, this extraordinary but ultimately tragic double-act died—a victim of a truly unique case of fatal attraction.

Such a dire situation is made even more so, however, if the dicephalous snake in question belongs to a venomous species. One such example, with a finale as sad but unequivocally final in every sense as that which befell Dudley-Duplex, was recorded by Irish-born South African herpetologist F.M. [Frederick William] Fitz-Simons in his book *Snakes* (1932). The events occurred during his time as the director of a snake farm that he had founded in 1918 at the Port Elizabeth Museum, South Africa, and here is his account of this poignant but powerful tale of serpentine treachery and lethal revenge:

> We once had a freak snake of this sort [dicephalous], with three inches of neck to each head. . . . One day Johannes gave the two heads a frog apiece and left them to dispose of the food. The following morning he looked into the box to see if all was well, but to his amazement he noticed one head had swallowed the other down to where the body divided. Being hastily summoned, I discovered the head that had

been swallowed was not dead. After gentle massaging the tangle was straightened out, but the heads were subsequently not as friendly as formerly, and one day the end came. The brain which had temporarily become a meal, seemingly never forgave the other. The indignity of being swallowed rankled. What the immediate provocation actually was I do not know, but it had evidently attacked the other head with full intent to kill, because both heads and body were found cold and dead. The snake was of the Back-fanged species, it being one of the Schaapsteker [colubrid sand snake] genus (*Psammophis*). The aggressive head had bitten the other repeatedly and injected sufficient venom to cause death; and the other had retaliated. This we verified by a post-mortem.

As also noted in the longstanding study of a two-headed eastern black rat snake *Pantherophis alleghaniensis* documented in the newspaper report quoted by me at the beginning of this chapter, it is certainly clear that in spite of a dicephalous snake's two heads being intimately related to one another genetically speaking, they exhibit no degree of altruism towards one another that is often seen between closely-related non-conjoined individuals especially (but by no means exclusively) in a wide range of higher vertebrate species.

A particularly unusual dicephalous snake was captured on 13 May 1975 at Salta, Argentina. This specimen's single body not only sported two heads but also possessed two tails. An individual that displays duplication of its anterior and posterior ends whereas its body region remains a single entity is referred to as a dicephalus dipygus (or, less commonly nowadays, an anakatadidymus). Measuring 18 in long, Salta's two-headed two-tailed snake was also unusual in that only one head ingested food (albeit voraciously), the other not functioning at all. In view of the Dudley-Duplex and South African sand snake sagas, however, this may have been no bad thing—two heads are not always better than one after all!

The October/November 1990 issue of a British magazine entitled *The Countryman* contained a very interesting article by Andrew Allen concerning two-headed specimens of the barred grass snake *Natrix helvetica*. He notes that the occurrence of these

7 | TWO HEADS OR MORE

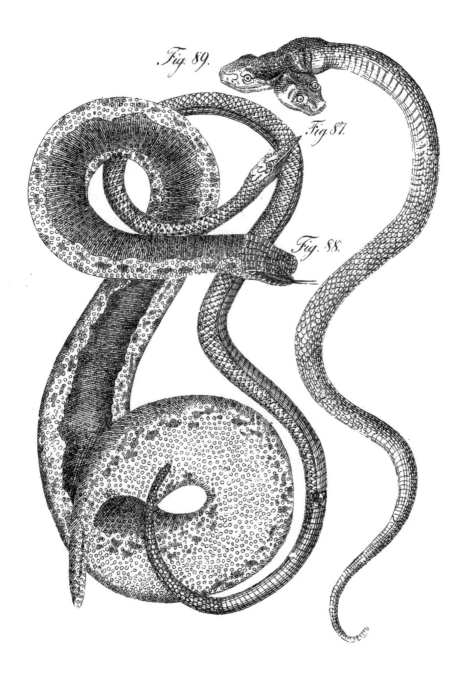

Vintage engraving of a two-headed or bicephalic snake

freak individuals, to which this particular snake species seems particularly prone, is temperature-related. To avoid risks posed by the notoriously uncertain, fickle nature of the British weather, it ensures that its eggs are exposed to continual warmth and thereby a high rate of successful hatching by laying them inside compost heaps. Sometimes, however, the heat inside such heaps fluctuates dramatically, and according to Allen this causes grass snake dicephaly:

> . . . the temperature inside a manure heap can fluctuate violently, sometimes reaching levels more like an oven than an incubator (hayricks sometimes burst into flame of their own volition, as a result of internal combustion). These thermal fluctuations—of much greater amplitude than those recorded in ordinary soil, at the depths where other oviparous lizards and snakes lay their eggs—disrupt the development of embryos, and are responsible for the abnormalities, such as double-heading, which plague the grass snake.
>
> It is easy to reproduce this effect in the laboratory. If grass snake eggs are incubated at a constant 29-33°C (the average temperature inside a clump of eggs in a manure-heap), the hatching rate is up to 95 per cent with no abnormalities. If the eggs are incubated at a fairly constant 29-33°C but with fluctuations up to 40, 45 or 50°C (mirroring more closely the real environment as recorded by microthermometers inserted into a clump of grass-snake eggs deep inside a compost heap), the hatching rate falls to about 80 per cent and up to 1 per cent of the newborn grass snakes are dicephalous.

Finally: according to a brief but highly intriguing reptile-based aside by Dr James F. Gemmill in his classic tome *The Teratology of Fishes* (1912), in the older records a snake with *three* heads is stated to have been seen at Lake Ontario in the USA. There is also an account reported by the eminent Italian naturalist Ulisse Aldrovandi (1522-1605) of a three-headed snake that was killed in the Pyrenees. Confirming that at least the embryological occurrence of tricephalic

7 | TWO HEADS OR MORE

A TWO-HEADED SNAKE is a curiosity at Kansas State University's Fairchild museum these days. The 14-inch long bull snake was found accidentally about three weeks ago by Robert Mortimer, a farmer living near Delphos. The snake is being studied by K-State scientists. In this photo it can be seen that the heads join about an inch down the spine.

Two-headed bullsnake found at Delphos, Kansas (Manhattan, KS, *Mercury,* December 7, 1960)

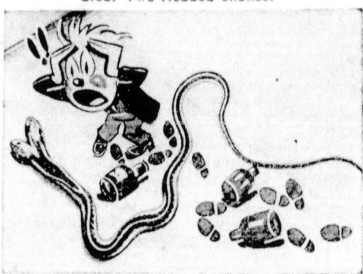

Photo of a two-headed garter snake (with comic elements added), found in California (Waterloo, IA, *Courier,* July 16, 1944)

Ornate gilded statue of a naga at the Wat Phra Kaew in the Royal Palaces at Bangkok, Thailand (© Dr Karl Shuker)

snakes is not impossible, in a paper published by the Swiss scientific journal *Anatomischer Anzeiger* in 1900, Berlin-based biologist G. Wetzel figured a very early stage in the development of a European grass snake *N. natrix* in which there were three centres of segmentation on the yolk, and one of the centres was itself double.

And speaking of alleged multi-headed snakes . . .

MODERN-DAY NAGAS—OR PHOTOSHOPPED FRAUDS?

According to Hindu and Buddhist mythology, nagas are ancient serpent deities that can take human or semi-human form, and in Buddhist mythology a naga can have several heads (see also Chapter 6 of the present book). They are most often represented as huge cobras with expanded hoods.

One famous legend tells of how the Lord Buddha was shaded from the searing rays of the sun while asleep by the hoods of the multi-headed naga king Muchilinda. In another version of this story, Muchilinda protects him in this same manner from a severe rainstorm while he is meditating under the Bodhi tree.

Needless to say, however, no such thing as a multi-headed cobra exists in the realm of zoology. True, there are some fully-confirmed cases of two-headed cobras, but nothing more dramatic. This is why, when several different people forwarded me the following photograph at the beginning of March 2012, I was intrigued—but only for a moment.

Closer observation made it readily apparent to me that this three-headed cobra owed its additional heads not to the fickle fortune of teratology but rather to the deft digital manipulation of Photoshop. For whereas a bona fide three-headed snake (assuming that such an entity could ever survive to adulthood anyway) would hold its heads at differing angles and heights, the "three little maids in a row" orientation of this photographed specimen clearly exposed its Photoshopped origin, in which the head of a normal cobra had simply been triplicated and the overlapping edges deftly blended to yield this eye-catching if wholly fake naga lookalike.

But don't take my word for it. Readily accessible online is a selection of other three-headed and also some five-headed Photoshopped cobras. And if five heads aren't enough, there's even an impressive twelve-headed specimen!

124 SECRET SNAKES AND SERPENT SURPRISES

Fake three-headed cobra created via digital manipulation (USC Title 17 § 107)

Fake twelve-headed cobra created via digital manipulation (USC Title 17 § 107)

Finally, if you want a modern-day naga of your own, this is how to obtain one—a YouTube video produced by a Photoshop crafter with the YT user name Rijil kv and presently accessible at https://www.youtube.com/watch?v=_czlKY0jDK4 shows precisely how to create a five-headed cobra with Photoshop in just two minutes!

And then people wonder why I don't have much faith any more in photographic evidence alone when attempting to determine the validity or otherwise of a cryptozoological case!

8
SECRETS OF THE SNAKE-STONES—CHARTING THEIR HISTORIES AND MYSTERIES

> A very curious subject . . . is the power of extracting venom from a wound inflicted by reptiles, attributed to the 'snake-stone,' which the Hindoos and Cingalese usually carry with them.
>
> Philip H. Gosse—*The Romance of Natural History, Second Series*

Snake-stones and their alleged powers of extracting venom from ostensibly fatal snakebites have generated substantial debate for centuries. Many adamantly deny that there is any truth to the numerous accounts on record, but there are others who believe just as firmly that the prompt application of one of these strange objects has saved them from certain death. Nowadays, they scarcely rate a mention in wildlife books, but many pre-20th-Century works contained detailed accounts, including the following selection. Read them now, and consider for yourself the extraordinary case of the snake-stones.

The use of snake-stones and their supposed properties have been reported from many parts of the world harbouring highly venomous snakes, but in particular from those frequented by arguably the most famous venomous snake of all—*Naja naja,* the Asian spectacled cobra or cobra de capello ('hooded cobra'), a name commonly applied to it prior to the 1900s but not so widely used today. Some of the most familiar accounts of snake-stone use in relation to cobra bites are those included in Sir James Emerson Tennent's book *Sketches of the Natural History of Ceylon* (1861), where the snake-stone is referred to as the pamboo-kaloo. These incidents featured some impeccable eyewitnesses. For example:

> On one occasion, in March, 1854, a friend of mine was riding, with some other civil officers of the Government, along a jungle path in the vicinity of Bintenne, when he saw one of two Tamils, who were approaching the party, suddenly dart into the forest and return, holding in both hands a cobra de capello which he had seized by the head and tail. He called to his companion for assistance to place it in their covered basket, but, in doing this, he handled it so inexpertly that it seized him by the finger, and retained its hold for a few seconds, as if unable to retract its fangs. The blood flowed, and intense pain appeared to follow almost immediately but, with all expedition, the friend of the sufferer undid his waist-cloth, and took from it two snake-stones, each of the size of a small almond, intensely black and highly polished, though of an extremely light substance. These he applied, one to each wound inflicted by the teeth of the serpent, to which they attached themselves closely; the blood that oozed from the bites being rapidly imbibed by the porous texture of the article applied. The stones adhered tenaciously for three or four minutes, the wounded man's companion in the meanwhile rubbing his arm downwards from the shoulder towards the fingers. At length, the snake-stones dropped off of their own accord; the suffering of the man appeared to subside; he twisted his fingers till the joints cracked, and went on his way without concern.

The second incident related by Tennent is no less astonishing:

In another instance, in 1853, Mr. Lavalliere, then District Judge of Kandy, informed me that he saw a snake-charmer in the jungle, close by the town, search for a cobra de capello, and, after disturbing one in its retreat, the man tried to secure it, but, in the attempt, he was bitten in the thigh till blood trickled from the wound. He instantly applied the *Pamboo-Kaloo,* which adhered closely for about ten minutes, during which time he passed the root which he held in his hand backwards and forwards above the stone, till the latter dropped to the ground. He assured M. Lavalliere that all danger was then past. That gentleman obtained from him the snake-stone he had relied on, and saw him repeatedly afterwards in perfect health.

The root used by the snake-charmer seems to have been either the stem of an *Aristolochia* (a woody vine called Dutchman's pipe) or that of some other form of jungle vine. As for the snake-stone's composition, Tennent later submitted one to the famous research chemist Prof. Michael Faraday for analysis. In reply, Faraday stated that in his belief it was:

> . . . a piece of charred bone which has been filled with blood perhaps several times, and then carefully charred again. Evidence of this is afforded, as well by the apertures of cells or tubes on its surface as by the fact that it yields and breaks under pressure, and exhibits an organic structure within. When heated slightly, water rises from it, and also a little ammonia; and, if heated still more highly in the air, carbon burns away, and a bulky white ash is left, retaining the shape and size of the stone.

Predictably, the ash proved to be largely calcium phosphate in composition. Continuing with Faraday's comments:

> . . . if the piece of matter has ever been employed as a spongy absorbent, it seems hardly fit for that purpose in its present state; but who can say to what

treatment it has been subjected since it was fit for use, or to what treatment the natives may submit it when expecting to have occasion to use it?

Summing up the case, Tennent concluded, quite reasonably:

> The probability is, that the animal charcoal, when instantaneously applied, may be sufficiently porous and absorbent to extract the venom from the recent wound, together with a portion of the blood, before it has had time to be carried into the system; and that the blood which Mr. Faraday detected in the specimen submitted to him was that of the Indian on whose person the effect was exhibited on the occasion to which my informant was an eye-witness.

Sir James Emerson Tennent

Many snake-stones used in Sri Lanka apparently originate from India, brought to the island by travelling snake-charmers from India's Coromandel coast. Moreover, according to Dr John Davy's book *An Account of the Interior of Ceylon, and of Its Inhabitants* (1821), they also reach Sri Lanka via Indian merchants who purchase them from the monks of Manila, Philippines. Davy described three main types: one composed of partially burnt bone and slightly absorptive, a second manufactured from chalk, and a third made from plant material and resembling bezoar; the latter two are not absorptive.

In view of the plenitude of venomous snakes inhabiting tropical Africa, it should come as no surprise to learn that the use of snake-stones is prevalent here too. As far back as 1772, Swedish naturalist Carl Peter Thunberg described seeing snake-stones used by the Boers in South Africa's Cape Province (as he duly documented in his extensive work *Travels at the Cape of Good Hope, 1772-1775*). Once again these were mostly imported from India, particularly from Malabar, although at such extortionate prices that few of the South African farmers could afford to purchase them. Examining one of these stones, Thunberg described it as being black in colour (hence its alternative name, black-stone), convex on one side, and so porous that bubbles rose out of it when it was plunged into water.

Moreover, a modern-day Kenyan teaching leaflet produced by the organisation REAP (Rural Extension with Africa's Poor), commended the efficiency of black-stones in treating snake bites and scorpion stings, even providing a 'recipe' for creating such stones from sections of cattle thigh bones, at: https://reap-eastafrica.org/wp-content/uploads/2018/04/Black-Stone.pdf. This demonstrates that belief in their powers is still prevalent in Africa.

Snake-stones are also known widely in Latin America. In Peru, they are called the piedra negra, which once again translates as 'black-stone', and are still often utilised. Mexican snake-stones had been brought to popular attention in 1829, by Lieutenant R.W.H. Hardy of the British Royal Navy in his book *Travels in the Interior of Mexico* . . . Three decades later, on 30 January 1860, he communicated some further details, received by Tennent, regarding their preparation. In Mexico, the snake-stone is called the piedra ponsona ('venom-stone'), and according to Hardy is prepared as follows:

> Take a piece of hart's horn [stag antler] of any convenient size and shape; cover it well round with grass

or hay, enclose both in a thin piece of sheet copper well wrapped round them, and place the parcel in a charcoal fire till the bone is sufficiently charred. When cold, remove the calcined horn from its envelope, when it will be ready for immediate use. In this state it will resemble a solid black fibrous substance, of the same shape and size as before it was subjected to this treatment.

USE—The wound being slightly punctured, apply the bone to the opening, to which it will adhere firmly for the space of two minutes; and when it falls, it should be received into a basin of water. It should then be dried in a cloth, and again applied to the wound. But it will not adhere longer than about one minute. In like manner it may be applied a third time; but now it will fall almost immediately, and nothing will cause it to adhere any more. These effects I witnessed in the case of a bite of a rattlesnake at Oposura, a town in the province of Sonora, in Mexico, from whence I obtained my recipe.

Deer antlers, popularly used for making snake-stones (PD)

8 | SNAKE-STONES

This detailed but wholly unsensationalised account aroused the curiosity of English naturalist Rev. J.G. Wood. He decided to follow Hardy's recipe to see if he could indeed manufacture a snake-stone in this manner, and recounted his experience in his multi-volume *Illustrated Natural History* (1859-1863):

> Being desirous of testing the truth of this recipe, I procured a piece of stag's-horn, cut it into proper shape, and exposed it to the heat of a fierce charcoal fire for an hour and a half. On removing it from the copper, the hay had been fused into a black mass, easily broken, and forming a complete cast of the inclosed horn, which fell out like an almond from its shell. On comparing the charred horn with the veritable Snake-stones, I find them to be identical except in the polish. The fracture of both is the same, and when exposed to a white heat in the air, my own specimen burned away, leaving a white ash precisely as related of the real specimen [analysed by Faraday], and the ashes of both are exactly alike, saving that my own is of a purer white than that specimen calcined by Mr Faraday, which has a slight tinge of pink, possibly from the absorbed blood. On throwing it into water, it gave out a vast amount of air from its pores, making the water look for a few seconds as if it were newly opened champagne, a peculiarity which agrees with Thunberg's description of the Snake-stone used at the Cape. The rather high polish of the Cingalese Snake-stone I could not rightly impart to my own specimen, probably for want of patience. I found, however, that by rendering the surface very smooth with a file, and afterwards with emery paper, *before* exposing it to the fire, it could be burnished afterwards by rubbing it with polished steel. Even in the original objects, the polish is not universal, the plane side being much rougher than the convex.

So far, only the application of snake-stones to snake-bites has been mentioned, but in some localities they have wider uses. In Sri Lanka and India, for instance, they are also said to be highly efficacious in the is extraction of venom from scorpion stings, as demonstrated by the following incident, reported by Major-General Edward Napier in his book *Scenes and Sports in Foreign Lands, Vol. 2* (1840):

> These people generally have for sale numbers of *snake-stones,* which are said to be equally an antidote against the bite of the serpent and the sting of the scorpion. For the former I have never seen it tried; and to prove its efficacy with the latter, the samp-wallah generally carries about in small earthen vessels a number of these animals, one of which he allows to wound him with his sting. The snake-stone, which is a dark, shining, smooth pebble, about the size and shape of a French bean, on being applied to the wound, instantly adheres to it, and by a power of suction appears to draw out the poison, which is supposed to be contained in the small bubbles which, on the immersion of the stone into a glass of water, are seen in great numbers to rise to the surface.
>
> My first idea on beholding the samp-wallah allow himself to be stung by the scorpion was, that the latter had by some means been rendered harmless. However, not wishing voluntarily to put this to the test by personal experience, I purchased some of the stones, resolved on the very first opportunity to try their efficacy. Shortly after this, happening to be marching up the country with a detachment, we pitched our camp on some very stony ground, in clearing which one of the English soldiers happened to be bit [stung] in the hand by a large scorpion. As soon as I heard of this circumstance, I sent for the sufferer, who appeared to be in great pain, which he described as a burning sensation running all the way up his arm to the very shoulder.
>
> I applied one of the snake-stones to the puncture; it adhered immediately, and during about eight minutes that it remained on the patient, he by degrees became easier; the pain diminished, gradually coming down from the shoulder, until it appeared entirely

confined to the immediate vicinity of the wound. I now removed the stone: on putting it into a cup of water, numbers of the small air-bubbles rose to the surface, and in a short time the man ceased to suffer any inconvenience from the accident.

In 1927, black, porous 'scorpion-stones' were shown to Dr Graham Netting by the monks of Trinidad's Mount St Benedict. When analysed, they were found to be composed of animal bone charcoal, and when placed upon moistened skin they remained attached until they had absorbed some moisture, after which they dropped off, suggesting that they may indeed be of use in drawing out venom from a freshly inflicted scorpion sting wound. And in rural areas of the USA, so-called 'madstones', created from a variety of substances (including bone, deer antlers, certain porous minerals, and sometimes even semi-precious stones), have been used against scorpion stings, as well as bites from rabid dogs.

One of the most unusual incidents in which a snake-stone was employed was described by D. Hervey (*Nature*, 24 May 1900):

> A good many years ago, when sea-bathing in the Old Straits of Singapore (i.e. those separating the island from the Malay Peninsula), I put my foot in a slight muddy hollow in the sandy sea-bed; the moment I did so, I received an agonising stab near the ankle (from some red-hot poisoned blade, it seemed) which drove me in hot haste ashore, where a Malay constable on hearing what had happened, and on examining the wound, pronounced my assailant to be the 'ikan sembilang' (sembilang fish), *Plotosus canius,* one of the siluroids [catfishes], I am informed by Mr Boulenger of the British Museum. The fish is armed with three powerful spines on the head, one projecting perpendicularly from the top, and one projecting horizontally from each side. The Malay lost no time in running to the barracks near by, whence he shortly returned with a little round charcoal-like stone about the size of a small marble. This he pressed on to the wound, to which it adhered, and remained there by itself, without any continuation of pressure, for a

Plotosus canius, the 'ikan sembilang' catfish

minute or more. Then it fell off, and black blood began to flow, which, after a little, was succeeded by blood of normal colour. The pain, which had been excessively acute, began to diminish soon after this, and in an hour had practically disappeared. The wound gave me no further trouble, but a fortnight afterwards I noticed a hole about the size of a pea where the wound had been. . . . The black stone applied by the Malay to the wound came, he alleged, from the head of a snake, and claimed, therefore, to be a bezoar stone. It was, no doubt, a snake-stone, probably made of charred bone, and therefore porous in character, which would account for the adhesive and absorptive powers it displayed in my case.

The curious Malay belief recalled by Hervey, that snake-stones were derived from the heads of snakes, is immediately reminiscent of the toadstone (bufonite) myth—". . . the toad, ugly and venomous, wears yet a precious jewel in his head", as Shakespeare wrote in *As You Like It.* In reality, however, such 'stones' or 'jewels' were the button-like fossilised teeth of *Lepidotes* (aka *Lepidotus*), an extinct genus of actinopterygian (ray-finned) fish from the Jurassic and Cretaceous Periods but related to the modern-day gars or garpikes. In a parallel scenario, stones or jewels were once thought to exist in the heads of frogs too; these were called batrachites.

As for the snake-stone equivalent, this is not confined to Malaysia. In a short *Nature* report (26 July 1900) responding to Hervey's, and based upon information received from a Mr E.H.L. Schwarz of Cape Town, it was disclosed that South African farmers also hold this belief. However, as the report commented, it may have reached

8 | SNAKE-STONES

there via the Malay slaves obtained from Batavia (now Jakarta), Java, by the early Dutch.

In *Venomous Reptiles* (1971), Sherman and Madge Minton reported that in India it is believed that some cobras bear in their hood a dark brown, luminous stone termed a *mun*, which heals snake-bites instantaneously. Those that the Mintons examined proved to be bezoar stones, or enteroliths (stones swallowed by various animals to aid digestion), or, in most cases, samples of heat-treated agate.

A similar myth was documented by Tennent from Sri Lanka:

> One curious tradition in Ceylon embodies the popular legend, that the stomach of the cobra de capello occasionally contains a precious stone of such unapproachable brilliancy as to surpass all known jewels.

Supposed toadstone extraction, depicted in a 1497 woodcut by Johannes de Cuba

> This inestimable stone is called the *nāga-mānik-kya*; but not one snake in thousands is supposed to possess such a treasure. The cobra, before eating, is believed to cast it up and conceal it for the moment; else its splendour, like a flambeau, would attract all beholders. The tales of the peasantry, in relation to it, all turn upon the devices of those in search of the gem, and the vigilance and cunning of the cobra by which they are baffled; the reptile itself being more enamoured of the priceless jewel than even its most ardent pursuers.

Nevertheless, and needless to say, unless such folk-beliefs originate from the (remote) possibility that snakes have occasionally been found in the wild that were inflicted with some kind of tumour or other abnormal growth, there is no evidence for the existence of jewels or any other kind of stone present inside the heads or stomachs of snakes. Once all folk-beliefs of this latter kind appertaining to such objects are cast aside, however, can there still be room for doubt that at least those snake-stones composed of charred bone or horn (and which are almost exclusively termed black-stones nowadays) can really alleviate the effect of venomous bites and stings? In fact, very appreciable doubt continues to be expressed in scientific circles.

Modern-day sceptics find it difficult to believe that such an object can generate sufficient powers of suction quickly enough to draw the venom out of the wound before the victim's blood circulatory system begins to transport it further into the body. Moreover, a fairly recent Bolivian study by Dr J.P. Chippaux and two co-workers (*Toxicon*, April 2007), testing the effectiveness of black-stone application upon mice following intra-muscular injection of venom from the puff adder *Bitis arietans*, West African carpet viper *Echis ocellatus*, and black-necked spitting cobra *Naja nigricollis*, failed to demonstrate any positive envenomation effect. Comparable criticism had been voiced over a century earlier, by Sir Joseph Fayrer in his book *The Thanatophidia of India* (1872), and also by other snake-stone sceptics of the late 19th Century, when interest in snake-stones had reached its zenith.

However, in defence of the snake-stone's abilities, it must be pointed out that accounts describing its actions generally state specifically that it was (or should be) applied *straight after* the bite or sting had occurred (if it were to exert its full effect), i.e. well *before* the venom had begun to pervade the victim's system. Hence the Bolivian study, featuring direct intramuscular injection of venom, is hardly relevant after all. In contrast, a second, more detailed snake-stone published later that same year by Chippaux provided an interesting dichotomy in results obtained from two different procedures:

> The results showed the absence of effectiveness of the black stone when applied on wounds after venom injection. However, the direct contact between the black stone powder and the venom did reduce venom toxicity, as if black stone fixed venom proteins and removed the venom from the inoculum. The mechanical effectiveness of black stone can thus be shown. However, its efficacy in treating envenomation seemed very doubtful because of it is very nonspecific and because the venom diffuses rapidly from the wound.

In addition, we must consider the educated, reliable nature of many of the eyewitnesses whose testimonies have been presented here. Indeed, in some cases they had even admitted to scepticism concerning the natives' claims regarding snake-stones prior to witnessing with their own eyes the startlingly effective results obtained with them. Can we really justify choosing to discount all of this testimony as fraudulent or mistaken, as we must do if we are to deny the capability of snake-stones?

Furthermore, if snake-stones *are* impotent, is it not a quite extraordinary coincidence how similar are all of the cases reported here, despite having occurred independently of one another and in many different parts of the world and involving very dissimilar forms of animal? Unless there is at least some degree of truth to the snake-stone belief, it is highly unlikely that localities so distant from one another as those cited in this chapter could yield such similar accounts, corresponding with one another not just in general features but also in much more specific, ostensibly insignificant ones.

Consequently, the subject of snake-stones is one that I personally consider could certainly benefit from further investigation and experimentation. Folk remedies have frequently been tested scientifically and found to exhibit at least a degree of medical veracity. Might the same be true of snake-stones? Only time and further testing will tell for sure.

9
GIANT ANACONDAS AND OTHER SUPER-SIZED CRYPTOZOOLOGICAL SNAKES

> The slime with which the earth was covered by the waters of the flood produced an excessive fertility, which called forth every variety of production, both bad and good. Among the rest, Python, an enormous serpent, crept forth, the terror of the people, and lurked in the caves of Mount Parnassus. Apollo slew him with his arrows—weapons which he had not before used against any but feeble animals, hares, wild goats, and such game. In commemoration of this illustrious conquest he instituted the Pythian games, in which the victor in feats of strength, swiftness of foot, or in the chariot race was crowned with a wreath of beech leaves; for the laurel was not yet adopted by Apollo as his own tree.
>
> Thomas Bulfinch—*Age of Fable*

During the 1920s, Raymond L. Ditmars, Curator of Reptiles at New York's Bronx Zoo, offered $1,000 to anyone who could provide conclusive evidence for the existence of a snake measuring over 40 ft long. The prize has never been claimed. Yet there are many extraordinary eyewitness accounts on record asserting that gargantuan serpents far greater in length than anything ever confirmed by science are indeed a frightening reality in various regions of the world, as demonstrated by the fascinating selection of examples documented here.

THE GIANT SERPENT OF CARTHAGE AND OTHER OLD WORLD GOLIATHS

During the time of Rome's First Punic War (264-241 BC) with Carthage (which lay near present-day Tunis in Tunisia, North Africa), the Roman army, led by the renowned general Marcus Atilius Regulus, was advancing on Carthage, having reached the River Bagradas (aka Medjerda). As his battalions sought to cross this river, however, an enormous snake rose up before them from the reed beds, with great flattened head and glowing lantern-like eyes glaring malevolently at them as they cowered back at the sight of this monstrous reptile. Coil after coil in seemingly limitless extent emerged, and the soldiers estimated its vast length to be at least 120 ft!

Deciding that discretion may well be the better part of valour, Regulus's army retreated further down the river bank, hoping to cross far away from its ophidian guardian. And when they looked back, the giant snake had seemingly vanished. Yet no sooner did they attempt to cross at this new location than, without warning, the huge flattened head rose up from below the water surface and seized a nearby soldier in its mighty jaws, enfolding and crushing his body in its vice-like constricting coils, before mercilessly drowning him. And each time another soldier tried to cross, this grisly scene was re-enacted.

In fury, Regulus ordered his men to wheel forward and arm their siege ballistae—massive catapults used for hurling immense rocks at fortresses. Missile after missile was duly fired at the snake, bombarding it unceasingly until, wounded and dazed, the huge creature finally began to retreat into the river. But before it could submerge itself completely, a well-aimed rock hit it squarely between its eyes, shattering its skull and killing outright this veritable leviathan of the serpent world. Afterwards, the soldiers skinned its colossal body, and records preserved from that time claim that its skin did indeed measure a tremendous 120 ft.

Yet even if this skin had been artificially stretched (it is well known that snake skins can indeed be stretched quite considerably), it must still have been a truly exceptional specimen—always assuming, of course, that it really was a snake skin! I have uncovered a fascinating article from 1901, published by the French periodical *Le Naturaliste*, in which the author, a Dr Bougon, suggested that the specimen in question was not the snake's skin at all, but was instead its preserved intestine—noting that a 30-ft python would have a 120-ft intestine. Sadly, however, Bougon's undeniably thought-provoking notion can never be scientifically investigated, for the following stark reason.

Notwithstanding its anatomical identity, this stupendous trophy and also the snake's formidable jaws were eventually brought back to Rome and placed on display inside one of the temples on Capitol Hill. Here these spectacular relics remained until 133 BC, when, towards the end of the Numantine War against the Iberian Celts, they mysteriously disappeared, and were never reported again.

Always assuming that this Carthaginian mega-serpent's size had been recorded accurately and that it was its skin rather than its intestine that had been salvaged, what could its species have been?

Albertus Seba's engraving of a rock python, the likely identity of Carthage's giant snake

A rock python *Python sebae* is the most popular identity, but this species is not thought to have existed at any time in that particular area of Africa. And even where it *is* known to exist, no specimen even remotely as long as Regulus's antagonist has ever been chronicled. The longest confirmed specimen, measuring 32 ft, was shot in school grounds at Bingerville, Ivory Coast, by Mrs Charles Beart in 1932.

Nevertheless, and quoting from my book *Dragons in Zoology, Cryptozoology, and Culture* (2013), some classic myths and legends featuring worms and other mighty serpent dragons did unquestionably stem from sightings of very large snakes, notably pythons and boa constrictors. Indeed, modern-day pythons actually derive their name from the colossal serpent dragon Python, battled by the Greek sun god Apollo (see this present chapter's opening quote). And boas derive theirs from a monstrous Italian version known as the boas, which sucked countless cows dry of both their milk and their life.

Unlike those of many other snakes, the heads of pythons and boas are very well-delineated, just like those of serpent dragons. Their huge lengths are also very comparable with those reported for some serpent dragons, and in cases where the latter are even bigger, fear-induced exaggeration can certainly be implicated.

The world's longest species of snake alive today is the reticulated python *Python reticulatus* of southeast Asia, which regularly attains a total length of up to 20 ft, and sometimes more. One specimen, shot in 1912 on the north coast of Sulawesi (Celebes), Indonesia, supposedly measured an astonishing 30 ft after having been accurately measured by a team of civil engineers using a surveying tape. In summer 1907, however, a dark cane-coloured python estimated at 70 ft long had been observed through binoculars swimming in the Celebes Sea by Third Officer S. Clayton of the China Navigation Company's vessel *Taiyuan*.

Encounters by Western travellers with serpentine monsters such as these, and their much-embroidered retellings concerning them when safely back home, could have swiftly and very readily engendered all manner of far-fetched yarns concerning vast limbless dragons existing in exotic, far-off realms of swamp and jungle. From this, it would have been only a short step to relocating them in much closer, more familiar lands by imaginative storytellers. And if a few living specimens of such snakes were brought back to Europe from time to time for display in menageries and travelling sideshows, an occasional escape would have been more than sufficient to give rise to further lurid stories and local folklore.

In addition to their great size, another characteristic of serpent dragons linking them to giant snakes is their noxious breath, claimed in various folktales to be so toxic that it can kill livestock and spread infectious diseases. This is clearly nothing more than an exaggerated account of the foetid stench exhibited by the breath of giant meat-eating snakes such as pythons and boas—a quality also reported from other carnivorous animals, such as wolves and big cats.

Giant python, 1867, from *The Bestiarium of Aloys Zötl 1831-1887*

Equally, the glowing eyes of serpent dragons correspond well with the phosphorescent appearance of the eyes of anacondas and other very large constricting snakes, especially when viewed in dimly-lit surroundings. And it is probably no coincidence that many stories featuring serpent dragons tell of how they were encountered lying upon bright sunlit hills or stretched out in hot wastelands—because this is exactly what one would expect from huge snakes, which sunbathe in order to maintain their body temperature and metabolic rate. Snakes, like other reptiles, are poikilothermic ('cold-blooded'), and are therefore unable to regulate these aspects of their physiology internally, so are dependent instead upon external heat sources to achieve this.

Of course, myths and legends tell of serpent dragons far greater in size than even the largest known specimens of modern-day snake. Whereas this is no doubt due at least in part to exaggeration and storyteller licence as already noted, it is also true (and not merely with snakes) that in earlier times any exceptional, freakishly large specimens would be favoured targets for hunters looking for spectacular trophies. This selective decimation means that down through the centuries, the maximum size of giant snake species would eventually diminish, surviving in their original stature only within old tales of confrontation passed down in ever more distorted, embellished form from generation to generation, until finally the colossal serpent dragons that never actually existed were born.

Extra-large specimens of known snake species may well explain stories of alleged serpent dragons that were maintained in temples and caves to be venerated as oracles or deities in ancient Greece and Rome. One excellent example was chronicled by Sextus Propertius, a Latin poet-scholar of the 1st Century BC, in his *Elegies*:

> Lanuvium [on the Appian Way, roughly 25 miles from Rome] is, of old, protected by an aged dragon; here, where the occasion of an amusement so seldom occurring is not lost, where is the abrupt descent into a dark and hollowed cave; where is let down—maiden, beware of every such journey—the honorary tribute to the fasting snake, when he demands his yearly food, and hisses and twists deep down in the earth. Maidens, let down for such a rite, grow pale, when their hand is unprotectedly trusted in the snake's mouth. He snatches at the delicacies if offered by a maid; the very baskets tremble in the virgin's hands; if they are chaste, they return and fall on the necks of their parents, and the farmers cry 'We shall have a fruitful year.'

This clearly refers to some very large specimen of snake, and as the maiden was not poisoned even when she placed her hand in its mouth, it is obviously not a venomous species, but almost certainly

9 | SUPER-SIZED SNAKES

An 1825 print of warrior Matsui Tamijiro
battling a giant snake, by Utagawa Kuniyoshi

a python. Similar accounts featuring venerated serpent dragons living in groves in Rome and being fed barley cakes by sacred virgins appear in *De Natura Animalium*, by Rome-based Greek scholar Aelian (c.175-c.235 AD).

Such creatures may again have been African rock pythons. Common in much of sub-Saharan Africa, specimens of this very sizeable snake species were probably brought back to Rome, because it is certainly depicted in Roman mosaics.

An escapee venerated python may explain the account of a boa form of serpent dragon that, when killed upon Rome's Vatican Hill during Emperor Claudius's reign (41-54 AD), was reputedly found to contain an entire child inside its hugely distended gut.

Generously-embroidered reports of constricting pythons in India are undoubtedly at the root of this fanciful account in Pliny's *Natural History* (c.77-79 AD):

> Africa produces elephants, but it is India that produces the largest, as well as the dragon, who is perpetually at war with the elephant, and is itself of so enormous a size, as easily to envelop the elephants with its folds, and encircle them in its coils. The contest is equally fatal to both; the elephant, vanquished, falls to the earth, and by its weight crushes the dragon which is entwined around it.

In more recent times, giant snakes have been reported from Algeria. One of the most memorable incidents occurred on 6 or 7 January 1967, when a serpent allegedly measuring roughly 30 ft long and bearing a crest upon its head was spied on the construction site of the Djorf Torba dam east of Béchar by Hamza Rahmani, one of the site's workers. He succeeded in wedging this huge snake against some rocks with his bulldozer, and later reports claim that its teeth were hooked and were approximately 2.5 in long.

Apparently, however, neither its body nor any portion from it (not even one of its notable teeth) was preserved. This shows how even a mystery creature as sizeable as a giant snake can readily elude formal scientific examination!

The same applies with regard to an astonishing report from tropical Africa featuring an extremely reliable eyewitness. In 1959, an ostensibly immense python reared up towards a helicopter

9 | SUPER-SIZED SNAKES

passing overhead at an alleged altitude of 500 ft in Katanga (within what is now the Democratic Republic of the Congo), flown by the highly-acclaimed, much-decorated Belgian pilot and World War II flying ace Colonel Remy Van Lierde DFC (1915-1990), on his way back to his Katanga airbase. A colleague on board actually managed to snap a photograph of the creature, and using the size of background bushes and other topographical features in the photo as scale determinants, van Lierde estimated that the python appeared to be around 50 ft long—once again far greater than any scientifically-confirmed specimen.

The gargantuan Katanga mystery snake photographed by Colonel Remy Van Lierde's colleague from a helicopter (USC Title 17 § 107)

An interview with Van Lierde featured in an episode of the early 1980s UK television series *Arthur C. Clarke's Mysterious World*, and can currently be viewed online at: https://www.youtube.com/watch?v=v2UodhbP9Fw (the interview begins at around 7 min 36 sec into the video). Just in case it is no longer accessible by the time that this book is published, however, here is a verbatim transcript of Van Lierde's testimony from that episode:

So as we had a camera on board, I decided to make several passes over the hole where the snake was in, in able [sic] to let the man take a picture of it, and I made certainly between four and six passes right over the hole where the snake was in. By then I was already flying for 25 years, so I've a very good experience of measuring things. And I would say the snake I saw there was close to 50 foot, close to 50 feet—I don't know, you say 50 foot, or 50 feet?—but very close to, certainly. And it was moving inside the hole, and looking very dark green, deep green-brown, with his belly white. Now when I came down on that snake in his hole, and I would say at about 25-30 foot up, the snake raised up, by about, I would say, 10 foot, and I could very clearly, closely, see the head, it was looking, and I could not make a better comparison [than] with a very large horse, with big, very very big jaws, looking triangular. And you're just standing up like there to me, and I feel and I'm convinced if I had been in its range it would have struck at me, it would have been striking me. And yet I would say it was certainly at least, at least over 42 foot wide [sic—he meant long] and 3 ft long [sic—he meant wide]. It could have easily eaten up a man.

Giant pythons are apparently well known to local inhabitants of this region of Africa, who even accord them their own special name, the pumina. Having said that, there has been much controversy as to whether, notwithstanding his considerable experience in making field observations, Van Lierde may have over-estimated the snake's length. Several different investigators have utilised topographical features in the photograph, most notably a number of termite mounds near the hole into which it supposedly vanished, in an attempt to determine independently the latter's size, but no conclusive result has yet been obtained.

9 | SUPER-SIZED SNAKES

THE SUCURIJU GIGANTE—SOUTH AMERICA'S SUPER-SIZED ANACONDA

According to the official record books, although sometimes exceeding 440 lb in weight and therefore far heavier than Asia's reticulated python, South America's common or green anaconda *Eunectes murinus* rarely exceeds 20 ft in length. Yet there are numerous reports of specimens far bigger than this. Indeed, such monsters even have their own local names, such as the sucuriju gigante in Brazil and the camoodi in Guyana. Sometimes they are also said to bear a pair of horns on their head.

Perhaps the most (in)famous encounter with a purported sucuriju gigante occurred in 1907, when, while leading an expedition through the Amazonian rainforest in Brazil's Acre State, the celebrated, subsequently-lost explorer Lieutenant-Colonel Percy H. Fawcett shot a massive anaconda as it began to emerge from the Rio Abuna and onto the bank. In his book *Exploration Fawcett* (1953), he claimed that as far as it was possible to measure the body, a length of 45 ft lay out of the water, with a further 17 ft still in it, yielding a total length of 62 ft. Even though Fawcett was known

Fawcett shooting the giant anaconda

for his meticulous observations, this claim is nowadays viewed with scepticism by many zoologists.

On 22 May 1922 at around 3 pm, priest Father Victor Heinz witnessed a sucuriju gigante while travelling home by canoe along the Amazon River from Obidos in Brazil's Pará State. He and his petrified crew saw about 90 ft away in midstream a huge snake, coiled up in two rings, and they gazed in awe as it drifted passively downstream. Fr Heinz estimated its visible length at just under 80 ft, and stated that its body was as thick as an oil drum.

Moreover, on 29 October 1929 he encountered another specimen, this time while he and his crew were travelling by river to Alenquer in Brazil's Pará State at around midnight. Approaching them in the dark from the opposite direction, its eyes were so large and phosphorescent that he initially mistook them for a pair of blue-green navigation lights on a steamer! Happily, this monstrous serpent paid no attention to its terrified observers!

The following photograph depicts an alleged 130-145-ft-long sucuriju gigante that according to Tim Dinsdale's book *The Leviathans* (1966) was originally captured alive on the banks of the Amazon and towed into Manaos by a river tug before being subsequently dispatched via a round of machine-gun fire. However, does the photo depict a genuine giant anaconda, or just a well-executed hoax involving forced perspective? The question remains unanswered.

Alleged sucuriju gigante (USC Title 17 § 107)

Sucuriju gigante encountered by Father Heinz and his crew (© William Rebsamen)

A giant anaconda coming ashore (© William Rebsamen)

Equally enigmatic is this second photo, snapped in 1948, of a supposed 115-ft sucuriju gigante, which reputedly came ashore and hid in the old fortifications of Fort Abuna in western Brazil's Guaporé Territory before being machine-gunned to death and pushed into the Abuna River.

Supposed 115-ft-long sucuriju gigante floating dead in the Abuna River within Brazil's Guaporé Territory
(USC Title 17 § 107)

More recently, on 19 August 1997, a veritable behemoth of a snake, jet-black and supposedly almost 130 ft long, reputedly raided Nueva Tacna, a village near the Rio Napo in northern Peru. Its five eyewitnesses were later interviewed by no less eminent a person than Jorge Samuel Chávez Sibina, mayor of the Municipalidad Provincial de Maynas, who, in the company of radio journalist Carlos Villareal, flew over the village and afterwards stated that in his opinion: "There really is something to the villagers' stories". Moreover, a track supposedly left behind by this goliath measured about 1600 ft long and 30 ft wide. Incidentally, this report should not be confused (but often is) with the following phoney, photoshopped picture depicting just such a beast that has been circulating online for many years:

Fake online photograph of a supposed giant black anaconda
(USC Title 17 § 107)

Also worth noting is the following short communication posted by American cryptozoological author Matt Bille to the online cz@ egroups cryptozoological chat site on 27 August 2000:

> I should pass along the fact that missionary/naturalist Peter Hocking reports many people in wild areas of Peru say there are two kind of anacondas—the "green" (the standard type) and the "black" which is larger, darker, and has a different head shape. He shared with me the account of a man named Jamie Torres, whose veracity and familiarity with anacondas Peter vouches for. Torres claims a huge black anaconda went under his canoe in February 1999—he estimated the snake's length at 25 meters [82 ft]. Hocking notes he commonly hears stories of 15-20 meter [50-65 ft] snakes, but no one has been able to provide him with any hard evidence.

Were it not for its supposed head shape difference, I'd suggest that the black anaconda form was merely a melanistic version of the normal green anaconda, especially as in a wide range of different species melanistic specimens tend to be bigger than their normal counterparts. The local name given to the black anaconda is the yacumama, which translates as "mother of the water".

Traditionally, mainstream herpetologists have spoken out in favour of the physical impossibility (or at least the very considerable improbability) of giant snakes, noting that even in prehistoric times there were no known species significantly larger than those existing today. However, this line of conjecture suffered a major blow in early 2009, when Canadian biologist Dr Jason J. Head and a team of co-researchers announced that 28 specimens of a hitherto-unknown fossil snake of truly gargantuan proportions had been discovered in the Cerrejón Formation within coal mines at La Guajira, Colombia.

Life-size model of *Titanoboa* (© Dr Karl Shuker)

This new species, which existed 58-60 million years ago during the Mid-to-Late Palaeocene Epoch, was christened *Titanoboa cerrejonensis* (*Nature*, 5 February 2009). By comparing the sizes and shapes of the vertebrae of its eight largest specimens to those of modern-day snakes, Head and co confidently estimated that the aptly-named *Titanoboa* had attained a maximum length of 40-50 ft, weighed around 2500 lb, and boasted a girth of about 3 ft at its body's thickest portion. Snakes could indeed attain huge proportions after all.

Indeed, since its discovery some cryptozoologists have daringly suggested that perhaps South America's mysterious serpent giants actually constitute living specimens of *Titanoboa*—but as noted above, this immense ophidian died out approximately 60 million years ago . . . didn't it?

NORTH AMERICAN BOSS SNAKES

Also very deserving of review here in relation to giant New World serpents are boss snakes. Little known outside North America, 'boss snake' is a non-specific, non-scientific term that was used quite commonly across the latter continent up until the end of the 19th Century to denote any snake that appeared to be much larger than officially recognised forms in the area where it had been encountered. Numerous reports of exceedingly sizeable yet ostensibly unidentified serpents to which this loose term can be applied have been documented, but these had never been compiled and analysed within a single volume devoted to them until 2008, the year that saw the publication of *Boss Snakes: Stories and Sightings of Giant Snakes in North America*, written by American herpetological enthusiast and cryptozoological researcher Chad Arment.

At almost 400 pages long, and including an extensive state-by-state compendium of boss snake accounts from the USA, this fascinating book contains an unrivalled array of reports, which collectively show that the diversity of boss snakes described is immense, indisputably involving many different species. So what can they be, and how can such diversity be explained?

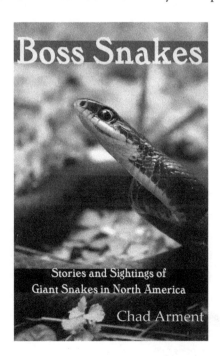

Boss Snakes
(© Chad Arment/
Coachwhip Publications)

Chad has created three primary categories that collectively house all such reports. These are: False Stories; Recognized Snakes; and Unknown Snakes.

Within False Stories, he includes newspaper hoaxes (as also revealed in this present book of mine, reports of unusual snakes were a common theme of such hoaxes prior to modern times), pranks, misidentifications, campfire tales, rumours, showman's hype (at sideshows, travelling carnivals, etc), and even social control (fake stories involving big snakes spread deliberately in order to scare and manipulate people, including property deterrents).

Within Recognized Species, he includes reports of native species that contain size exaggerations, specimens of native species exceeding their recognized size, and out-of-place, non-native escapees/releases.

And within Unknown Species, he includes reports of unusual snakes that may actually constitute species currently undescribed by science.

It goes without saying that known fakes, frauds, hoaxes, pranks, tall tales, and campfire yarns, not to mention misidentifications and infamous sideshow hyperbole, effectively combine to yield a vast range of morphological descriptions, but all of them of little if any zoological value—quite the contrary, in fact, if we consider how significantly they may have contributed to the near-protean nature of the boss snake and strewn confusion in their wake.

The maximum confirmed length for North America's longest native non-venomous species is 8 ft 9 in, for the bullsnake *Pituophis catenifer sayi*; and for its longest native venomous species is 8 ft 3 in, for the eastern diamondback rattlesnake *Crotalus adamanteus*. As noted earlier in this chapter, however, hunting inevitably involves the largest, most spectacular specimens of a given hunted species being favoured targets, with their decimation eventually leading to an overall diminution in size for that species.

Consequently, as Chad acknowledges, it is not beyond the realms of possibility that in earlier centuries, certain truly exceptional specimens of some of this continent's common snake species were genuinely encountered and killed, in so doing wiping out the genes responsible for their great size if this were a genetically-induced characteristic, and thus explaining why such sizeable specimens are not met with today. Local isolating factors yielding a small, inbred population might also result in gigantism, via the phenomenon of genetic drift.

Some instances of boss snakes may actually feature established populations of non-native species originating from escapee/released captive specimens. The explosive population growth of Burmese pythons *Python bivittatus* in the Florida Everglades is a dramatic, fully-confirmed modern-day example.

But what of bona fide unknown, scientifically-undescribed species existing in North America? Chad readily concedes that this is the least likely category within his boss snake classification scheme, and he rules out on the grounds of too great a diversity of reported morphological descriptions any possibility that a single such species might explain all boss snake reports. However, he does not entirely discount the prospect of one or more small, localised, existing populations of one or more unknown species, whether or not closely related to known species. Needless to say, however, until (if ever) any tangible, physical evidence for such latter creatures' reality is obtained and formally examined, their presence among the herpetological fauna of North America remains unproved.

MEGA-CONSTRICTORS DOWN UNDER?

Expanded from an earlier article of mine published by the British mysteries magazine *Fortean Times*, in my 2010 book *Dr Shuker's Alien Zoo: From the Pages of Fortean Times* I documented a mystifying giant snake said to inhabit parts of Australia but which as far as I'm aware had never previously been brought to cryptozoological attention. My information source for this ophidian cryptid was Australian herpetologist Richard Wells, who kindly permitted me to document in my book, so here is what I wrote about it:

> Back in the 1970s, while Richard was working for the Northern Territory Museum in Darwin, an amateur naturalist brought in an extremely sizeable python, roughly 4 m long, of a previously unknown species, which was later formally described and named *Liasis* [now *Morelia*] *oenpelliensis*, the Oenpelli python. Subsequent specimens of this new snake have been

recorded that vie in size with the mighty amethystine python *L. amethystinus* [now *Simalia amethistina*]—Australia's largest species of snake, and the fourth largest in the world, which can attain a total length of up to 7 m.

It seems remarkable that a snake as sizeable as *M. oenpelliensis* could remain undiscovered by science until as recently as the 1970s, and even more so if local aboriginal claims are correct—namely, that specimens greatly in excess of 4 m exist. Nor is the evidence for this dramatic prospect wholly anecdotal. According to Richard: ". . . the obvious tracks of a huge python have been found within vast underground caverns under Arnhem Land, and these were so large as to indicate that it may attain around 10 metres in length".

Moreover, Richard has received consistent reports from local tribes of a massive aquatic python-like snake, whose description leads him to consider that a bona fide prehistoric survivor may be the answer—*Wonambi naracoortensis*. This remarkable species was a giant 5-m-long [approx. 20-ft-long] constricting species of snake, but belonging to an ancient, primitive group known as the madtsoiids, and deemed to have been at least partially aquatic. At one time, madtsoiids existed on all continents formerly part of the southern super-continent Gondwanaland, but they all died out around 55 million years ago—except in Australia, where they continued to diversify, culminating in *Wonambi*, which became extinct only within the last 50,000 years, inciting speculation that it may have been contemporary with the first humans to reach Australia, and might even have inspired Dream-Time myths of the great Rainbow Serpent.

But could it still exist today? The concept of surviving madtsoiids is not restricted to Australian cryptids. As already noted in Chapter 6 of the present book, English cryptozoologist Richard Freeman has offered this identity as an explanation for reports of

Reconstruction of *Wonambi* (© Hodari Nundu)

gigantic water snakes inhabiting the Mekong River comprising Thailand's northeastern border with Laos, and known as nagas (not to be confused with the ancient snake deities of the same name). Until Richard Wells's above-documented account, however, there had been no reports of comparable aquatic mystery snakes in Australia.

Conversely, when I communicated with palaeontologist Dr Ralph Molnar, formerly Curator of the Queensland Museum and an expert in Australian fossil reptiles, concerning these cryptids, he favoured the modern-day carpet (diamond) python *Morelia spilota* as a more plausible candidate taxonomically. However, he was not surprised to learn that reports of extra-large constrictors have emerged here.

Personally, I look towards the amethystine python, a northern species already known to attain immense lengths, which is also a good swimmer and usually occurs near water. The prospect of exceptionally-large aquatic specimens, their huge size buoyed by their liquid medium, is not untenable.

Carpet python *Morelia spilota* (Haplochromis, CC BY-SA 3.0)

Amethystine python *Simalia amethistina*
(Cannibal Holiday, CC BY 2.0)

9 | SUPER-SIZED SNAKES

Frontispiece to garrison deserter John Browne's *Affecting Narrative* book from 1802, dramatically depicting an 'ibibaboka'—clearly a grossly-exaggerated anaconda, yet supposedly venomous, 27 ft long, with a 20-in circumference, which he reputedly confronted and gunned down in 1799 on the south Atlantic island of St Helena, not known by scientists to harbour *any* species of snake!

PROPORTIONS AND PREHISTORY

How reliable are such reports as those presented here? Obviously, human estimation of size, especially when dealing with elongate, coiling objects like snakes, is far from perfect, and much given to exaggeration. Preserved skins do not provide reliable evidence for giant snakes either, because it has been ably demonstrated that those obtained from heavy snakes like anacondas can be deliberately stretched by as much as 30 per cent without causing much distortion to their markings.

Researchers have also suggested that their great size could cause giant snakes to experience problems in maintaining stable blood pressure, and that they would need to remain submerged in water for their immense weight to be effectively buoyed. Furthermore, snake specialist Peter Pritchard has calculated that the maximum length of a snake species is 1.5-2.5 times its shortest adult length—which means that as small adult common anacondas measure 10-12 ft long, the greatest theoretical length for this species is only marginally above 30 ft.

Even prehistory—a domain replete with reptilian giants—once offered little support for serpent monsters. Traditionally, the largest species of fossil snake on record has been North Africa's *Gigantophis garstini*, which existed around 40 million years ago during the Eocene Epoch. It was believed to measure more than 30 ft, but not to exceed the minimum length needed to claim the Bronx Zoo's longstanding prize. And then, of course, in 2009 along came *Titanoboa* . . .

Suddenly, giant snakes were a myth no longer. Here was indisputable evidence that at least one such species had genuinely existed.

So could there be others too—still thriving in secluded swamps and rivers, their colossal forms in flagrant disregard of what should or should not be possible according to the laws of biophysics, lurking like primeval serpent dragons amid our planet's remotest, shadow-infested realms? Perhaps one day a future Fawcett will uncover the truth—provided, unlike the original Fawcett, he lives long enough to bring the required evidence back home with him!

10
THE MONGOLIAN DEATH WORM—A SHOCKING SURPRISE IN THE GOBI?

> Worms are the intestines of the earth.
>
> Aristotle—*De Generatione Animalium, Book III*

It's not every day—or every expedition—that begins with a request from a country's head of government formally requesting that a specimen be captured of a creature so elusive, and deadly, that western science does not even recognise its existence. Nevertheless, that is precisely what happened in 1922 when eminent American palaeontologist Prof. Roy Chapman Andrews met the Mongolian premier in order to obtain the necessary permits for the American Museum of Natural History's Central Asiatic Expedition to search for dinosaur fossils in the Gobi Desert. And the creature that the Mongolian premier instructed him to procure? None other than the lethal allghoi khorkhoi (sometimes spelled olgoj-chorchoj)—or, as it is nowadays commonly referred to throughout the world, the Mongolian death worm.

Although in the 1920s this extraordinary mystery beast was totally unheard of outside Mongolia, today it is one of the most (in)famous of all cryptozoological creatures—thanks to the series of pioneering expeditions to its southern Gobi homeland launched by Czech explorer Ivan Mackerle (d. 2013). The first of these

The late Ivan Mackerle (© Ivan Mackerle)

took place during June and July 1990, and subsequently attracted considerable interest internationally. During his searches, Ivan collected a very impressive dossier of information concerning the death worm, based upon eyewitness reports and other anecdotal evidence, which he very kindly made freely available to me to use as I wished in my own writings, and which can be summarised as follows.

Its local names—allghoi khorkhoi and allergorhai horhai—translate as 'intestine worm', because according to eyewitness testimony this mysterious sausage-shaped creature resembles a living intestine. Red in colour with darker blotches, it measures 3-5 ft long and is as thick as a man's arm, but has no discernible scales, mouth, nor even any eyes or other recognisable sensory organs. It is said to be truncated at both ends, but according to some accounts at least one end also bears a series of long pointed structures at its tip.

For much of the year, the death worm remains concealed beneath the Gobi's sands, but during the two hottest months—June and July—it can sometimes be encountered lying on the surface, particularly after a downpour of rain. Locals claim that it can also be found in association with the black saxaul *Haloxylon ammodendron*, a yellow-flowered desert shrub belonging to the amaranth family, whose roots are parasitized by the goyo or Central Asian desert thumb *Cynomorium songaricum*. This is a strange, cigar-shaped plant, one of only two members of the genus *Cynomorium*, seemingly most closely allied to the saxifrages.

According once again to local lore, the death worm is deadly for two very different reasons. If approached too closely, it is said to raise one end of its body upwards (as portrayed on the front cover of my book *The Beasts That Hide From Man*, 2003), and then squirt with unerring accuracy at its victim a stream of extremely poisonous, acidic fluid that burns the victim's flesh, turning it yellow, before rapidly inducing death. It is claimed that the death worm derives this highly toxic substance externally—either from the saxaul's roots or from the goyo attached to them (and thereby reminiscent of how South America's deadly arrow-poison frogs derive their skin toxins, from certain small arthropods that they devour). During my own researches, however, I have uncovered no evidence to suggest that the saxaul's roots are poisonous, and I have revealed that the goyo is definitely not poisonous (it is eaten as famine food, and used widely in Chinese herbalism). So if the death worm truly emits a toxic fluid, it presumably manufactures it internally, rather than deriving it externally.

Artistic reconstruction of the Mongolian death worm's possible appearance when rearing upwards, based upon eyewitness descriptions (© Ivan Mackerle)

Goyo *Cynomorium songaricum* (© Ivan Mackerle)

10 | MONGOLIAN DEATH WORM

Even more shocking—in every sense!—is the death worm's second alleged mode of attack. Nomadic herders inhabiting the southern Gobi tell of how entire herds of camels have been killed instantly merely by walking over a patch of sand concealing a death worm beneath the surface. Moreover, one of Ivan Mackerle's local guides recalled how, many years earlier, a geologist visiting the Gobi as part of a field trip was killed when he began idly poking some sand one night with an iron rod—as he did so, he abruptly dropped to the ground, dead, for apparently no reason. But when his horrified colleagues rushed up to him, they saw the sand where he had been poking the rod suddenly begin to churn violently, and from out of it emerged a huge, fat death worm.

The camels presumably died from coming into direct physical contact with the death worm hidden beneath their feet, but the geologist only touched it indirectly, via the metal rod. Consequently, the only conceivable way that this action could have caused his death is by electrocution—which would obviously explain the camels' instant deaths too. Although there are several different taxonomic groups of fish containing species that can generate electricity via the activity of special organs—including the famous electric eels and gymnotids, as well as the electric catfish, electric rays, mormyrids, rajid skates, and electric stargazers—no known species of terrestrial creature possesses this ability. So if the native claims concerning the camels and the geologist are correct, and always assuming of course that it really does exist, the death worm must be a very special animal indeed. But what precisely could it be?

Despite its English name and superficially similar external appearance, it is highly unlikely that the death worm could be a bona fide earthworm or related invertebrate. For although some earthworms do grow to prodigious lengths, and certain species known aptly as squirters even spurt streams of fluid from various body orifices, none exhibits a water-retentive cuticle, which would be imperative for survival in desert conditions to avoid drying out. Of course, there may be a highly-specialised earthworm in the Gobi that has indeed evolved such a modification, but with no precedent currently known, the chances of this seem slim. In addition, if the death worm's powers of electrocution are real, this would require even more modification and specialisation for an earthworm to fit the bill.

Caecilians constitute a taxonomic order of limbless amphibians that are deceptively worm-like in appearance and predominantly subterranean in lifestyle. Certain species can also attain a total length matching the dimensions reported for the death worm. As with true worms, however, caecilians' skin is water-permeable, so once again even a giant caecilian would soon dry out in the arid Gobi, unless, uniquely among these particular amphibians, it had evolved a water-retentive skin.

If the death worm is genuine, it is almost certainly some form of reptile. To my mind, the likeliest solution is an unusually large species of amphisbaenian. On account of their vermiform appearance (most species are limbless), these little-known reptiles are also called worm-lizards, even though, taxonomically speaking, they are neither. As with caecilians, they spend much of their lives underground, rarely coming to the surface except after a heavy fall of rain. This all corresponds well with the death worm's reported behaviour. Furthermore, unlike real worms and caecilians the skin of amphisbaenians is water-retentive, so a giant species would not dry out in the Gobi.

Conversely, whereas the death worm is said to be smooth externally, amphisbaenians are very visibly scaly, and they also have a readily-observed mouth. In addition, they are all completely harmless, which wholly contradicts the twin death-dealing talents attributed to the Gobi's most feared denizen. Naturally, it is conceivable that these abilities are entirely apocryphal, nothing more substantial than superstitious fancy. After all, several known species of amphisbaenian, and also caecilian, are fervently believed by their local human neighbours to be deadly poisonous even though in reality they are wholly innocuous.

Much of what has been proposed for and against an amphisbaenian identity for the Mongolian death worm applies equally to the possibility of its being an unknown species of very large legless true lizard—akin perhaps to the familiar slow worm and glass snake, or even to the skinks, some species of which are limbless. However, these lizards are much less worm-like and subterranean than amphisbaenians, so overall the latter provide a more satisfactory match with the death worm.

Last, but by no means least, is the thought-provoking prospect that the death worm may be a highly specialised species of snake. Not only do most of the above-noted physical and behavioural

10 | MONGOLIAN DEATH WORM

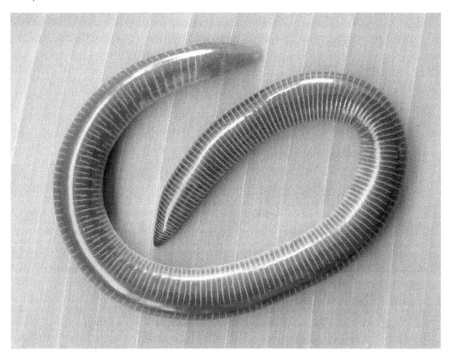

Uraeotyphlus narayani, a caecilian (Venu Govindappa, CC BY 3.0)

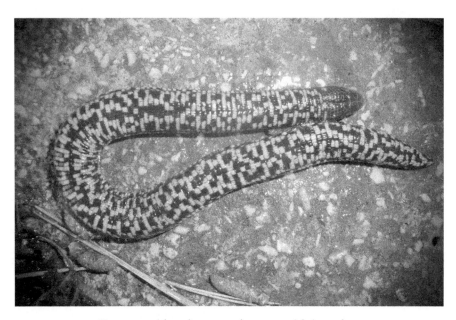

Trogonophis wiegmanni, an amphisbaenian
(Aissa Djamel Filali, CC BY-SA 4.0)

similarities between the death worm and the amphisbaenians and legless lizards apply here too, but spitting cobras also offer a famous precedent for an elongate creature that can eject a stream of corrosive venom with deadly accuracy at a potential aggressor. Moreover, the spine-bearing tip described for the death worm recalls a genus of cobra-related species known as death adders *Acanthophis* spp., which possess a spiny worm-like projection at the tip of their tail that acts as a lure for potential prey.

Their name recognises the fact that although, like cobras, they are elapids, the death adders have evolved to occupy the ecological role filled elsewhere by true vipers. Could there be a specialised, unknown species of death adder that has evolved the venom-spitting ability of its spitting cobra relatives? If so, this would vindicate the locals' testimony concerning the death worm's emissions. But what about its alleged powers of electrocution?

Remarkably, this too may be more than just a myth. For if the death worm were indeed a snake and perhaps sported such smooth, fine, tiny scales that they were not readily discernible, when it was crawling through sand these scales may be able to generate a weak electrical current via friction—a process known as triboelectricity, which has already been documented from certain sand-dwelling snake species. Indeed, to quote from a *Nature* article of 1994 on triboelectricity in snakes, authored by W.T. Vonstille and W.T. Stille III:

> Snakes were not blessed with the voltage-generating organs of electric fish, but the simple act of slithering along the ground can generate potentials of 100-1,000 volts. In fact, their dry skin seems adapted to generating and retaining electrical charge. Even more curious, laboratory experiments with snake rattles demonstrate that they can generate 75-100 volts when shaken!

If this electrostatic ability in turn gave rise to exaggerated descriptions of the death worm's electrical potency, it is easy to see how, over the course of several generations of ever more fanciful retellings, the entirely false belief in a creature that kills by electrocution could ultimately arise.

10 | MONGOLIAN DEATH WORM

A second, very different snake identity from that of the death adder was put forward five years ago, but has received little publicity since then. It seeks to explain the Mongolian death worm as a real yet wholly harmless ophidian species, with all of this cryptid's allegedly lethal capabilities being a figment of folklore, nothing more. A multi-authored volume entitled *The Amphibians of Mongolia* (2017), edited by Sergius L. Kuzmin and published in Moscow but written in both Russian and English, contains the following short yet very thought-provoking paragraph:

> Zoologist Yu K Gorelov, who worked extensively in Mongolia in the 1970s, decided to know the truth [re the Mongolian death worm] and found out that the prototype of the Olgoi-Khorkoi was the Tartar Sand Boa (*Eryx tartaricus*). . . . Later, Gorelov said that when he was showing a specimen of the boa to the Mongols in the Gobi, they confirmed that it was Olgoi-Khorkoi and that they were afraid of it. An individual once was put in a jar with a disinfectant [preservative?] and was exhibited for a few days during a

Death adder *Acanthophis antarcticus*
(Queensland Museum, CC BY 4.0)

holiday in Dalaanzadgad Town (Yu K. Gorelov, personal communication).

Is it possible, therefore, that despite the death worm's initially unlikely form and behavioural proclivities, there is indeed a real, scientifically-undescribed species at the heart of this longstanding mystery, albeit one far less flamboyant and formidable than the version described in local testimony? Could it even be true, as suggested by Gorelov's testimony, that the entire death worm scenario is nothing more than native folklore?

Of course, the latter claim signally fails to explain the report collected by Ivan Mackerle of how a geologist was instantly killed by a death worm simply by touching it indirectly with an iron rod. Also needing to be taken into account here is the misleading practice by locals of readily agreeing with suggestions put to them by Western visitors in order to ingratiate themselves with the visitors—an occurrence often reported in cryptozoological investigations.

In recent times, several expeditions other than those of Ivan have also searched the southern Gobi's vast terrain for its purported 'monster', but none has met with any success so far. Well worth noting, as some of these later expeditions were startled to discover, the newest generation of Gobi nomads are as likely to be riding desert motorbikes as camels, and some even carry mobile phones inside the folds of their traditional desert robes. So perhaps they are also heeding less and less the traditional stories and beliefs of their elders.

Having said that, there may be another, very different reason why these expeditions have returned empty-handed. Some locals claim that death worms have been seen far less frequently in recent years than in the past. Who knows—perhaps, just as the rest of the world has finally started to learn about and become interested in it, the Mongolian death worm has begun slipping inexorably into extinction.

How ironic that would be—almost as ironic, in fact, as Prof. Roy Chapman Andrews's straight-faced promise to the Mongolian premier back in 1922 that if his expedition did encounter a death worm during their search for dinosaur fossils in the Gobi, they would do their best to secure its capture using a pair of long steel collecting forceps. In view of what reputedly happened to the hapless geologist who poked one of these fearful creatures with a metal rod, it's probably just as well that Prof. Andrews and his team never did find any!

EPILOGUE

I have recently been considering a new potential explanation for the Mongolian death worm's reputed power of electrocution, one that as far as I am aware has not been previously proposed. If it truly exists, might this elusive creature bear fine, venom-producing hair-like spines over its outer surface, comparable to the urticating hairs borne by certain caterpillars and spiders, for example, which when touched elicit such extreme pain that it feels like having received an electric shock? This precise description is frequently cited for Japan's aptly-dubbed denkimushi or electric bug—the brightly-coloured but greatly-feared hairy caterpillar of *Monema flavescens*, a species of limacodid or cup moth.

Alternatively, perhaps its corrosive venom is not just actively sprayed forth when the death worm is threatened, but is also passively secreted over its outer surface even under normal conditions, keeping it moist, thereby preventing desiccation, but also protecting the animal at all times from would-be attackers, and inducing extreme pain so swiftly as to create the illusion of having delivered an electric shock?

Lastly, here is a fascinating snippet of potentially relevant information kindly brought to my attention by correspondent Keith Baker on 24 October 2012. He noted that Thomas Rymer Jones's book *A General Outline of the Animal Kingdom* (1841) contains the following short but intriguing statement about a certain centipede species (since renamed *Geophilus electricus*):

> Some Scolopendrae . . . emit in the dark a strong phosphorescent light; and one species (*S. electrica*) is able to give a powerful electrical shock to the hand of the person who inadvertently seizes it.

This centipede species is bioluminescent too, but I haven't obtained any independent corroboration regarding an ability to give electric shocks. However, the venomous bite of certain large species is excruciatingly painful, so once again this might give the illusion of having delivered an electric shock.

How ironic it would be if we have been looking in entirely the wrong direction all along when seeking to explain the Mongolian death worm's alleged ability to electrocute.

11
SNAKES WITH WINGS—AND OTHER STRANGE THINGS

> I went once to a certain place in Arabia, almost exactly opposite the city of Buto, to make inquiries concerning the winged serpents. On my arrival I saw the back-bones and ribs of serpents in such numbers as it is impossible to describe: of the ribs there were a multitude of heaps, some great, some small, some middle-sized. The place where the bones lie is at the entrance of a narrow gorge between steep mountains, where there open upon a spacious plain communicating with the great plain of Egypt. The story goes that with the spring the winged snakes come flying from Arabia towards Egypt, but are met in this gorge by the birds called ibises, who forbid their entrance and destroy them all. The Arabians assert, and the Egyptians also admit, that it is on account of the service thus rendered that the Egyptians hold the ibis in so much reverence.
>
> Herodotus—*The History, Book II*

Despite their common name, the five species of so-called flying snake (genus *Chrysopelea*) of southeast Asia cannot actively fly. However, it is well known that these distinctive species can glide for up to 300 ft through the air by launching themselves from a tree while simultaneously spreading their ribs and flattening their body, until their undersurface is concave, thereby transforming themselves into a ribbon-shaped parachute.

Yet according to some remarkable reports filed away within the bulging archives of cryptozoology, there may be some currently-undescribed species of snake that are capable of true flight, i.e. achieved with the aid of wings or comparable means of active propulsion.

THE NAMIBIAN FLYING SNAKE

One such mystery beast is the supposed flying snake that has been reported not only by the native Namaqua people but also by a number of European eyewitnesses within the Namib Desert of southern Namibia. According to their generally consistent accounts, it has a brown or yellow body mottled with dark spots, an inflated neck, and a notably large head bearing a pair of short backward-pointing horns—plus, very remarkably, a glowing 'torch' in the centre of its brow. Most astonishing of all, however, is the pair of membranous bat-like wings allegedly emerging from the sides of its neck or mouth.

Eyewitnesses have stated that this extraordinary snake launches itself from the summit of a high rocky ledge, then soars down to the ground, landing with an appreciable impact and producing scaly tracks in the dusty earth. In 1942, while tending sheep in the mountains at Keetmanshoop, teenager Michael Esterhuise threw a stone at what he had assumed to be a large monitor lizard lurking inside a rocky crack. When it emerged, however, it revealed itself to be a big snake with a pair of wing-like structures projecting from the sides of its mouth.

On a separate occasion, moreover, one of these serpents soared down towards Esterhuise after having launched itself from a rocky ledge. When it landed, hitting the ground with great force, Esterhuise fainted, and when he was later found (unharmed, although still unconscious) by a search party, the snake had gone but its tracks remained. They were subsequently examined by no less celebrated a naturalist than Marjorie Courtenay-Latimer—curator of South Africa's East London Museum and immortalised zoologically as the discoverer of that famous 'living fossil' fish the coelacanth *Latimeria chalumnae* in 1938. In her opinion, these tracks, containing the clear impression of scales, were indeed consistent with the marks that a snake would make.

11 | SNAKES WITH WINGS

Namibian flying snake based upon eyewitness descriptions (© Philippa Foster)

Second representation of the Namibian flying snake's possible appearance (© Tim Morris)

A South African television documentary by Angus Whitty Productions, entitled *In Search of the Giant Flying Snake of Namibia* and first broadcast in 1995, contained testimony from a number of alleged eyewitnesses, which provided estimates of this mystery serpent's total length that ranged from 9 ft to 15 ft. The programme also specially prepared and featured on-screen a detailed drawing of the latter snake's alleged appearance based upon such testimony.

Well worth noting is that Namibia is a former German colony, so it is not impossible that Teutonic legends of lightning snakes retold here by German settlers may have infiltrated and influenced native Namibian lore. However, such legends cannot leave physical, tangible tracks like those examined by Miss Courtenay-Latimer, so perhaps a real snake is indeed present but one whose appearance has been exaggerated or distorted in the telling, due to shock, by those who have unexpectedly encountered it.

If so, the Namibian flying snake may still be an undescribed species, but one that in reality merely sports a pair of extensible lateral membranes similar to those of the famous Asian gliding lizard *Draco volans* (although whether such structures would be sufficiently adept, aerodynamically, to bear so sizeable a snake through the air is another matter), plus a pair of horny projections resembling the 'eyebrow' horns of certain African vipers. As for its glowing 'torch', this may be nothing more mysterious than a highly-reflective patch of shining scales on its brow.

THE TL'IISH NAAT'A'I OF ARIZONA

For a number of years, American cryptozoologist Nick Sucik has been investigating reports of an equally mystifying but even more obscure aerial anomaly of the serpentine kind—the tl'iish naat'a'í (pronounced 'kleesh-not-ahee' and translated as 'snake that flies'). Also known as the Arizona flying snake, apparently this bizarre reptile is a familiar creature there to the Navajo Nation, and to the Hopi Nation as well (who refer to it by names translating as 'sun snake'). They all describe it as being fundamentally serpentine in form, generally around 6 ft long, and dull grey in colour (although sometimes said to have a red belly), but possessing a pair of retractable and virtually transparent wing-like membranes. These emerge from behind its head, run laterally along much of its body's length,

11 | SNAKES WITH WINGS

can flap vigorously and very rapidly, and are thus used for active flight (rather than passive gliding).

Some eyewitnesses have stated that these membranes sparkle in the sun when illuminated at certain angles. They also claim that this mysterious reptile constructs a kind of nest from twigs, located along the sides of cliffs or among rocks; and that when airborne, its flying membranes make a hissing sound, likened by some witnesses to a passenger jet's noise when passing by overhead. Comparable reports have also emerged from both the Texan and the Mexican sides of the Rio Grande, including one claimed sighting of a supposed snake-like entity flying amid a group of bats there that was videoed at 4 am one morning by a security camera at Lajitas, Texas.

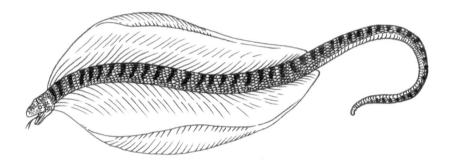

Reconstruction of the Arizona flying snake's possible appearance (© Tim Morris)

The video can presently be accessed on YouTube (at: https://www.youtube.com/watch?v=F-T9lnJDfVg), where it was posted by a Gil Bartee on 26 June 2008. Sadly, however, the alleged serpent is only glimpsed very briefly (I assume that it is the entity appearing at 0:54 minutes into the video—Bartee provides no details), and even then not clearly. Some viewers have opined that it may itself have been a bat (albeit a much larger one) or even an owl, but Nick is not convinced by such identities.

A somewhat different version has also been reported from Arizona. Known as the arrow snake or via a Navajo name written phonetically as kleesh-kaw, it is said to be black with white stripes, and more frequently sighted than the tl'iish naat'a'í.

On 10 November 2016, British cryptozoological researcher Richard Muirhead posted in *Facebook*'s Cryptozoology Herpetological

Research Group a hitherto-obscure newspaper article dealing principally with one of the afore-mentioned, long-known Asian flying snake species (*Chrysopelea*), but whose final paragraph contained information that is definitely of cryptozoological interest. Published in the *Oregonian* on 15 March 1942, the paragraph in question reads as follows:

> A western prototype [i.e. of *Chrysopelea ornata*] is reputed to exist somewhere in Southern Mexico, although snake experts have made many fruitless expeditions into the interior for living specimens.

Might this be a previously-unpublicised reference to the tl'iish naat'a'í? If so, however, it indicates that this mystery snake, or something comparable, exists further south in Mexico than the Rio Grande.

In 2004, Nick Sucik prepared a detailed paper documenting traditional folklore and contemporary sightings relating to the tl'iish naat'a'í, which can presently be accessed online (at: https://www.yumpu.com/en/document/read/377836/exploring-the-prospect-of-an-unidentified-species-of-reptile-within-). It contains a number of fascinating eyewitness accounts of this truly extraordinary, zoologically-unknown snake.

On 26 September 2021, Tim Swartz kindly posted the following information on my *ShukerNature* blog regarding a couple of flying snake reports from Indiana that were new to me:

> The state of Indiana in the U.S. has had its fair share of winged snake accounts over the years. The *Ft. Wayne Gazette* ran a tantalizingly short article on May 27, 1883 that referred to "A vast quantity of mammal fossils were found in Wabash County. This is near the same location where Justice of the Peace, Lewis Keagle, of Laketon, saw a large flying serpent a few years ago. The squire has lost his interest in all science and attends strictly to his office affairs."
>
> I conducted a little research on Justice Lewis Keagle, he was a veteran of the Civil war, serving in Company E, 130th Infantry Regiment Indiana. He served in the capacity of Justice of the Peace in

Wabash County starting in 1876 and passed away in 1897. Unfortunately, I couldn't find any other references about Justice Keagle and his flying serpent.

Another flying serpent was seen in September 1883 near Greensburg, Indiana. According to the *Decatur Review* (Decatur, Illinois—October 17 1914) Mrs. Joseph Groswick and Mrs. Casper were out in a buggy when a seven-foot-long winged serpent flew out of a tree and chased the pair for almost a mile. Luckily, a pair of hunters and their dogs managed to chase the creature away before it did any damage. In addition to its wings, the two women claimed the snake also had a beak like an eagle.

In addition, an 18-20-ft-long luminous white 'sky eel' with flapping side fins was seen wriggling and hovering in the sky above Crawfordville, Indiana, for two successive nights during 4-5 September 1891, which its numerous eyewitnesses felt sure was a living creature. This is just one of a number of reports published during the 1800s and earlier concerning enormous snake-like entities observed writhing through the sky over the USA and elsewhere around the world. However, as further investigations indicate that these so-called sky serpents are more likely to have been meteorological than zoological in nature, I have not included them here, but details can be found in a chapter dealing with supposed sky beasts and other aerial anomalies in my book *Dr Shuker's Casebook* (2008).

CONTINENTAL EUROPEAN WINGED SNAKES

Remarkably, some intriguing but thoroughly mystifying, modern-day reports of aerial snakes have even been filed from Europe. For instance, one day during 1930 or 1931, the mother of André Mellira was preparing lunch in a hut deep within the forest at the mountain village of La Bollène-Vésubie, close to Nice, southern France, when she looked out of the window and saw what looked like a green snake with wings! Moreover, this amazing creature promptly flew down from the branches of a tree close by and landed upon the hut's window sill. When Mellira's mother cried out in fear and alarm, however, her unexpected winged visitor dived down into a bush and vanished. Intriguingly, there is a longstanding tradition of winged snakes inhabiting the southern Alps, but these have always been discounted by scientists as myths.

An illustration from a 1723 publication by Swiss scholar Johann Jakob Scheuchzer depicting an alleged alpine winged snake

A 12-year-old Bulgarian girl called Hazel Göksu was walking towards a spring very near her home one summer evening in 1947 in order to fill two buckets with water. Suddenly, however, she noticed what initially looked like some branches lying on the path ahead, but as she drew nearer she realised that they were thin snakes. Black, grey, and white in colour, and 3-6 ft long, they abruptly emitted a peculiar cry—and then launched themselves into the air, flying 6-10 ft above the ground in a straight line to the spring, about 500 ft away, before vanishing behind some trees. Hazel was so frightened by what she had seen that she ran back to her home immediately, and never visited the spring again alone.

GLAMORGAN'S PLUME-WINGED POULTRY PREDATORS

British mythology is replete with folktales and legends of fabulous beasts, including many that feature dragons and other reptilian monsters. Surely the most remarkable of these, however, are the jewel-scaled, plume-winged wonders that were reportedly still existing in Wales as recently as the 1800s.

Marie Trevelyan brought these exquisite creatures to widespread attention in her book *Folk-Lore and Folk Stories of Wales* (1909), and her description of them is so vibrant and uniquely detailed for such an ostensibly implausible type of beast that it deserves quoting here:

> The woods round Penllyne Castle, Glamorgan [in southern Wales], had the reputation of being frequented by winged serpents, and these were the terror of old and young alike. An aged inhabitant of Penllyne, who died a few years ago [c.1900], said that in his boyhood the winged serpents were described as very beautiful. They were coiled when in repose, and "looked as if they were covered with jewels of all sorts. Some of them had crests sparkling with all the colours of the rainbow." When disturbed they glided swiftly, "sparkling all over," to their hiding places. When angry, they "flew over people's heads, with outspread wings bright, and sometimes with eyes too, like the feathers in a peacock's tail." He said it was "no story invented to frighten children," but a real fact. His father and uncle had killed some of them, for they were "as bad as foxes for poultry." The old man attributed the extinction of the winged serpents to the fact that they were "terrors in the farmyards and coverts."

An old woman, whose parents in her early childhood took her to visit Penmark Place, Glamorgan, said she often heard the people talking about the ravages of the winged serpents in that neighbourhood. She described them in the same way as the man of Penllyne. There was a "king and queen" of winged serpents, she said, in the woods round Bewper. The old people in her early days said that wherever winged serpents were to be seen "there was sure to be buried money or something of value" near at hand. Her grandfather told her of an encounter with a winged serpent in the woods near Porthkerry Park, not far from Penmark. He and his brother "made up their minds to catch one, and watched a whole day for the serpent to rise. Then they shot at it, and the creature fell wounded, only to rise and attack my uncle, beating him about the head with its wings." She said a fierce fight ensured between the men and the serpent, which was at last killed. She had seen its skin and feathers, but after the grandfather's death they were thrown away. That serpent was as notorious "as any fox" in the farmyards and coverts around Penmark.

A Glamorgan feathered snake with wings from the front cover of my book *From Flying Toads To Snakes With Wings* (© Dr Karl Shuker)

11 | SNAKES WITH WINGS

In 1812, very similar beasts were also reported in the Vale of Edeirnion, northern Wales.

What could have inspired such astonishing accounts? Remarkably, it has been suggested by certain folklorists and cryptozoologists that these truly exceptional creatures were pheasants. As the ring-necked pheasant *Phasianus colchicus* (the only species present in Wales during the early 19th Century) was introduced into Britain back in Roman times, however, it seems unlikely that a species so well-established here by the 1800s could be mistaken for anything as exotic as a plumed serpent with wings.

Even less likely is the prospect that they represented an unknown species of pheasant, one perhaps that was more elongate in form than usual (possessing a longer-than-typical neck and tail perhaps?), so as to present a vaguely serpentine appearance. For if this were indeed so, there is no doubt whatsoever that many specimens of such a distinctive and extremely eye-catching bird would have been diligently preserved as prized taxiderm exhibits in country manors and museums. Such a striking form of game bird would also have been extensively documented and depicted in countryside magazines or those devoted to hunting and shooting—sports that were extremely prevalent and popular throughout Britain two

A pair of ring-necked pheasants

centuries ago, and obviously it would have been instantly recognised by hunters, poachers, and gamekeepers alike as a mere bird, not some bizarre reptilian entity more akin to the Aztecs' deified Quetzalcoatl!

In short, if such a spectacular, impossible-to-overlook bird had ever inhabited Wales as late in time as the 1800s, it would have been formally discovered and described long before it was ultimately exterminated. Instead, it is conspicuous only by its absence from natural history tomes and from any other wildlife publications, being solely confined to the pages of Trevelyan's book and to scant mentions elsewhere in other works of British mythology.

Equally difficult to explain if these bedazzling beasts were genuinely pheasants (known or unknown species notwithstanding) is their appetite for the farmers' chickens, earning them the reputation of being as troublesome on this score as foxes. Whereas male pheasants can be aggressive, it hardly need be pointed out that they do not feast upon chickens. Ditto for the possibility that they constituted escapee peacocks. And there is no known bird of prey native to Britain (or, indeed, anywhere else in the world for that matter) that matches the multicoloured, glittering appearance described for the thoroughly baffling albeit very beautiful creatures under consideration here.

The same situation also arises when seeking parallels outside the confines of recognised natural history, by venturing forth instead within the more flexible boundaries of zoomythology. An association with buried treasure or similar hoards of riches is of course a familiar theme in dragon myths, but otherwise there is nothing even vaguely comparable between Wales's winged feathered serpents and any other beast of British legend and folklore on record. For not only is their morphology exceptional, so too are their surprising erstwhile abundance and the acceptance of them by the local people as relatively mundane members of the area's fauna.

If only the skin and feathers of that killed specimen had been preserved and submitted for scientific examination instead of being discarded. After all, it's not every day that the opportunity to examine the mortal remains of a winged, feathered, serpent arises!

11 | SNAKES WITH WINGS

A COUPLE OF WINGED WHATSITS AROUND LONDON

Perhaps the most unexpected flying snakes on record from England were reported from just outside its capital city—London. For according to a correspondent writing as 'SB' in *The Gentleman's Magazine* on 20 April 1798, a truly remarkable animal was observed during early August 1776 just a few miles west of London:

> The strange object was of the serpent kind: its size that of the largest common snake; and as well as it could be discovered from so transient a view of it, resembled it by a kind of grey mottled skin. The head of this extraordinary animal appeared about the size of a small woman's hand. It had a pair of short wings very forward on the body, near its head; and the length of the whole body was about two feet. Its flight was very gentle; it seemed too heavy to fly either fast or high; and its manner of flying was not in an horizontal attitude, but with its head considerably higher than the tail; so that it seemed continually labouring to ascend without ever being able to raise itself much higher than seven or eight feet from the ground.

This same magazine subsequently published a second, more recent report, by a correspondent signing only as 'JR'—describing a sighting by a friend of the same (or a very similar) flying snake encountered at 10.30 pm on 15 July 1797 on the road between London's Hammersmith and Hyde Park Corner:

> The body was of a dark colour, about the thickness of the lower part of a man's arm, about two feet long. The wings were very short, and placed near the head. The head was raised above the body. It was not seven or eight feet from the ground. Being an animal of such uncommon description, I was particular in noticing the day of the month, and likewise being the day preceding a most dreadful storm of thunder and lightning.

If we are willing to accept that these reports are neither outright hoaxes (worth noting, however, is that neither of the authors supplied their name) nor even some abstruse example of 18th-Century political satire, we can only assume that the observers were not zoologically-informed, and had mistaken some other, less bizarre creature for a flying snake. For example, might these two accounts have been grotesque exaggerations of some large insect like a damselfly or robber fly (both of which when in flight sometimes hold their body in a similar pose to that described for this winged serpent)?

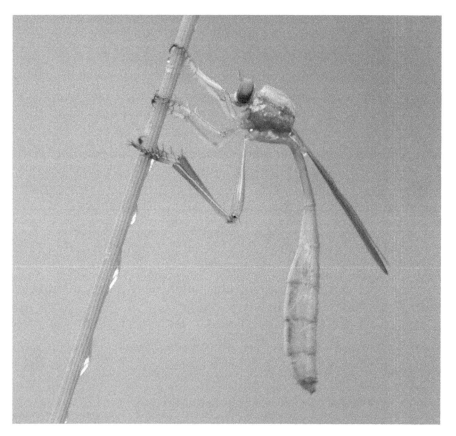

Robber fly (Vengolis, CC BY-SA 4.0)

Indeed, this particular case reminds me of those occasions on which I have been asked to remove 'baby horned snakes' from neighbours' gardens during the summer, only to discover time and time again that they are actually the quite sizeable, very distinctive caterpillars of the large elephant hawk moth *Deilephila elpenor*.

11 | SNAKES WITH WINGS

Having said that, however, and having read many times the two authors' respective descriptions quoted above from *The Gentleman's Magazine* of what they allegedly saw, I still do not have even the slightest notion of what this enigmatic creature may have been.

The same applies to this short but thoroughly perplexing report, hitherto unpublicised in the cryptozoological literature, of a supposed winged snake encountered in a garden in the Welsh village of Cefn on 16 June 1858:

> On the morning of the 16th inst., Mrs. Mary Richards, landlady of the Cefn Inn, Cefn, near Rista, states that she, being at the time in her own garden, heard a rustling noise, similar to the shaking of a leather apron, and on looking up distinctly saw an animal body shaped like a snake, with wings about the size of a common bellows, flying about 14 feet from the ground!

A 'baby horned snake' that is in reality the very distinctive caterpillar of the large elephant hawk moth (AnemoneProjectors, CC BY-SA 2.0)

This report appeared on 23 June 1858 in the *Worcester Chronicle* newspaper, where it had been quoted directly from another newspaper, the *Bristol Mercury*.

EGYPT'S PLAGUE OF FLYING SERPENTS

Finally: no discussion of aerial snakes could be complete without considering the very curious case of Egypt's supposed plague of flying serpents.

In early times, small but highly venomous snakes of many different colours but all possessing membranous bat-like wings reputedly existed in Arabia, and congregated in great throngs upon those prized trees that produced the much-sought-after frankincense resin. According to the celebrated Greek historian Herodotus of Halicarnassus (c.484-c.425 BC):

> [The Arabians] gather frankincense by burning that storax [styrax resin] which Phoenicians carry to Hellas; they burn this and so get the frankincense; for the spice-bearing trees are guarded by small winged snakes of varied colour, many around each tree; these are the snakes that attack Egypt. Nothing except the smoke of storax will drive them away from the trees.

So numerous were they, in fact, that during their springtime migration from Arabia towards Egypt, the very air resounded with their incessant hissing and the unceasing beating of innumerable wings. Happily, however, as described in another Herodotus quote, which opens this present chapter of my own book, Egypt's sacred ibises soon decimated these toxic ophidian locusts, devouring them in such vast quantities that none remained.

Many scholars believe that these winged wonders really were locusts, whose 'transformation' into snakes was due merely to exaggerated, elaborated retellings by successive storytellers down through the ages. Others claim that they were genuine snakes, but that their wings were either hearsay or fictitious additions purposefully supplied later by chroniclers anxious to enhance their tomes' dramatic content.

Alternatively, the great piles of bones claimed by Herodotus to be those of Arabian winged snakes may in reality have been fossils, possibly of the elongate, superficially snake-like early Cretaceous salamander *Ramonellus longispinus*, proposed in 2007 by London-based researcher Karen Radner. Its fossils have been found in great quantities at Makhtesh Ramon—a huge erosion crater (the world's largest) in Israel's Negev Desert.

Whatever the explanation, it can be said with certainty that in spite of Herodotus's first-hand observation of what he claimed to be masses of piled-up skeletons of these creatures, no such snakes exist in the Middle East today. Presumably, therefore, the skeletons seen by him were not from snakes at all (with no detailed description or illustrations of them to examine, it is impossible to know for sure)—or perhaps they truly were once real, but their macabre mode of reproduction explains their demise.

Bestiary engraving of Arabian flying snakes and ibis

For according yet again to the writings of Herodotus (and those of several other ancient historians too), at the very height of passion the female Arabian winged snake would bite her unfortunate partner's head off, rather like a serpentine praying mantis. And when the young snakes developing inside her afterwards had attained the required size for emerging into outside world, they would gnaw their way out of their mother's body, chewing through her uterus and gut, thereby killing her in the process.

Consequently, even if such fanciful creatures really did exist at one time, cursed with such a deadly mode of reproduction and birth it is perhaps little wonder that Arabia's flying serpents became extinct!

In reality, however, it seems far more plausible that such claims were based upon misinterpretations of skin sloughing in snakes, with observers of such activity wrongly assuming that a matured snake offspring was bursting out through the skin of a dead parent. Or, to put it another way: in addition to being a highly influential scholar, Herodotus was nothing if not an imaginative one!

12
COURTING THE COBRA

> "Who is Nag?" said he. "I am Nag. The great god Brahm put his mark upon all our people when the first cobra spread his hood to keep the sun off Brahm as he slept. Look, and be afraid!"
>
> Rudyard Kipling—'Rikki-Tikki-Tavi', from *The Jungle Book*

Since time immemorial, humans have been irresistibly fascinated by snakes—but most especially by cobras, nurturing an innate, inexplicable desire for close interaction, and even intimacy, with these large, highly venomous, and ostensibly imperious entities. This arcane aspiration has attained expression by all manner of different means. They include: fear-infiltrated veneration and handling by acolytes of Indian snake cults that perceived cobras as reincarnations of bygone leaders and referred to them as nagas; the fragile balance of respect and control achieved in authentic cobra charming; and even highly-emotive displays of devoted, unreserved love for these regal reptiles, fervently believed by many to bestow blessings upon their homes and lives.

Yet for many Westerners, cobra cults and other manifestations of humankind's mystical inter-relationship with these serpents are totally alien concepts—exhibiting facets of human and reptilian behaviour that seemingly transcend traditional explanation or rationalisation.

THE SERPENT GOD AND THE SNAKE PRIESTESS

One particularly dramatic case, recorded in his book *On Safari* (1963), was witnessed by no less an authority than Armand Denis, the pioneering wildlife film-maker and author. In 1939, during a filming expedition to the Far East, Denis was in northern Burma (now Myanmar), investigating whether ophiolatreia (snake worship) was still practised there, when he met an old Buddhist priest who told him to travel to a remote mountainous village, where he would be shown all that he hoped to see—and more! Two days later, Denis had arrived, and the next morning he found himself sitting in a flower-decorated oxcart alongside the village's snake priestess, a beautiful young woman in her early 30s, at the head of a procession containing most of the other villagers, who were bearing gifts for the serpent god and providing enthusiastic musical accompaniment with an ample supply of bells and gongs.

After a sedate journey along a winding mountain path, Denis and company finally neared a small cave, the journey's destination. Quite a while later, during which time the villagers had busied themselves strewing assorted offerings to the serpent god on either side of the path leading to the cave, the snake priestess walked steadily towards the cave's opening, accompanied for part of the way by Denis. At the opening the priestess paused, and called into it. A few minutes later an enormous snake emerged, and coiled itself at her feet. It was a cobra—but no ordinary one, for this was nothing less than *Ophiophagus hannah*, the king cobra. As thick as a man's arm and sheathed in olive-green scales imparting a deep, velvet-like sheen, complemented by a superimposed series of pale-yellow cross-bands down its body's length and more distinct ones upon its neck, with a total length of up to 18.5 ft the king cobra is the world's largest venomous snake. It is also one of its most deadly, and most aggressive—so much so that the preferred diet of this most macho of mega-serpents is other snakes (*Ophiophagus* translates as 'snake-eater').

Even as the priestess stood there, absolutely motionless, the huge snake rose up with hood outstretched, standing erect and poised to strike. Able to hold its head 3 ft or more above the ground, and positioned less than 4 ft away from her, it was well within range. Yet in answer to the cobra's challenge, the priestess merely bowed her own head towards it, slowly, deferentially, and seemingly without

12 | COURTING THE COBRA

fear. Responding immediately, the snake lunged forward, striking at the level of her knees, but in the same instant the woman had moved slightly to one side, so that the cobra's deadly fangs made harmless contact with the fabric of her pure-white skirt. This macabre dance of would-be death between snake and woman, or deity and priestess, was repeated many times, and on each occasion the woman succeeded in avoiding the powerful reptile's fatal fangs—recalling a skilful matador deflecting the terrible horns of a charging bull, but equipped with a skirt of snow rather than a cloak of crimson.

Suddenly, however, the snake priestess's performance reached its particular climax in a manner never mirrored by that of any matador. With her hands placed behind her back, she moved a little closer to her lethal god, and during a moment when it remained erect but immobile, she leaned forward and lightly kissed the king cobra on top of its head! Drawing back instantaneously, she countered the inevitable strike that ensued, after which she promptly kissed the cobra again, and, after deflecting its consequent lunge, kissed it a third time too. The ceremony thus concluded, she simply turned her back on the cobra, and walked away, slowly but apparently untroubled, towards Denis and the waiting villagers. Nor was her confidence betrayed by the cobra—instead of striking her from behind, it merely turned aside and slid swiftly from sight into its cave.

If, during the journey back to the village, Denis had suspected that he had been hallucinating, and that this astonishing ritual had never happened, one could surely have forgiven him, because it certainly seems almost beyond belief that such a performance could ever take place. However, he had conclusive evidence for its reality right before his eyes. Clearly visible on the woman's white skirt were many damp, amber-hued stains—the potent venom of a king cobra, the legacy of her audience with her ophidian deity.

This astonishing performance has been witnessed over the years by other Western observers too, and behavioural zoologist Dr Desmond Morris's book *Men and Snakes* (1965) includes photographs of an even more incredible variation on its macabre theme—in which the snake priestess is shown kissing the king cobra not on top of its head but directly on its mouth! This terrifying deed was also regularly performed by celebrated Burmese snake charmer Saya Hnin-Mahla as the climax of her act with her co-performer, an adult king cobra.

King cobra *Ophiophagus hannah* (Rushen, CC BY-SA 2.0)

Burmese snake charmer Saya Hnin-Mahla kissing a king cobra

12 | COURTING THE COBRA

SPITTING IN THE FACE OF DANGER—LITERALLY!

Narrating a selection of his varied wildlife experiences on an LP record album but again entitled *On Safari*, Armand Denis recalled a second, no less extraordinary encounter that he had witnessed between king cobra and human. Just before World War II, Denis was in Singapore on a filming assignment, and in order to complete the wildlife film that he had been working upon he advertised locally for a number of king cobras, a common species in that area. Eventually, he received about a dozen, all adult and extremely belligerent, which he maintained in a securely-fastened crate with a fine wire-netting top, whose mesh they profusely drenched with their potent venom as they struck at it repeatedly in their fury at finding themselves held captive in this manner.

One day, a young Chinese boy, dressed in a strange white garb with deep sleeves, arrived at Denis's hotel, and gravely volunteered his services to Denis as a snake-handler, provided that Denis would give him one of the king cobras at the end of the filming sessions. Although he naturally doubted the boy's capability to handle such dangerous snakes as these in safety, Denis was sufficiently intrigued by his serious demeanour and outlandish offer to allow him to take a look at the cobras, while they writhed irritably but impotently within the confines of their locked crate. The boy soon focused his attention upon one especially large and aggressive specimen, which he considered to be very beautiful, and which, he assured Denis, he would have no problem in handling. Needless to say, Denis swiftly reminded him that this was a lethal creature that no-one would dare to handle in its current, highly emotional state. Not until it had quietened down during several days of captivity could it be considered in any way safe to deal with, and only then for filming purposes.

The boy merely smiled, however, and asserted confidently that it would be very easy for him to handle it now—straight away—and in complete safety. He then began to prise up one corner of the crate, and Denis, very much alarmed, implored him to leave the snake alone. In response, the boy paused, and withdrew from the folds of one of his long sleeves a small vial of strange green liquid, which, when uncorked, released a fragrance vaguely reminiscent of freshly-cut grass. He poured some of this into his mouth, and then leaned down to the crate, until his face was well within the cobra's striking range. Hardly daring to look, Denis could only stand and await the inevitable, instantaneous strike that would swiftly bring death to this foolish child. Instead, it was the boy who acted first, and in a very unexpected manner.

Leaning even closer to the crate, he suddenly spat the liquid out of his mouth, spraying it liberally all over the face, head, and body of his chosen cobra! The boy waited for about a minute, and then—to Denis's even greater surprise, and absolute horror!—he casually reached into the crate and lifted the cobra out, his hands around the middle of its body's great length, holding this huge deadly serpent with no more concern than any other child might display when holding a length of cord or a skipping rope. By some uncanny means, the green liquid appeared to have rendered the cobra almost totally passive; true, it reared its ebony-scaled, fist-sized head upwards to gaze evenly at its young captor, but it made no attempt to strike at him.

After a time, the boy placed the cobra back into the crate, bowed solemnly to a still-stupefied Denis, and walked out of his room, promising to come back the following morning, and handle all of the cobras in the crate—but he did not return, and Denis never saw his mysterious visitor again.

REPELLING RATTLESNAKES

Science has yet to offer a satisfactory explanation for the phenomenal spectacle witnessed by Denis that day, but it is widely asserted that certain substances will successfully repel various snakes, including some of the most venomous species. For example, there is a longstanding belief in parts of Ohio that rattlesnakes are effectively repelled by the leaves of the white ash *Fraxinus americanus*. As he reported in the *American Journal of Science* in 1823, Samuel Woodruff once had the opportunity to test this belief, when he unexpectedly encountered a large *Crotalus* rattlesnake near northeastern Ohio's Mahoning River.

Searching for a white ash to assess its effects upon this snake, Woodruff soon found one nearby, and cut a wand from it, bearing a quantity of its leaves. He then returned to the snake, and, when it coiled and made ready to strike him as he approached, Woodruff

12 | COURTING THE COBRA

leaned forward and placed the leaves on its body. The snake immediately threw its body into violent contortions, writhing and twisting upon its back as if in great agony. Not until Woodruff lifted the wand off its body did the snake assume its former pose, ready to attack.

When obtaining his wand of white ash, Woodruff had also cut a wand from another species of tree, the sugar maple *Acer saccharum*, to serve as a control. He now placed this wand on the snake, but it had no effect at all—instead, the snake struck fiercely at it, its head momentarily becoming obscured among the wand's leaves. Woodruff repeated this ploy with the sugar maple wand several times, always with the same outcome, but when he subsequently applied the white ash wand once more, the snake again threw itself into anguished contortions upon its back, which only ceased when the wand was removed. At around this same time, the renowned American zoologist Prof. Benjamin Silliman tested this response of rattlesnakes to the leaves of the white ash, and he obtained comparable results.

Are rattlesnakes repelled by white ash?
Timber rattlesnake *Crotalus horridus* (Peter Paplanus, CC BY 2.0)

NULLA PAMBU—THE GOOD SNAKE

During the late 1960s, naturalist Harry Miller was privileged to witness one of the most mystical, and mystifying, of all cobra rituals—the festival of Naga Panchami, held at Shirala, a village in Maharashtra, western India (*National Geographic*, September 1970). Taking place each July (on the fifth day of the moon in Sawan, according to snake symbolism researcher J.H. Rivett-Carnac, quoted in Tudor Press's *Serpent Worship*, 1980), it celebrates *Naja naja*, the familiar spectacled cobra—which the Shirala villagers call Nulla Pambu, the Good Snake, and deem to be a manifestation of the god Shiva.

For days before the festival, cobras were assiduously collected from the surrounding countryside and placed inside earthenware pots, which were then sealed to restrain their occupants from emerging prematurely. On the morning of the festival, the pots were carried in a joyful if noisy procession through the village, and onwards to a small temple, into which the reptiles were released—but the ceremony was far from over.

On the contrary, the cobras were frequently handled devotedly by their former captors, displayed to the deity, worshipped by throngs of villagers, sprinkled deferentially with confetti-like showers of rice, exhibited in brightly-bedecked mobile carts, crowned with coronets of single flowers, and then returned to their pots overnight, awaiting release into the countryside the following morning.

Yet never once, through all of this, and with hundreds of cobras at large and freely handled by the villagers, was a single person bitten! Moreover, when Miller's assistant examined many of the participating cobras prior to their release, he discovered to his great surprise that they all possessed their venom fangs intact—none had been removed or tampered with in any way. The cobras were therefore fully able to bite, and to kill—yet they did neither. True, the spectacled cobra can often be essentially docile and rather reluctant to bite; also, from a very early age the Shirala villagers are taught how to handle snakes correctly, beginning with harmless species and eventually graduating to the cobras themselves and other venomous species. Even so, can these factors really be enough to explain such astonishingly intimate yet apparently wholly safe interaction with these potentially lethal reptiles?

12 | COURTING THE COBRA

THE TEMPLE VIPERS OF PENANG

A comparably close association between human and snake is the standard feature at one of the most unusual yet popular tourist attractions in the Far East—the Snake Temple of Penang, Malaysia. Here, amidst the sultry half-light and heady fumes of burning incense, countless numbers of lethargic serpents repose languorously upon branches planted in ceremonial urns, placed reverentially before the altar of this extraordinary Buddhist shrine.

Wagler's pit viper or temple viper *Tropidolaemus wagleri* (Rushen, CC BY-SA 2.0)

Bright emerald green with encircling bands of gold, and belonging to the highly venomous species known as Wagler's pit viper *Tropidolaemus wagleri*, these sacred snakes never leave their temple abode. Instead, they spend their days feeding upon eggs conveyed to them in baskets by obeisant human attendants, and gazing inscrutably with ever-open eyes upon the congregation of Eastern worshippers and Western sightseers visiting the shrine every year—compelled by an intrinsic, inexplicable desire to experience the mystical union of fear and fascination that snakes have so effortlessly aroused in humankind from the earliest times.

AZTEC ADORATION

Of course, snake worship and snake handling are by no means limited to cobras, but few other examples involve such feats of raw courage and hair-trigger emotional control upon the part of the worshipper as those exhibited by the Burmese *Ophiophagus* priestesses and by the villagers participating in Naga Panchami. Perhaps the most comparable, paradoxically, is one involving a non-venomous species—the boa constrictor *Boa constrictor*, from Mexico, the Caribbean, and South America.

Numerous snake temples existed during the great Aztec civilisation, and their priests traditionally carried living boas, often of great size, wreathed around their bodies, in order to inspire fear, wonder, and obedience among the general populace. Needless to say, however, if the boas were not treated with great care during such performances their innate instincts for constriction would instantly be triggered, and their hapless servitors would suffer the dreadful consequences of their remiss conduct. Notwithstanding this, it is possible that on occasion the priests derived some very positive benefits from their hazardous profession—the inspiration for an electrifying segment of Robert Southey's famous poem *Madoc: The Curse of Kehama* (1810), in which Neolin, the snake god's priest, is a prisoner of Madoc and his party . . . when suddenly:

> Forth, from the dark recesses of the cave,
> The Serpent came; the Hoamen at the sight
> Shouted; and they who held the Priest, appalled,
> Relaxed their hold. On came the mighty Snake,
> And twined, in many a wreath, round Neolin,
> Darting aright, aleft, his sinuous neck,
> With searching eye and lifted jaw and tongue,
> Quivering, and hiss as of a heavy shower
> Upon the summer woods. The Britons stood
> Astounded at the powerful reptile's bulk,
> And that strange sight. His girth was as of man;
> But easily could he have overtopped
> Goliath's helmed head, or that huge King
> Of Basan, hugest of the Anakim.
> What then was human strength, if once involved
> Within those dreadful coils! The multitude
> Fell prone and worshipped.

12 | COURTING THE COBRA

As well they might, since heretics were generally sacrificed!

The Aztecs were not the only worshippers of constricting snakes. Danh-gbi, the serpent god venerated by tribes in the West African country of Benin (formerly Dahomey), is represented in corporeal form by the African rock python *Python sebae*. It was the arrival of this creed in the West Indies (especially Haiti) with the transportation of Benin natives during the terrible years of the slave trade that gave rise to the mysterious religion nowadays referred to as voodoo. This initially involved the continuing worship of Danh-gbi, but under the new name of Damballah-wèdo, and featured living specimens of boa (these specimens were the actual Voodoo), the New World counterparts of pythons.

MACABRE PLAYMATES

There are many cases on record of interactions between cobras and people in which the human participants had no experience whatsoever in snake handling, yet have nonetheless survived their close encounters of the serpentine kind wholly unharmed.

One of the most outstanding of these was reported by the Sri Lankan wildlife journal *Loris* (December 1967). After leaving her baby alone in a room for a short time one morning, its mother returned just before noon to feed it—and discovered that it was no longer alone. Her child now had a playmate, with whom it was enjoying a happy game—the playmate was stroking the baby's face with its head, and the baby was pushing the playmate's head away, a simple game that was being repeated over and over. Indeed, the game was so innocuous that the mother would not have been in any way concerned—had it not been for the terrifying fact that the baby's playmate was an adult cobra!

The cobra was coiled around the child's body, and its hood was fully expanded, yet it seemed totally disinclined to strike the child. If anything, and at the risk of sounding anthropomorphic, it actually appeared to be enjoying the game! In contrast, the mother was almost demented with fear, but wisely decided to remain perfectly still and hope that the snake would leave of its own accord, without biting the baby. Happily, the cobra did finally depart, and when the frightened mother examined her child she found it to be completely unharmed and no worse for its extraordinary encounter.

That same issue of *Loris* also contained another startling example of an apparently benign child-serpent inter-relationship. Taking place in Port Elizabeth, South Africa, it featured a two-year-old boy called Allan Jonker, who went off to play in his parents' garden each morning with what his parents innocently assumed to be an imaginary friend—a friend that Allan always referred to as his baby. One day, out of sheer curiosity, Allan's older brother went along too—to see what type of game Allan played, and to find out whether there really was someone, or something, that he played with. To his horror, the brother discovered that Allan's 'baby' was not imaginary but was very real—only too real, in fact, because it proved to be a fully-grown adult *Bitis arietans*, Africa's notoriously deadly puff adder!

As soon as Allan's father learnt of this, he raced up to the infant, diverted his attention using a bouncing ball, and, once the child was out of harm's way, dispatched the snake with a spade. He later discovered that his young son had been affectionately squeezing the puff adder between his hands; yet, incredibly, the snake—belonging to a species noted for its belligerent temperament—had never attempted to bite him. Indeed, the boy had become so attached to his bizarre 'baby' that he cried all night long after learning of its death.

SNAKE CHARMING AND COBRA COOLING

In the dim half-light she sits, a motionless statue veiled in shadow—but all is not entirely still. Out of the shadows a sibilant hissing pervades the silence, and her long dark hair writhes and coils, just like living serpents—which is not at all surprising, because this is precisely what they are. Recalling a latter-day Medusa, this exotic, mesmerising figure is Aasha, daughter and accomplished protégé of Yogi Raj Bengali—one of the world's most celebrated modern-day snake charmers. Festooning her hair with animate cobras as other young women might decorate theirs with ribbons, and adorning her fingers with living scorpions in the way that her peers wear rings, is all part of her extraordinary vocation in life, to emulate her esteemed father in their sensational shows held in Rajasthan, and are all facets of her extraordinary talent for handling these potentially deadly beasts.

Although he hails from Rajasthan, Yogi Raj Bengali has performed at all of the major Indian festivals, and at the special

12 | COURTING THE COBRA

request of many eminent dignitaries, in Asia and overseas, during a lifetime of snake charming—thereby maintaining an extraordinary traditional spectacle whose origins are shrouded in the mists of far-distant ages.

Just like snake worship, snake charming has been taking place for thousands of years and has featured the cobra very prominently—for good reason. No other type of serpent can engender the tangible aura of menace personified by the erect cobra, swaying before the pipe-playing snake charmer with its hood expanded and its slender forked tongue flickering.

Indian cobras and snake charmers, 1890 lithograph

The two principal species used are the Asian spectacled cobra *Naja naja* and the Egyptian cobra *N. haje* in North Africa—although Bengali and Aasha also regularly defy death by incorporating a king cobra in their spectacular act. Most Asian snake charmers are Indian, who travel as far afield as Nepal and Sri Lanka to perform. The most famous and accomplished of these are ones who, like Bengali, use 'hot' cobras in their act, i.e. specimens that have not been tampered with to render them harmless. Hence their very lives depend entirely upon the consummate skill and detailed knowledge regarding the safe handling of such snakes that these performers acquire during their hazardous careers. Moreover, the importance of acquiring such skills extends beyond the requirements of their specified performances. Once a snake charmer has become well known for his prowess in handling dangerous serpents, he will also be regularly called upon to rid houses and villages of snakes—i.e. wholly wild specimens that have never been tampered with and thus are able to inflict potentially lethal bites.

Indeed, as I learnt during a conversation with Mark O'Shea, an internationally-renowned herpetologist and snake handler based at the West Midlands Safari Park in England, there are certain tribes in India, most notably the Jogi, whose entire lives are focused exclusively upon the capture and exhibition of snakes. In fact, as Mark pointed out to me, it is very likely that in many instances snake charming began as a flamboyant advertisement by snake catchers seeking to attract customers and to reveal their skills in serpent subjugation.

Yet for every snake charmer who uses hot cobras, there are any number of fraudsters and tricksters who prefer to employ 'cold' versions in their acts, particularly in North Africa. More concerned with cajoling coins from the pockets of gullible tourists than with enticing serpents from their baskets, these charlatan charmers use cobras that have been 'cooled'. Also known as venomoids, cooled cobras are ones that have been rendered harmless by any one of several different means, which include removing or destroying the venom fangs and reserve fangs, sometimes the venom sacs too, and cauterising the sockets. Tragically, however, the snakes do not always survive such ill-treatment (unless the fangs have been removed via skilful surgical techniques and replaced by specially-manufactured harmless counterparts—an expensive procedure beyond the finances of many snake charmers). Some charmers will even resort to sewing up the snake's mouth—a barbarous practice inevitably resulting in the snake's death from starvation. However, the callous attitude prevailing among such unscrupulous showmen is that as cobras are common in Africa, dead specimens can easily be replaced.

Sometimes a snake charmer does not tamper with his cobra's mouth, but secures its tail inside its basket instead, so that the cobra cannot reach the charmer if he sits beyond its striking range. Once again, however, this can be lethal for the cobra, because

Promotional poster for appearance of snake charmer Nala Damajanti at the Folies Bergère, probably from 1886

infections arising from such treatment can readily set in—particularly gangrene, if the blood supply to the tail is restricted or cut off by the tightness of the rope tying the tail to the basket.

As for the charming process itself, there is more to this than meets the eye—or ear, bearing in mind that as snakes neither possess eardrums nor external ears, they cannot detect many airborne noises and are therefore virtually deaf (but see also Chapter 16 for some notable exceptions). Consequently, it is not the music played by the snake charmer on his familiar bheen (snake pipe) that stimulates the cobra to dance. Instead, it is the charmer's actions, such as the tapping of his knee or toe, and the overt swaying movements of his pipe (often bearing a light-reflecting mirror at its tip), that serve this function—inducing the cobra to sway in synchrony with hood erect as it strives to keep the pipe in view, and sometimes even strikes at its tip if feeling threatened.

CATALEPTIC COBRAS?

A truly astonishing feat can be achieved by some of the more accomplished Egyptian cobra handlers, as described in *The World of Wonders* (1881-1882), edited by A. Taffs:

> The Egyptian conjurers know how to render this serpent stiff and immovable by pressing the nape of the neck with the finger, and thus throwing it into a sort of catalepsy. The serpent is thus apparently converted into a rod or stick. Traces of this trick occur in Scripture, and it affords a striking illustration of the passage where Pharaoh's wise men cast down their rods, which were turned into serpents, but were devoured by the serpent of Aaron.

In my files, I have many well-attested records of animals being rendered prone by human hypnotists, including a wide range of mammals, birds, reptiles, and even arthropod invertebrates—to place a lobster in a trance, for instance, simply balance it vertically on its head, i.e. stand it in a perpendicular orientation on its claws with its rostrum ('beak') touching the ground, to yield a tripod.

Hence the above-claimed technique with snakes is not as improbable as it might otherwise seem.

THE FASCINATION OF SNAKE HYPNOTISTS

Speaking of humans hypnotising snakes: there are also many highly intriguing accounts on record describing various predatory animals, including foxes, stoats, and snakes, performing ostensibly similar acts of hypnotism or 'fascination' upon prey individuals.

Snakes seem particularly adept, as there are numerous reports of snakes performing this direct, eye-to-eye version of fascination. Reverend Henry Bond, a 19th-Century vicar, witnessed one such instance in Dorset, southwestern England, which he documented in the scientific journal *The Zoologist* via a letter dated 14 August 1860:

> Up the hill above Tyneham, towards the sea, I was struck by the shrill cry and fluttering agitation of a common hedgesparrow, in a whitethorn bush. Regardless of my presence, its remarkable motions were continued, getting, at every hop from bough to bough, lower and lower down in the bush. Drawing nearer, I saw a common snake [i.e. grass snake] coiled up, but having its head erect, watching the sparrow; the moment the snake saw me it glided away, and the sparrow flew off with its usual mode of flight.

A similar case was recorded in *The Zoologist* by John Henry Belfrage of Muswell Hill, a suburban district of north London, in a letter dated 12 February 1861:

> When proceeding down the avenue here one morning, at a turn in the path I saw a robin, which appeared to me spell-bound, so much so as to allow a much closer approach than is usual even with that boldest of the feathered tribe. On going nearer I perceived what I took to be the cause, in a large common snake, which was lying coiled up on one side of

the path, with its head a little raised. My appearance broke the spell, and the robin flew away; at the same time, the snake dropped its head and assumed a perfectly inert appearance.

Some sceptics explain cases of supposed snake fascination as nothing more mysterious than eyewitnesses failing to realise that snakes invariably have fixed gazes, simply because they have no eyelids and therefore cannot blink, but this 'solution' totally ignores the victim's abnormal behaviour. Others claim that in cases when the victim has been rendered immobile, the snake (if venomous) has already injected it with venom. However, instances where the victim has fled when the snake's gaze was momentarily broken negate this theory.

A rattlesnake purportedly fascinating its rabbit prey victim

In reality, assuming the validity of eyewitnesses' testimony, it seems more plausible that the victim is so traumatised by the sight of the predator in such close proximity that its normal instincts for escape are inhibited, but not its natural curiosity, which may even induce it to move ever closer in order to observe more clearly its fear's source. Even so, there is clearly much still to be uncovered within this highly speculative area of animal behaviour.

12 | COURTING THE COBRA

FAVOURED BY THE GODS?

The ancient legend encapsulated in this chapter's opening quote from Rudyard Kipling's story 'Rikki-Tikki-Tavi', of how the first cobra used its hood to shade the god Brahm from the sun's hot rays, has given rise to the long-lasting Indian belief that if a cobra should raise its hood over someone without displaying aggression, that person is destined for great fortune and success. This prophecy has been dramatically verified on more than one occasion.

During the mid-1870s, a tyrannical maharajah had been deposed by the British in the Indian state of Baroda, but as he had no sons to continue the royal line, a search was instigated for a suitable youngster to become his official heir. Time passed, yet no-one could be found anywhere in the land, until the searchers began to despair of ever succeeding in their quest—and then they saw him, surely the unlikeliest future ruler of all time.

There, in a clearing alongside a dusty road, lay a scruffy beggar boy, fast asleep, but across his prone body a tall shadow had fallen—the shadow of a huge cobra. The snake had raised itself erect, and was swaying slowly back and forth over the sleeping child, its outstretched hood shielding his face from the sun, but it did not try to strike him.

To the searchers, this mesmerising scene was unequivocal proof that their quest was finally at an end—in spite of his humble appearance, the boy had clearly been revealed by divine intervention as their land's true future maharajah. Eventually, the cobra sank to the ground, and glided away—and as soon as it had done so the searchers awoke the boy, informed him of his new, exalted status, and took him with them, back to the royal palace.

The cobra-mediated prophecy had transformed fairy tale into fact, turning a ragged pauper into a regal prince. Moreover, when he was of age, he did indeed become the ruler of Baroda and, as such, one of the world's richest men—but he was also a very benevolent, enlightened monarch, under whom the country flourished and his people prospered.

As Jacqueline Mudie revealed in her absorbing book *Early Years: The Childhood of Famous People* (1966), a similar case history began one day in 1916 when, while lying on the grass outside the house where she was staying during a visit to Kashmir, a 16-year-old girl found herself face to face with a cobra. The cobra reared upwards,

Vijayalakshmi Pandit

12 | COURTING THE COBRA

extended its hood, and swayed backwards and forwards over her head for a moment, but did not try to harm her, then lowered its head to the ground again and slipped away through the grass. When an Indian soothsayer learnt of this, she informed the girl's family that it signified the gods' special favour.

Her prophecy was certainly fulfilled—for the girl, born as Swarup Kumari Nehru (and sister to future Indian prime minister Pandit Nehru), but changing to Mrs Vijayalakshmi Pandit when married, ultimately became Ambassador to the USA and to the then USSR, Indian High Commissioner in London, and President of the 8th General Assembly of the United Nations in an illustrious career, retiring in 1961.

When asked during an interview with a British newspaper some years ago to disclose the secret of successful snake training, Yogi Raj Bengali merely smiled, and stated that although some do become accustomed to a certain touch and are quite placid, for the most part snakes cannot be trained; they simply do whatever they want to do.

As these are the words of an expert in the handling of potentially lethal snakes, clearly the mystical links between cobras and their contemporary human courtiers have far from vanished, and there is evidently a great deal still to be comprehended in this most perilous but potent of partnerships.

13
GOOSEBERRY WIVES, HAIRY VIPERS, AND HAZELWORMS

> It is curious to note the old sea-margins of human thought! Each subsiding century reveals some new mystery; we build where monsters used to hide themselves.
>
> Henry Wadsworth Longfellow—*Kavanagh*

Furry snakes seem like a contradiction in terms, because all known ophidians are demonstrably scaly—which makes the following selection of little-known serpentine cryptids all the more surprising, and fascinating, as they are united by a shared surfacing of hair.

GREETING THE GOOSEBERRY WIFE

An amusing piece of folklore peculiar to the Isle of Wight (IOW) is that this southern English island is home to a giant hairy caterpillar known as the gooseberry wife that lurks amid gooseberry bushes waiting to devour any naughty children who try to steal the berries. Remarkably, however, there are a few reports on file from beyond this isle's boundaries that describe allegedly real mystery creatures that bear more than a passing resemblance to this supposedly mythical bogey beast.

In 2007, Neil Powney from Basildon, Essex, wrote to the UK magazine *Fortean Times* revealing that during the 1970s, when she was 7-8 years old and living in the Corringham area of Essex, his girlfriend Lyn saw what she claims to have been a serpentine mystery beast that resembled a huge furry caterpillar crawling up a lavender tree in her parents' back garden. Observing it from less than 5 ft away, she could see that it was covered in 4-in-long hairs, was dark brown-green in colour, as thick as a rolling pin, and about 1 ft long.

As Lyn observed it, this remarkable entity made its way up the trunk of the lavender tree, then moved across onto a panel of the fence next to the tree, crawling along the fence until it reached a gap that it squeezed through, taking it into their neighbour's garden. Looking over the fence, Lyn could see the creature crawling across their neighbour's lawn, at which point she then ran into her own house and fetched her mother to see it. By the time that they reached the fence and looked over, however, it had gone.

It is well known that children often judge objects, particularly unfamiliar ones, to be bigger than they actually are. Yet even if we downgrade her 1-ft estimate of the creature's length by as much as 50 per cent, to a much less dramatic 6 in, that would still be an immense caterpillar, especially when encountered in Britain. Consequently, it occurred to me that perhaps what Lyn had seen was a colony of caterpillars moving together in formation, as a column or procession like some species do—and, being only a child, she had duly mistaken them for a single, giant entity.

The caterpillar of the pine processionary moth *Thaumetopoea pityocampa* is a famous example that exhibits this phenomenon. The larvae of certain species of dark-winged fungus gnat (notably *Sciara militaris*) belonging to the taxonomic family Sciaridae also migrate in processions, which can be very lengthy. And as will shortly be revealed in this chapter, they already provide one very telling precedent in relation to sightings of elongate mystery beasts. Yet Lyn's view of the creature in her garden was at such close range that this does not seem a very satisfactory explanation for it.

Incidentally, the mysterious, extra-large gooseberry wife of IOW folklore should not be confused with either of the much smaller, familiar entomological species referred to as gooseberry caterpillars due to their feeding upon gooseberry leaves. One of these is a genuine caterpillar, the larva of the magpie (currant) moth *Abraxas*

Pine processionary caterpillars *Thaumetopoea pityocampa*
(PD / Jürgen Appel)

grossulariata. The other is the tiny larva of the sawfly *Nematus ribesii*, but although it is commonly referred to as a gooseberry caterpillar (because it does closely resemble a minute caterpillar in outward appearance), its sawfly identity means that it is in fact a hymenopteran, and therefore much more closely related to bees, wasps, and ants than to lepidopterans.

ALGERIA'S ANOMALOUS HAIRY VIPER AND A JAVAN GIANT

But what relevance do hairy caterpillars, giant or otherwise, have in relation to snakes (secret or otherwise)? The answer is that they may provide an explanation for what is otherwise a truly anomalous snake report published during January 1852 in London's highly respected Sunday broadsheet newspaper *The Observer* and subsequently reproduced in English naturalist Frank Buckland's book *Curiosities of Natural History* (1857), which is where I first saw it many years ago:

> In the Algerian paper we read that a hairy viper was seen a few days ago near Drariah, coiled round a tree. It resembled an enormous caterpillar, and was of a brownish-red colour; its length was about twenty-two inches. The moment it saw that it was observed, it glided into the brushwood, and all attempts to discover it were unavailing. The authorities of the Museum of Natural History of Paris have sent off orders to their agents in Algiers to get a specimen of this viper.

No further details appear to have been published concerning Algeria's uniquely hirsute vipers, however, so we can only assume that the museum's agents failed in their task. As it happens, Central Africa is home to an unusual species of snake known as the hairy bush viper *Atheris hispida* due to its extremely keeled scales, whose long spiny projections give it a bristly, almost hairy appearance. But no such snake is known from North Africa.

13 | GOOSEBERRY WIVES

Hairy bush viper *Atheris hispida* (Bree Mc, CC BY 2.0)

Presumably, therefore—always assuming that it did truly exist in the first place!—Algeria's 'hairy viper' was actually either an enormous caterpillar or a caterpillar procession, the latter identity clearly being much more likely. After all, if it were indeed a single caterpillar, estimates of its size had obviously been greatly exaggerated. At least I hope so—because any butterfly or moth metamorphosing from a 22-in-long caterpillar would be a fearsome sight to behold! Something more akin, in fact, to a Wonderland caterpillar of Lewis Carrollian creation than anything expected from Algeria, or even, for that matter, the Isle of Wight.

Equally formidable if real would have been the inconnu Indonesian hairy snake of allegedly gigantic proportions that reputedly frequented the dense jungles of Java, at least according to the following brief but truly bizarre report that appeared in Michigan's *Kalamazoo Gazette* on 5 August 1911:

> Captain Watson said today that he would bring up a still more varied animal assortment next trip, for he has agents now working through the jungles in Java and on the Malay Peninsula looking up certain strange beasts, one of which is a hairy snake of huge proportions, which has been met with in Java and

which Captain Watson declares may possibly prove to be a surviving mammoth caterpillar of a prehistoric age.

It would be interesting to ascertain the identity of the above-cited Captain Watson (I have tried but so far failed to do so), if only to discover where he obtained his extraordinary notion of gargantuan caterpillars existing in prehistoric times, let alone persisting into modern ones! I strongly suspect that this report is an example of the notorious brand of lurid journalistic hoax story that was very common in American newspapers, especially local ones, during the 19th and early 20th Centuries. Certainly, nothing more concerning it, including the hairy ophidian mammoth itself, has emerged in subsequent years.

HAIRY SNAKES IN AMERICA

During the mid/late 1800s and early 1900s, it was infuriatingly commonplace for newspapers and magazines in the USA and elsewhere to invent lurid, fraudulent animal stories purely for entertainment purposes, but without actually stating that they were merely journalistic hoaxes. The regrettable but inevitable result of this chicanery is that some of these fake accounts have found their way into the cryptozoological literature, introducing further confusion and controversy into a subject already benighted by such issues.

A fair number of these wildlife-themed yarns feature bizarre serpents (see Chapter 24 for a diverse selection), including several hairy snakes. Most of the latter are evident frauds, but there are two examples that in my opinion may actually be genuine—yet if so, how can they be explained?

The first of these was documented in a letter penned by a Mr T.O. Russell, which was published in the February 1891 issue of a periodical entitled *Nature's Realm*. Here it is:

> In the fall of 1869 I was in La Crosse, Wis., and having some business in La Crescent, on the Minnesota side of the Mississippi, I crossed the river in a ferry boat. There is, or was, an arm of the river on the Minnesota side called, in western parlance, a 'slew.'

Over this there is a bridge; on going over it I saw a snake coiled on a 'butt' that had been sawed off a tree of about two feet in diameter, and it was floating in the water. The snake was so different from any animal of the kind I had ever before seen that I gazed on it for fully five minutes. It was evidently asleep and within ten feet of me—was, in fact, directly under me as I leaned over the side of the bridge. The 'slew' had no current in it, for the water was very low; I had, therefore, ample opportunity to observe the snake. It was red, and, more extraordinary still, it was thickly covered with hair. It resembled no snake I had ever seen before. It was exactly like a red cow's tail. The hair on it was fully an inch long and as thick as that growing on a cow's tail. Having no means of capturing the snake, I determined to make it show itself and flung a piece of stick at it. It awoke at the splash in the water, uncoiled itself and dived into the slough. It was certainly 6 feet long or more. I have told some dozens of people in La Crosse about it, among them Mr. Davidson, of the Clyde house, but none of them remembered to have even seen such a snake. Mr. Davidson is the best known sportsman in La Crosse, and it is strange that he never should have seen any snake like it.

The second example featured in a number of Oklahoma-based newspaper reports published during September 1908. They told of an extraordinary snake that had recently been captured by young farmer W. Gilbert and his visiting cousin Luther Naylor in a pond of water on Gilbert's farm, 16 miles south of Lawton. The most detailed description of it that I have seen appeared in Lawton's *Daily News-Republican* on 12 September:

[Its] body is covered with a fine coat of hair fully a half inch in length.
 The snake measures thirty inches in length and with the exception of its heavy growth of hair is closely similar to an ordinary serpent in both size and actions. Its head alone is free from the hair-suit and

> this closely resembles the head of a "copper-head." The growth extraordinary is brown in color, and almost as soft as moleskin but with much longer hair."

Curiously, however, it was described quite differently in a shorter account published by Lawton's *Constitution-Democrat* newspaper on 17 September:

> It is about eighteen inches in length and is covered with a black growth of hair or moss, which is possibly a quarter of an inch in length.

Irrespective of its length and hair colour, the two men had successfully captured this hairy snake in a bucket, then transferred it into a glass jar. On 11 September, they brought their captive, still very much alive and active inside its transparent prison, to Lawton and exhibited it there, whereupon, according to the *Daily News-Republican*:

> . . . hundreds of people here have examined it but none have ever seen anything similar or are able to explain the freak.

According to the latter newspaper's account, the most popular explanation offered by this snake's observers was that it was a specimen of some ordinary species but with diseased skin that had become covered in a fungal growth of hair. Conversely, in the *Constitution-Democrat's* report, a Mr Hub Crawford was quoted as saying that the hairy growth was nothing but a coating of moss.

Gilbert and Naylor were reputedly offered sizeable sums of money from various persons interested in owning this mystifying snake, but the two men turned them all down, and were said to be planning to build an aquarium in which to maintain their distinctive discovery—after which both they and their hairy snake simply vanished from the headlines.

If we assume that these two cases are indeed genuine (bear in mind that *Nature's Realm* was a respectable natural history periodical, and the Lawton hairy snake was publicly displayed and viewed by numerous people), worth noting is that both cases involved snakes of an aquatic nature. When reading them, especially the second one, I too wondered if a fungal infection of the snake's skin was responsible, with its hair in reality constituting a mass of very fine, filamentous fungal hyphae (i.e. a mycelium). Injured fishes can become infected with an aquatic cotton mould fungus known as *Saprolegnia,* and do look as if they are covered in white hair (not to be confused, however, with the fur-bearing trout, a humorous man-made hoax created by combining a fish's head and fins with the white fur of some small rodent or rabbit).

Moreover, snakes (particularly North American ones) are susceptible to a fungal infection called SFD (Snake Fungal Disease), caused by *Ophidiomyces ophiodiicola*. However, this causes lesions in their skin rather than covering it with hyphae. Also, I am not aware of any fungal infections in snakes caused by *Saprolegnia,* nor any fungal infections of any kind that generate red, brown, or black hair-like hyphae.

The fact that both hairy snakes were aquatic suggests to me that they may have somehow become entangled in a mass or mat of freshwater algae or, alternatively, moss (as opined by Hub Crawford). Certainly, not all algae and mosses are green or yellow—some are deep red in colour, others are brown or even black. In addition, when I was communicating recently with renowned British snake expert Mark O'Shea concerning this subject, he mentioned that some sea-snakes have had marine algae growing upon them that made them look hairy.

HAIRY HUBERT

I found the following interesting snippet of information a while ago in William Brockie's book *Legends and Superstitions of the County of Durham* (1886), which warrants a mention here:

> HAIRY HUBERT
> If you throw a hairy worm, in the North called Hairy Hubert, over your head, and take care not to look to see where it alights, you are sure to get something new before long.

County Durham is in the northeast of England, and although I had never heard of Hairy Hubert before, I suspected that it was probably a local name used there for some form of hairy caterpillar. And sure enough, when I investigated it, I discovered that the creature in question was none other than the woolly bear, the famously furry caterpillar of the garden tiger moth *Arctia caja*, a common species in Great Britain.

HEARKENING BACK TO THE HAZELWORM

One of the most extraordinary creatures to straddle the boundaries of mythology and reality must surely be the European hazelworm, and yet its fascinating history is all but forgotten today. High time, therefore, to resurrect it from centuries of zoological neglect and present its very curious credentials to a modern-day audience at last.

Back in the Middle Ages, the Germanic folklore of Central Europe's alpine regions contained many tales of a terrifying dragon of the huge, limbless, serpent-like variety known as the worm. But this particular worm was set apart from others by its sometimes hairy rather than scaly outer surface, and above all else by its proclivity for inhabiting areas containing a plenitude of hazel bushes. Consequently, it duly became known as the hazelworm (aka Heerwurm and Haselwurm in German, but not to be confused with a known species of legless lizard, the slow worm *Anguis fragilis*, which is also sometimes referred to as the hazelworm).

Additionally, Leander Petzoldt reported in his *Kleines Lexikon der Dämonen und Elementargeister* (2003) that according to some traditional beliefs, the hazelworm was nothing less than the Eden Serpent that had tempted Adam and Eve with fruit from the Tree of Knowledge of Good and Evil in the Garden of Eden, and was therefore also accorded such alternative names as the Paradise Snake and the Worm of Knowledge. After God had cursed it and banished it for its treachery, however, the Serpent supposedly sought sanctuary in hazel bushes outside Eden, where it feeds to this day upon their foliage, and winds its elongated body around their roots. Moreover, it subsequently became passive in nature, and can readily be recognised by its whitish colouration, thus yielding for it a further name—the white worm or Weisser Wurm. And because it is said to surface just before the onset of a war, yet another name given to this contentious creature is the war worm.

Early retellings of its legends ascribed to the hazelworm an immense body length. Perhaps the most famous example is a local account penned by Rector and Pastor Heinrich Eckstorm (1557-1622) that appeared in *Chronicon Walkenredense*. Printed in 1617, this was the Latin chronicle of his monastery, Walkenried Abbey, situated in what is today Lower Saxony, Germany. Here is what he wrote.

One day in July 1597, a woman hailing from Holbach ventured into Lower Saxony's Harz mountain range to collect blueberries, but as she ascended she encountered an enormous hazelworm, which scared her so much that she promptly abandoned her basket of diligently-picked berries and fled to the village of Zorge. There she met a woodcutter named Old William, and pleaded with him to give her shelter, which he did, although he and his wife laughed heartily and disbelievingly when the woman told them about the hazelworm.

Eight days later, however, when inadvertently finding himself in the vicinity of where she had claimed to have seen the monster, Old William himself encountered it, lying across the road up ahead, and so big that he had initially mistaken it for a fallen oak tree—until it began to move, and raise its hitherto-concealed head from out of some nearby hazel bushes. He too duly fled to Zorge, where he told everyone what he had seen.

Old William estimated that the hazelworm had been around 18 ft long, was as thick as a man's thigh, was green and yellow in colour, and, of particular interest, possessed feet on its underparts, rather than being limbless. Several notable personages were present to hear his testimony, including lawyers Mitzschefal from Stöckei and Joachim Götz from Olenhusen, and doctors Johannes Stromer and Philipp Ratzenberg.

Two centuries later, in 1790, Blankenburg-based chronicler Johann Christophe Stübner, a major sceptic of hazelworm reports, nonetheless recorded that the skeleton of a charred hazelworm was supposedly discovered in Wurmberg, a Lower Saxony forestry village near Braunlage. He also noted that in 1782 a lengthy hazelworm could apparently still be found in Allröder Forest.

Conversely, as noted by renowned South Tyrolean folklorist Hans Fink in his book *Verzaubertes Land: Volkskult und Ahnenbrauch in Südtirol* [*Enchanted Land: Folk Art and Alpine Life in South Tyrol*] (1969), stories concerning the hazelworm that still abound today in the autonomous South Tyrol (occupying a region formerly part of Austria-Hungary but annexed by Italy in 1919) aver that it is no bigger than a cradle-fitting child in swaddling clothes. (This in turn has led to some confusion with another herpetological alpine cryptid, the tatzelworm.) There are even claims that it has the head of a child too and can howl like a baby crying.

Also, it was once greatly sought after. As documented by Claudia Liath in *Der Grüne Hain* [*The Green Grove*] (2012), this was because anyone eating the flesh of a hazelworm would supposedly become immortal, remaining forever young, handsome, and healthy, and would also gain all manner of other ostensibly desirable but otherwise unobtainable benefits, such as the ability to talk to and understand the speech of animals, to discover hidden treasures, and to be fully versed in the healing properties of plants. Indeed, some of his envious, less gifted contemporaries actually avowed that the extraordinary scholarly abilities of Swiss physician, alchemist, and astrologer Theophrastus Paracelsus (1493/4-1541) must surely be due to his having secretly consumed the meat of a hazelworm.

In *Hexenwahn: Schicksale und Hintergründe. Die Tiroler Hexenprozesse* [*The Witch Delusion: Fates and Backgrounds. The Tyrolean Witch Trials*] (2018), Hansjörg Rabanser recorded that during one such trial—that of the alleged sorcerer Mathaus Niderjocher, held at the Sonnenburg district court in 1650/51—the defendant claimed that he and a locksmith named Andreas had once hunted a hazelworm by magical means. After consulting a book of sorcery, they had drawn a magical circle around a hazel bush, then dug out the bush itself, and found at knee-deep level in the earth a stony plate, beneath which was a hazelworm that was very long, thick, and white in colour. Despite recourse to evocation spells from the book of sorcery, however, they were unable to control or capture the hazelworm, which bit Andreas in the hand before disappearing.

If such claims as those presented above were factual, there may even be opportunities to repeat them in the present day, judging at least from some tantalising reports of hazelworms having been killed in modern times, as collected and presented in an extensive online article on this subject by Swiss chronicler Markus Kappeler.

For example, not far from Ilfeld monastery in Honstein county at the foot of the Harz Mountains are the ruins of a castle named Harzburg, where a hazelworm was reputedly seen for three consecutive years around half a century ago, until killed by two woodcutters there, after which its body was hung from a tree, attracting many interested viewers coming from near and far. It was said to be 12 ft long, with a head reminiscent of a pike's in general form. (Back in 1703, within his major opus *Hercynia |Curiosa oder Curiöser Hartz-Wald*, Dr Georg H. Behrens had claimed that very large, hideous-looking hazelworms inhabited these very same castle ruins.) The skin of another slain hazelworm was allegedly exhibited at one time in Schleusingen, a city in Thuringia, Germany.

Even today, locals inhabiting what was formerly the Duchy of Brunswick-Lüneburg in northwestern Germany (now the Kingdom of Hanover and Duchy of Brunswick) claim that this rangy reptile is still quite common, that it sucks the milk from the udders of cows and poisons the meadows, and that they therefore still go out at certain times of the year to hunt young specimens measuring 3-4.5 ft. Make of that what you will!

For in reality, the mysterious hazelworm has long since ceased to be a mystery, at least for zoologists. Indeed, as far back as the 1770s, physician August C. Kühn documented that sightings of supposed hazelworms were actually based upon observations of long moving columns of army worms—a popular name given to the black-headed, white-bodied larva of *Sciara* (=*Lycoria*) *militaris* and several other dark-winged species of fungus gnat, as mentioned earlier in this chapter. Subsequent studies by other naturalists swiftly confirmed his statement.

Columns or processions of these insect larvae moving in a nose-to-tail manner, i.e. each larva following immediately behind another, can measure up to 30 ft long and several inches in diameter (as such columns can each be many larvae abreast). Accordingly, such a procession might well be mistaken for a single enormously lengthy, elongate snake-like entity if seen only briefly or during poor viewing conditions (e.g. at twilight, during mist or fog), and especially if unexpectedly encountered by a layman too terrified to stay around for a closer look!

Similarly, sightings of noticeably hairy hazelworms were ultimately discounted as columns of hairy caterpillars walking in single file and belonging to the pine processionary moth *Thaumetopoea pityocampa*, again mentioned earlier in this chapter. The hazelworm was no more, merely a closely-knit procession of insect larvae, not a single, uniform entity in its own right after all.

An extremely lengthy procession of fungus gnat larvae, nowadays deemed to be the identity of the very long, white-bodied hazelworm of traditional alpine lore

Of course, the above identification does beg the question: if this is truly all that the hazelworm ever was, how can we explain the reports of exhibited hazelworm skins, a charred hazelworm skeleton, and other physical evidence purportedly originating from this officially non-existent creature? Nothing more than tall tales and baseless folklore—or a bona fide cryptozoological conundrum still awaiting a satisfactory solution?

STOP PRESS: GREEN FURRY SNAKE CAPTURED IN THAILAND

In early March 2022, numerous websites were reviewing a *Tik-Tok* video posted on 27 February by user @firstminimini of a bizarre-looking freshwater snake captured alive by local man Tu in a swamp within Thailand's Sakon Nakhon province that seemed on first sight to be covered in long green fur (see https://tinyurl.com/5f2jcxyn). In fact, its 'fur' was profuse algae attached to this 2-ft-long snake's dorsal and lateral scales (its belly was unaffected). Taxonomically, it was apparently a *Homalopsis* water snake, a mildly venomous Asian colubrid that typically lurks motionless inside rocky crevices in still, stagnant water to seize prey, but where, as a result, algal growth upon it can occur.

Although this specimen is an extreme case, algal biofouling in snakes is not scientifically unprecedented. In 2010, for instance, an extensive paper by Sydney University biologist Dr R. Shine and two co-researchers documenting it in sea-snakes was published *(Proceedings of the Royal Society B: Biological Sciences)*. In 2013, algal fouling was formally recorded for the first time from a homalopsid species, the dog-faced water snake *Cerberus rynchops (Herpetology Notes)*.

Also, wildlife friend Sally Watts informed me that the aquatic southeast Asian tentacle snakes *Erpeton tentaculatum* at Chester Zoo, England ". . . sported amazing weed growth . . . though not as much as this. Hidden in plain sight, as it were. Apparently when they shed skin they were 'bald', then regrew their camouflage". Sadly, they later died in a fire.

14
A BIPEDAL SNAKE IN THE GARDEN OF EDEN? WHAT DID THE PRE-CURSED SERPENT LOOK LIKE?

> And the Lord God said unto the serpent, Because thou hast done this, thou art cursed above all cattle, and above every beast of the field; upon thy belly shalt thou go, and dust shalt thou eat all the days of thy life:
> And I will put enmity between thee and the woman, and between thy seed and her seed; it shall bruise thy head, and thou shalt bruise his heel.
>
> The Book of Genesis (3: 14-15)—*The Holy Bible*

An early passage in the Bible is responsible for one of the classic herpetologically-relevant sources of longstanding theological speculation and controversy among scholars of Scripture, as now revealed and comprehensively explored here.

When God learnt that the serpent in the Garden of Eden had successfully tempted Eve and thence Adam to eat the fruit from the Tree of Knowledge of Good and Evil, He cursed the serpent, as described in the above quotation from Genesis that opens this present chapter. According to that account, therefore, the serpent only acquired its present-day form, as a limbless creature slithering upon its ventral surface, *after* it had been cursed—which begs the oft-posed theological question: "What did the serpent look like *before* it was cursed?"

The Bible itself offers little in the way of clues. Apart from revealing that it could converse directly with Adam and Eve, the only reference to the pre-cursed Eden serpent (Genesis, 3: 1) states: "Now the serpent was more subtil [sic] than any beast of the field which the Lord God had made". Even so, theologians and artists have offered many putative answers down through the ages.

Some theologians have been in no doubt that the serpent was physically transformed by God's curse. Thus, in their *Biblical Commentary on the Old Testament, Vol. 1: The Pentateuch* (1866), Drs Carl F. Keil and Franz Delitzsch unequivocally stated:

> The punishment of the serpent corresponded to the crime. It had exalted itself above the man; therefore upon its belly it should go, and dust it should eat all the days of its life. If these words are not to be robbed of their entire meaning, they cannot be understood in any other way than as denoting that the form and movements of the serpent were altered, and that its present repulsive shape is the effect of the curse pronounced upon it, though we cannot form any accurate idea of its original appearance. Going upon the belly (=creeping, Lev. xi. 42) was a mark of the deepest degradation; also the eating of dust, which is not to be understood as meaning that dust was to be its only food, but that while crawling in the dust it would also swallow dust.

Notwithstanding the above authors' claim, rabbinical tradition formulated a number of ideas regarding the serpent's appearance before it received God's curse. According to the *Zohar* (*Book of Splendour*), which constitutes the main text of the Jewish Qabalah (Kabbalah) and provides a vast commentary upon the Pentateuch, in its pre-cursed form it had stood upright on two hind legs, just like Adam and Eve, and other subsequent humans, and was as tall as a camel.

Similarly, certain ancient Egyptian carvings depict the pre-cursed serpent as an exceedingly slender biped with a long neck and tail, a pair of lengthy arms, and standing slightly taller than a human on two elongate hind legs, offering Adam a fruit with one of its paws. When it was cursed, however, God (or St Michael, according to St Barnabas's apocryphal gospel) cut off its arms and legs, thereby yielding the limbless snake known today. God also took away its power of human speech by splitting its tongue, so that it could only hiss thereafter, and must have rendered its fangs venomous, because no venomous creature would surely have existed in Eden before the Fall.

Bipedal long-tailed humanoid Eden serpent with Adam and Eve, from an unidentified 15th-Century manuscript

In the *Aggadah*, an ancient compendium of Jewish (rabbinic) texts, this contentious reptile's pre-cursed form is described as follows:

> Among the animals, the serpent was notable. Of all of them, he had the most excellent qualities, in some of which he resembled man. Like man, he stood upright on two feet, and in height he was equal to the camel. . . . His superior mental gifts caused him to become an infidel.

Nor is that the only eye-opening reptile-related claim made in the *Aggadah* texts concerning Eden's serpent and this garden's two human inhabitants. In detailing the fateful consequences experienced by Adam and Eve after eating the forbidden fruit from the Tree of Knowledge, American mysteries researcher Dr Joe Lewels has noted that the *Aggadah* texts imply that they were originally very different outwardly from humans today:

> The first result was that Adam and Eve became naked. Before, their bodies had been overlaid with a horny skin and enveloped with the cloud of glory. No sooner had they violated the command given them than the cloud of glory and the horny skin dropped from them, and they stood there in their nakedness and ashamed.

This suggests that the first two humans were initially covered in a shining scaly skin, and part of their punishment for consuming the forbidden fruit was to lose their scales. Continuing that line of speculation: if Adam were indeed created in the image of his maker, his maker must have been reptilian. And in the opinion of some scholars, this radical, revolutionary supposition is ostensibly substantiated by a passage in another early compendium—the *Nag Hammadi Library*, which constitutes a series of ancient Gnostic text scrolls found inside a clay jar in a small Upper Egyptian town of the same name during 1945. The passage reads:

> Now Eve believed the words of the serpent. She looked at the tree. She took some of its fruit and ate, and she gave to her husband also, and he ate too. Then their mind opened. For when they ate, the light of knowledge shone for them; they knew that they were naked with regard to knowledge. When they saw their makers, they loathed them since they were beastly forms. They understood very much.

The concept of reptilian creators as indicated in early texts such as these has also been extensively explored by American researcher R.A. Boulay in his book *Flying Serpents and Dragons: The Story of Mankind's Reptilian Past* (revised 1997). Based upon these texts'

14 | THE GARDEN OF EDEN

testimony, Boulay concludes: "The sad fact is that in the West we have created God in our image and not the other way around. In this way we have hidden the true identity of our creators". This is in stark contrast to Eastern traditions, in which humanity's supposed descent from reptilian ancestors is openly lauded. Early Chinese emperors, for instance, widely proclaimed their lineage from dragons, and noble Indian families even today claim descent from the revered Indian serpent deities or nagas.

As for the pre-cursed Eden serpent: noting that the Hebrew word for 'serpent' is 'nachash', in his book *The Genesis Record* (1976) Dr Henry M. Morris commented:

> There has been much speculation as to whether the serpent originally was able to stand upright (the Hebrew word *nachash*, some maintain, originally meant "shining, upright creature").

He then speculated:

> The body of the serpent, in addition, was altered even further by eliminating his ability to stand erect, eye-to-eye with man as it were.
> It is further possible that all these animals (other than the birds) were quadrupeds, except the serpent, who had the remarkable ability, with a strong vertebral skeleton supported by limbs, to rear and hold himself erect when talking with Adam and Eve.

And in response to the biblical account of God's cursing of the serpent, prominent German theologian Martin Luther stated:

> From this some obvious conclusions follow: that before sin the serpent was a most beautiful little animal and most pleasing to man, as little mules, sheep and puppies today; moreover, that it walked upright.

Another school of thought favoured the idea that the pre-cursed serpent was a winged snake. This theory has also been aired by certain scholars in relation to the order of angels known as seraphs or seraphim, variously deeming them to be fiery winged serpents of the arid deserts or even as flame-like reptilian beings. For instance: in his 6-volume *Complete Commentary Upon The Whole Bible* (1708), Welsh-born Nonconformist minister/author Matthew Henry opined as follows regarding the nature of Eden's serpent from *Genesis*, Chapter 3:

> Perhaps it was a flying serpent, which seemed to come from on high as a messenger from the upper world, one of the seraphim; for the fiery serpents were flying, *Isaiah* xiv. 29. Many a dangerous temptation comes to us in gay fine colours that are but skin-deep, and seems to come from above; for Satan can seem an angel of light.

Other scholars have speculated that the serpent's transformation may not have been physical at all, but merely figurative. In his *Commentaries on the First Book of Moses Called Genesis*, pioneering 16th-Century French theologian John Calvin suggested that there is:

> . . . no absurdity in supposing, that the serpent was again consigned to that former condition, to which he was already naturally subject. For thus he, who had exalted himself against the image of God, was to be thrust back into his proper rank; . . . he is recalled from his insolent motions to his accustomed mode of going, in such a way as to be, at the same time, condemned to perpetual infamy. To eat dust is the sign of a vile and sordid nature. This (in my opinion) is the simple meaning of the passage.

And Frank E. Gaebelein, editing *The Expositor's Bible Commentary* (1990), opined:

> This curse does not necessarily suggest that the snake had previously walked with feet and legs as the other land animals. The point is rather that for the rest of his life, as a result of the curse, when the snake crawls on his belly, as snakes do, he will "eat dust." The emphasis lies in the snake's 'eating dust,' an

expression that elsewhere carries the meaning of 'total defeat' (cf. Isa 65: 25, Mic 7: 17).

Yet another facet of this biblical event that has engendered considerable theological contention is whether the serpent was indeed merely a reptile, i.e. a corporeal animal, or whether it was Satan in the guise of a snake, or even a snake controlled by Satan. Leading on from this line of thought is whether, therefore, God's curse was indeed imposed upon the serpent, or whether it was actually imposed upon Satan. Quoting from a sermon written by Australian theologian Rev. Rayner Winterbotham (1842-1924) and entitled 'The Divine Sentence on the Serpent':

> 1. I lay down the position that no punishment in the way of physical degradation was inflicted by God in His sentence upon the serpent tribe . . .
>
> 2. I lay down the position, which I think no one will seriously dispute, that the real tempter was not the serpent at all, but the devil . . .
>
> 3. I conclude from the foregoing positions, and conclude with confidence, that the serpent was not really cursed at all, while the devil was.

A comparable diversity of views have manifested themselves in artistic representations of the serpent too. As already noted, early Egyptian carvings portrayed an erect, bipedal being, but early European painters tended to depict it as a normal, limbless snake coiled around the Tree of Knowledge.

By the 12th Century AD, however, a shift in opinion had occurred, and European artists began portraying a somewhat more humanoid version—often still with a snake's body but now with the head (and sometimes also the arms) of a woman—a trend that crossed from art into literature too. Indeed, even Charles Dickens alluded to it, as "the serpent with a woman's head which tempted Eve", in his book *Household Words*, and citing Northumbrian monk the Venerable Bede (c.672-735 AD) as his source.

One famous early example in European art, produced by Benjamin the Scribe in c.1280, portrayed Adam and Eve flanking a

Complete story of Adam, Eve, and their expulsion from Eden, with the serpent depicted as half-human half-lizard—illuminated manuscript, early 1400s

14 | THE GARDEN OF EDEN

serpent sporting a woman's head and a pair of forelimbs (with the paw of one of these limbs holding a fruit from the Tree of Knowledge). Another appeared in a lavishly illustrated edition from 1455 of *Speculum Humanae Salvationis* (*'Mirror of Human Salvation'*), an anonymous work of popular theology (but possibly penned by Ludolph of Saxony, a German Roman Catholic theologian), first published some time between 1309 and 1324.

This hybrid serpent-woman monster also gained its own name, the draconopides (aka draconiopides, draconcopedes, and draconipes). Yet this is actually a decidedly inappropriate name for a serpent-bodied entity lacking hind legs, bearing in mind that 'draconopides' translates as 'dragon-footed'! Intriguingly, moreover, the draconopides image was sometimes utilised by artists to depict Lilith. Rabbinical lore claims that Adam's first wife was not Eve, but Lilith, made by God from dust like Adam (rather than from one of Adam's ribs, like Eve), and who therefore refused to be subjugated by Adam, deeming herself to be his equal as they shared a common origin. Instead, Lilith deserted Adam, consorting with demons instead and eventually becoming one herself. Moreover, in

Temptation scene, Sistine Chapel Ceiling—Michelangelo, 1508-12

some texts she is made synonymous with the Eden serpent—tempting Adam and his new wife, Eve, with the fruit from the Tree of Knowledge, and thereby causing humanity's Fall.

By the 15th Century, certain painters had created even more complex, more elaborate pre-cursed Eden serpents. Dating from c.1473, François Fouquet's painting 'Le Péché Originel' ('The Original Sin'—a title also used by several other artists for their versions of this same scene) depicts the serpent with a typically elongate, snake-like lower body, wrapped around the tree, but also with the upper body, arms, and head of a woman, and a pair of extended bat-like wings. A comparable depiction of this enigmatic reptilian entity but without the wings also occurs in the temptation scene portrayed in one of the panels constituting Michelangelo's glorious series of paintings on the ceiling of the Vatican's Sistine Chapel, created by him during 1508-12.

Other draconopides portrayals were produced by the likes of Masolino da Panicale (in 'The Temptation of Adam and Eve', c.1425, a fresco in Brancacci Chapel at the Church of Santa Maria del Carmine, in Florence, Italy); Raphael (in two separate paintings, early 1500s); Hans Holbein the Younger (in the second woodcut of his 'Danse Macabre' series from the 1520s); and Cornelius van Haarlem (in 'The Original Sin', 1592). A much more recent example appears in 'The Temptation of Eve', painted by the English Pre-Raphaelite artist John Roddam Spencer Stanhope in c.1877.

'The Temptation of Adam and Eve'—Masolino da Panicale, c.1425

14 | THE GARDEN OF EDEN

'The Temptation'—Hugo van der Goes, 1470

'Peccado Originale' ('The Original Sin')—
Jacapo della Quercia, 1425-38

14 | THE GARDEN OF EDEN

During 1425-38, Jacapo della Quercia had meticulously sculpted a stunning relief of Adam, Eve, and a draconopides Eden serpent for Bologna's San Petronio Basilica. A comparable scene appears on the pedestal of 'Madonna With Child' at the Cathedral of Notre Dame in Paris, France. Medieval illuminated manuscripts contain draconopides depictions too, as seen, for instance, in the *Furtmeyer Bible*, dating from c.1465; in the *Hours of Joanna the Mad* (Joanna I of Castile), created in Bruges in c.1486-1506; and in the *Farnese Hours*, from 1546.

There have also been some very spectacular draconopides portrayed in stained-glass windows. One particularly impressive example, dating from 1420, can be found in Ulm Cathedral, Germany, and there is another one at the Cathedral of St Etienne, in Châlons-en-Champagne, France. A third, produced by Renaissance artist Arnaud de Moles, is at Auch Cathedral, also in France. Even more striking, however, is the pre-cursed serpent of Eden as portrayed in 'The Temptation' by Flemish painter Hugo van der Goes in 1470, constituting the left-hand panel of a diptych now housed at Vienna's Kunsthistorisches Museum. As seen here, van der Goes conceived it as a bipedal, web-footed lizard-like entity with a long tail but with a woman's head, whose hair was plaited into horns, leaning against the Tree of Knowledge alongside Adam and Eve. Indeed, it was the sight of this fascinating, thought-provoking artwork, reproduced in a book on animal folklore and legends that I read long ago, which first stimulated my interest in the whole pre-cursed Eden serpent controversy.

A less famous but again fully bipedal draconopides features in a painting of Adam and Eve in Eden produced by an unidentified Brussels-based artist or group of artists, active there during 1480-1510, and referred to only as the Master of the Embroidered Foliage (on account of the characteristically embroidery-reminiscent appearance of foliage portrayed in his/their paintings). Another one appears very prominently in a medieval illuminated manuscript from the 1400s, sporting a scaly reptilian tail and clawed feet but a human body and head. Conversely, a predominantly mammalian example stands peeping out at Adam and Eve from behind a tree in the *Grimani Breviary*, an illuminated manuscript created in Italy, and dating once again from the 15th Century.

Back in the days before Charles Darwin's explanation of limblessness in snakes, as a natural and advantageous evolutionary process, was accepted by the scientific community (which currently deems that snakes evolved either from burrowing lizards or, alternatively, from varanids, i.e. monitor lizards, either directly or via varanid-derived marine lizards called mosasaurs), some naturalists offered their own input into the long-running discussion as to the pre-cursed serpent's likely morphology. One of the most memorable suggestions was proffered by enthusiastic amateur naturalist Frank Buckland, who was very intrigued that boas and pythons possess vestiges of hind legs beneath their skin, as well as two hook-like claws near their tail. In his book *Curiosities of Natural History* (1858), he explained these as follows:

> Supposing, then, the pre-Adamite [i.e. pre-cursed] snake to have gone on four legs, we might explain the passage by saying that after the curse the legs were struck off, but that the undeveloped legs were left (concealed, however, from casual observers) as evidence of what it formerly had been, and a type of its fallen condition.

In other words, these were remnants of earlier fully formed limbs, exactly as postulated by evolution—thus providing an example of Science and Scripture in full agreement.

However, it was not until the early years of this current, 21st Century that perhaps the most extraordinary aspect of all concerning the serpent of Eden was brought to public attention, via a fascinating newspaper article that soon attracted worldwide media interest. Here is that aspect.

One of the most enigmatic yet hitherto-obscure zoological relics held in any scientific establishment must surely be the 8-inch by 4-inch piece of scaly rusty-red leathery skin contained inside Archive Box #1920.1714 within the very sizeable collection of the Chicago Historical Society. For according to its yellowing French label, this is supposedly a genuine piece of skin from the very serpent that tempted Eve in the Garden of Eden!

Indeed, the label goes on to say that the serpent was killed by Adam on the day after its treachery to Eve, using a stake whose traces can be seen on this skin sample, which was preserved by his family in Asia. Affixed to the skin is a document written on

14 | THE GARDEN OF EDEN

velum or similar hide in an Asian script. The society purchased this mystifying exhibit, along with many other items, in 1920 from the eclectic collection of Chicago confectioner Charles F. Gunther—a grand collector of curiosities.

Speaking of Asia, there is an intriguing theological notion that not only were Adam and Eve banished from Eden by God but so too was the serpent—expelled to India after it had attempted to kill them. Although not alluded to in any of the canonical biblical accounts, this noteworthy claim is included within a series of Old Testament pseudepigrapha (falsely or ambiguously attributed texts) entitled *The Forgotten Books of Eden*. Dating from the 5th or 6th Century AD, these were found in Ethiopia, were written in an ancient South Semitic language called Ge'ez (originating in southern Eritrea and northern Ethiopia), having been translated from an Arabic original, and have been translated into English by Rutherford H. Platt Jnr, in 1926. The relevant details concerning the serpent's murderous intentions are contained in Chapter 18 within the first of these works, *The First Book of Adam*, and read as follows:

> 1 When the accursed serpent saw Adam and Eve, it swelled its head, stood on its tail, and with eyes blood-red, did as if it would kill them.
>
> 2 It made straight for Eve, and ran after her; while Adam standing by, wept because he had no stick in his hand wherewith to smite the serpent, and knew not how to put it to death.
>
> 3 But with a heart burning for Eve, Adam approached the serpent, and held it by the tail; when it turned towards him and said unto him:—
>
> 4 "O Adam, because of thee and of Eve, I am slippery, and go upon my belly." Then by reason of its great strength, it threw down Adam and Eve and pressed upon them, as if it would kill them.
>
> 5 But God sent an angel who threw the serpent away from them, and raised them up.

> 6 Then the Word of God came to the serpent, and said unto it, "In the first instance I made thee glib, and made thee to go upon thy belly; but I did not deprive thee of speech.
>
> 7 "Now, however, be thou dumb; and speak no more, thou and thy race; because in the first place, has the ruin of my creatures happened through thee, and now thou wishest to kill them."
>
> 8 Then the serpent was struck dumb, and spake no more.
>
> 9 And a wind came to blow from heaven by command of God that carried away the serpent from Adam and Eve, threw it on the sea shore, and it landed in India.

The serpent's swelling of its head brings to mind the expanding of its hood by a cobra. However, I'm not at all sure how any now-limbless serpent could run after Eve, nor do I comprehend how it could stand on its tail. (Having said that, the Belgian painter Pierre Jean van der Ouderaa produced an extraordinary painting of Eve's temptation that featured a tall draconopides with human head and upper parts but coiled ophidian lower body rearing upright alongside a tree.) Nevertheless, this little-known account certainly makes unusual reading.

Returning to the skin fragment at the Chicago Historical Society: although the society's chief curator, Olivia Mahoney, has no doubt that it is a fraud (as opposed to a bona fide piece of snakeskin dating back to the dawn of time), no research has ever been conducted on it to ascertain its true nature. Moreover, Mahoney is very reluctant to permit any, in case the skin is damaged, and also because in her view it is so evidently a fake that no such research is needed. That may well be, but it still doesn't answer what—if not a sample of skin from the Eden serpent—this anomalous object actually is.

The *Chicago Sun-Times* newspaper's religion writer, Cathleen Falsani, viewed and then wrote about this highly contentious yet hitherto-obscure biblical(?) relic in an article published by that newspaper on 10 October 2003. In it, she passed the very memorable comment that after watching this specimen being carried back in its box to the society's archives: "I couldn't help thinking about that scene from 'Raiders of the Lost Ark', where the Ark of the Covenant, and all of its power, is crated up and wheeled into a military warehouse among thousands of other generic crates. I wonder what else might be hiding anonymously in a quiet corner of a museum archive somewhere else, waiting to shock us with its mystery". What else indeed?

I have documented in my trilogy of books on new and rediscovered animals a sizeable number and diversity of remarkable, hitherto scientifically-unknown species that were first brought to formal zoological attention by encountering them not in the living state within their natural habitat but rather as long-preserved yet previously-overlooked, ignored specimens in the collections of various museums and other scientific institutions around the world. Consequently, I am only too well aware of the ever-present potential for extraordinary, fascinating finds being made in this way. But whether these will ever include any bona fide remains from the infamous Eden serpent is another matter entirely. Let's just say that I'm not holding my breath . . .

15
A MELANISTIC MYSTERY SNAKE?

> One hot day in December I had been standing perfectly still for a few minutes among the dry weeds when a slight rustling sound came from near my feet, and glancing down I saw the head and neck of a large black serpent moving slowly past me. In a moment or two the flat head was lost to sight among the close-growing weeds, but the long body continued moving slowly by—so slowly that it hardly appeared to move, and as the creature must have been not less than six feet long, and probably more, it took a very long time, while I stood thrilled with terror, not daring to make the slightest movement, gazing down upon it. Although so long it was not a thick snake, and as it moved on over the white ground it had the appearance of a coal-black current flowing past me—a current not of water or other liquid but of some such element as quicksilver moving on in a rope-like stream. At last it vanished, and turning I fled from the ground, thinking that never again would I venture into or near that frightfully dangerous spot in spite of its fascination.
>
> W.H. Hudson—*Far Away and Long Ago*

Whereas some mysteries become less mystifying once investigated, others only become even more so—and the ophidian example under consideration here definitely belongs to the latter category.

As a child, I was bought a wonderful anthology entitled *Animal Stories*, published in 1967, whose contents had been chosen by Alan C. Jenkins. Within its covers, he had compiled a splendid collection of animal-themed fiction and non-fiction, including chapters extracted from a number of classic books, such as Gerald Durrell's *The Bafut Beagles* (1954), Jim Corbett's *Man-Eaters of Kumaon* (1944), Ernest Thompson Seton's *Lives of the Hunted* (1901), and W.H. Hudson's *Far Away and Long Ago* (1918).

My favourite story in the entire anthology was a chapter entitled 'A Serpent Mystery', from the above-mentioned book by W.H. Hudson (in which he recalled his early life during the mid-1800s in the Quilmes, a borough in Argentina's Buenos Aires Province). Reading it, the mystery in question, namely the identity of a very remarkable snake that he had encountered on three separate occasions, seemed to have been solved by him at the end of the chapter. However, after returning to this story many years later and investigating his claims concerning the snake, I have realised that the mystery may still be far from solved. Here is a summary of Hudson's 'A Serpent Mystery' chapter.

Even as a boy, Hudson was familiar with the various ophidian species native to his home region, none of which exceeded 4 ft long, and he spent many hours exploring a weed-infested piece of waste ground at the far end of his family's plantation. One hot December day, while standing amid this wilderness, he heard a soft rustling sound near his feet, and, looking down, was startled to see a very long, slender, coal-black snake moving very slowly past him. He estimated its total length to be at least 6 ft, probably more, and he stared at it intently, remaining motionless until it finally vanished from sight among some long grass. What could it have been? Neither its colour nor its size matched that of any species that he had ever known or heard of existing in this area.

Initially, Hudson vowed never to return to that dangerous site, but his fascination with its unexpected inhabitant ultimately won the day, compelling him to venture back—and after numerous days of failure, he finally caught sight of the mysterious ebony-scaled serpent again, gliding languorously through the weeds in the very same spot as before. This time, however, Hudson was able to spy its destination—a hole in the ground, into which it passed until it was totally hidden from view. On many subsequent visits to the waste ground, he deliberately stood quietly near to this hole in the hope

15 | A MELANISTIC MYSTERY SNAKE?

W.H. Hudson

that sooner or later he would once more see its enigmatic owner, but the long black mystery snake never made an appearance.

Then one day, after having stood there yet again, and for some considerable time, but still without success, Hudson became bored, and chose instead to interest himself in observing a bat hanging from a twig just overhead. Concentrating upon the bat, he at first paid no heed to a sensation of pressure upon the instep of his right foot, but when the pressure increased, until it seemed as if a heavy metal bar were resting upon it, he casually glanced down to see what was responsible for this odd sensation—and was shocked to discover that it was none other than his long-sought-after black mystery snake, which was actually drawing its lengthy inky-black coils leisurely across his foot!

By standing in his present position, Hudson's foot was inadvertently blocking the snake's passage to its hole, and so rather than moving *around* the offending obstacle it had decided simply to take the shorter course, and pass directly *over* it! Thrilled, terrified, and tantalised in equal measures, Hudson remained immobile as coil after coil rippled like a sable stream across his foot, until at last their sinuous owner had re-entered its den undisturbed and unalarmed.

Although Hudson returned many times afterwards, he never saw the snake again, and no-one whom he questioned about it had seen or heard of anything like it in that area of Argentina either. Subsequent investigations, however, led him to believe that it was a melanistic (all-black) specimen of a species that he referred to as *Philodryas scotti*. He claimed that this was a not-uncommon Argentinian species, although not in his home region, and that it did indeed grow to 6 ft or more.

In addition, Hudson noted that two years before his three meetings with the black snake, a normal-coloured *P. scotti* specimen—one that he described as "a pale greenish-grey, with numerous dull black mottlings and small spots"—had been encountered by his sister as a small child (and swiftly dispatched by their horrified father), but until now had not been identified.

As noted earlier, one might assume from the above account that Hudson had duly solved the mystery of his black snake—but in fact nothing could be further from the truth.

To begin with: when searching online for *Philodryas scotti*, I discovered that only a single publication referred to it—and that

15 | A MELANISTIC MYSTERY SNAKE?

publication was none other than Hudson's own book, *Far Away and Long Ago*. Could it be, therefore, that the name given by Hudson had been incorrect? Pursuing this possibility, I soon discovered that there was indeed an Argentinian species mentioned in numerous sources whose name differed by only a single letter—namely, *Philodryas schotti* (sometimes given as *schottii*). A species of venomous, rear-fanged colubrid, its common name is the Patagonian green snake, and nowadays it is referred to by many authorities as *Philodryas patagoniensis*.

Was this the true identity of Hudson's '*Philodryas scotti*'? Certainly, photographs of *P. patagoniensis* correspond closely with Hudson's description of the snake encountered by his baby sister. Moreover, there are also a number of photographs online of melanistic specimens that readily recall Hudson's black mystery snake. However, *P. patagoniensis* does not normally exceed 5 ft.

Consequently, if the two snakes reported by Hudson did indeed belong to this species, either they were unusually lengthy or their size had been over-estimated by him. Some mutant gene alleles responsible for melanism are known to increase body size too, so

Patagonian green snake *Philodryas patagoniensis*
(Frederico de Alcântara Menezes *et al.* (2018), CC BY-SA 4.0)

assuming that Hudson had not over-estimated its length, this could explain the black snake's extra-large size, but not the normally-coloured specimen's.

So were these two snakes truly *P. patagoniensis*, or did they belong to a different species—and, if they did, which one? Perhaps, more than a century after the publication of *Far Away and Long Ago*, the last word has still to be said on the subject of W.H. Hudson's intriguing serpent mystery.

16
BLEATING PYTHONS, CHIMING PUFF ADDERS, AND OTHER UNEXPECTED SERPENTINE VOCALISTS

Reports about vocal sounds produced by snakes are extremely rare. So far known to the author, there are records from India of a captive [Indian] python, *Python molurus molurus*, producing a sound resembling 'Umh' of a man in agony and of a 'dhaman' [India's rat snake], *Ptyas mucosus*, uttering several kinds of noises including a low whine and variations thereon while being carried after a rough handling during capture and of another Dhaman producing 'Umh' while being caught. [Malcolm A.] Smith on the authority of Wall states that a 'dhaman' when cornered raises the forebody, inflates the throat and gives vent to a "peculiar sound, something like the noise produced by a cat at bay." [N.L.] Corkill records that in Wad Medani in the Sudan, a young lined house snake, *Boodon* [now *Boaedon*] *lineatus*, when seized with a pair of metal forceps produced a squeaking noise something between the squeak of a mouse and that of a press-the-button toy animal. A captive boa is also known to produce sound resembling that of the python referred to above.

> B.K. Behura—*Journal of the Utkal University Bhunaneswar*, July 1962

Apart from their familiar hisses, snakes are traditionally thought to be mute, but as revealed here, this longstanding assumption may have little basis in fact.

The sibilant hissing sounds of snakes are produced by air being forced through the glottis (the opening from the back of the throat's pharynx into the windpipe); the pitch of the hiss is controlled by the width of the glottis's aperture. In addition, there are certain species, such as the North American bullsnake *Pituophis catenifer sayi* and kin, with an unusually well-developed glottis flap (epiglottis) that increases these sounds as air is blown against it. Indeed, so effective is this that the bullsnake's bovine grunt (hence its name) can be heard up to 100 ft away.

But what about the remarkable cock-crowing sounds allegedly produced by the highly controversial African mystery snake known as the crowing crested cobra, documented in Chapter 4 of this present book? Could such sounds, less alone such a snake itself, be plausible?

In his extensive report on North Rhodesian (now Zambian) fauna that I referred to in that latter chapter, longstanding African game warden Lieutenant-Colonel Charles Pitman offered a singularly original and quite unforgettable explanation—postulating as the likely answer what must surely be the most macabre form of ventriloquism ever conceived!

According to Pitman, in those incidents on record featuring a snake that seemed to its bemused observer to be crowing, the snake was not actually making the sounds itself; on the contrary, the sounds were the screams of a prey victim that the snake was in the act of swallowing alive! In support of this ghoulish hypothesis, in his book *A Game Warden Takes Stock* (1942) Pitman cited the case of an African naturalist who suddenly heard a strange squeaking cry nearby, and discovered to his great surprise that it was coming from a rhombic night adder *Causus rhombeatus* in the middle of a heap of stones. To his even greater surprise, however, he found that the adder contained a small toad, engulfed so recently that it was still alive, and which, in Pitman's opinion, was unquestionably responsible for the peculiar cries issuing from the adder's mouth.

Yet even if such an imaginative theory could be stretched to explain every single report of snakes that crow (which is itself highly unlikely, as the possibility of frequent encounters with snakes engaged in the very act of swallowing screaming prey victims must

16 | SERPENTINE VOCALISTS

Bullsnake *Pituophis catenifer sayi* (freeparking, CC BY 2.0)

Rhombic night adder eating a frog in Mlilwane Wildlife Sanctuary, Eswatini (=Swaziland) (Barnard Gagnon, CC BY-SA 4.0)

surely rate as exceedingly slim!), it is still unsatisfactory. This is because crowing cries are by no means the only unexpected type of sound to have been reported from African (and other) snakes. Also on file are accounts of snakes that bleat, roar, bellow, cough, purr, bark, and even emit metallic bell-like sounds.

A representative series of examples was presented during an interesting series of communications from readers published in the London *Times* newspaper during the second half of 1929. It began on 22 August, with a letter by Captain Tracy Philipps, reporting the existence in Kabale (in Kigezi, Uganda) of a snake allegedly able to produce a single, sustained bell-like note like that of some Ethiopian horns; the natives informed him that this animal was known locally as the nkweta. That elicited a largely sceptical response on 24 August from Alleyne Leechman (former Director of Tanzania's Agricultural Research Station at Amani), although he did concede that British zoologist Edward G. Boulenger (son of George A. Boulenger) had admitted that a snake might make a sound similar to the notes produced by a gently-struck tuning fork.

On 26 August, Jan H. Koens of the Royal Empire Society announced that he had seen a 24-ft-long python raise itself up like a young tree and produce a deer-like bleat, and had heard an 11-ft black mamba *Dendroaspis polylepis* cough like a monkey. He felt that they purposefully imitated the cries of their prey in order to entice them to approach. Worth noting here is that many years earlier, the famous African explorer David Livingstone had mentioned a snake in South Africa referred to by the natives as the nogo putsane ('kid snake'), because it reputedly bleats like a young goat.

Moreover, in a *BioFortean Review* article of May 2007, American herpetological enthusiast Chad Arment noted a comparable African report documented by Charles John Andersson in his book *Lake Ngami* (1856):

> The story of the cockatrice, so common in many parts of the world, is also found among the Damaras; but instead of crowing, or, rather, chuckling like a fowl when going to roost, they say it bleats like a lamb. It attacks man as well as beast, and its bite is considered fatal. They point to the distant north as its proper home. In Timbo's country it is termed 'hangara,' and is said to attain to twelve feet, or even

16 | SERPENTINE VOCALISTS

> more, in length, with a beautifully variegated skin. On its head, like the Guinea-fowl, it has a horny protuberance of a reddish colour. It dwells chiefly in trees. Its chuckle is heard at nightfall; and people, imagining that the noise proceeds from one of their own domestic fowls that has strayed, hasten to drive it home. But this frequently causes their destruction; for, as soon as the cockatrice perceives its victim within reach, it darts at it with the speed of lightning; and if its fangs enter the flesh, death invariably ensues. Timbo informed me that he once saw a dog belonging to his father thus killed. Moreover, the cockatrice, like the wild dog, wantonly destroys more at a time than it can consume.

I find this report someone baffling, inasmuch as Andersson begins it by stating categorically that the snake does *not* chuckle like a fowl but bleats like a lamb instead, yet goes on to state with equal authority that it does produce a chuckle, which people mistake for that of a domestic fowl.

Less ambiguous is a note by explorer Leonard Clark in his book *The Rivers Ran East* (1954) concerning the supposed existence in South America of a snake referred to by the local Indian people as the shushupe. This still-unidentified species allegedly emits a strange cry like that of a duck in distress in order to lure its prey within striking range.

Could the shushupe possibly be the formidable, highly-venomous South American bushmaster *Lachesis muta*? Certainly, as revealed in his book *More About Leemo* (1967), Stanley E. Brock had absolutely no doubt that this snake has vocal capabilities:

> In my experience the bushmaster is the only snake in South America that I have heard emit any vocal sound. The noise is a high pitched, "chee-chee-chee-chee," one, and awesomely common (after you have learned what it is made by) in some forest areas. In Guyana, in the Kuyuwini, Kassikaitu, and Upper Essequibo River jungles, it is especially notorious. No doubt I would never have known what the noise was, although I had heard it often, if I had not been

told by the Indians. They say it only makes the sound at dusk when it first moves off to hunt from its day-long sleep. I have never actually stood and watched a bushmaster chirp, but I suppose some hawk-eyed Indians must have in the past. Every time I hear it my Indians (very often different ones) call its name—*"nan-amat"* immediately, and so I am personally convinced that the fact is true.

Of course, bearing in mind that Brock admitted that he had never personally witnessed a bushmaster vocalising, it is possible that the chirping sound heard was made by some entirely different creature(s), and that the Indians were mistaken in their belief that the bushmaster was responsible for it. However, the bushmaster is far from unique as an alleged vocalising serpent.

Bushmaster *Lachesis muta muta* (Christopher Murray, PD)

On 27 August 1929, a letter by Sir Hector L. Duff reminded *Times* readers of an episode included in his book *Nyasaland Under the Foreign Office* (1903). It concerned a long, drawn-out mystery sound, like the rather metallic note of a wire in the wind, heard by him in the hills near the city of Zomba (in what is now southern

Malawi), and which his native servant declared to be the cry of a certain type of large snake.

On 31 August 1929, G.P.L. James recalled in *The Times* that he had encountered several cobras in India that would produce a deep cat-like purr just before striking at their prey or if disturbed. (In 1931, in his very authoritative book *Snakes of the World,* eminent American herpetologist Raymond Ditmars also noted this, describing the sound as a sharp sneeze-like hiss.) Then on 2 September, G.E. Davies suggested that the 'purr' was emitted to bemuse or 'fascinate' the prey victim—already mesmerised by the cobra's expanded hood. Worth noting is that three years later, on 27 September 1932, a letter to *The Times* by David Freeman recorded that in Malaya he had heard cobras uttering an exceedingly shrill note, which did not seem to have any warning purpose, but may have been related to mating.

On 30 December 1929, Captain Tracy Philipps expanded upon his earlier *Times* letter, adding that his mystery snake's local name, the nkweta, meant 'I-you-am-calling', and that after encountering it and hearing it produce a sustained bell-like sound, he had recognised it as a puff adder *Bitis arietans*. This corroborated a statement made by Captain G.B. Ritchie, who had noted in an article published by the periodical *East Africa* in September 1929:

> Puff adders calling their mates at breeding time emit a beautiful bell-like note, audible for about 200 yards. Dr. G. Prentice, whose attention I drew to this matter, personally proved it.

In a letter to *The Times* of 7 September 1932, Philipps provided more details regarding this. He also noted that similar sounds produced by snakes had been heard by L.M. Nesbitt when crossing Ethiopia's Danakil desert lands in 1928—and as documented by Nesbitt two years later in the *Geographical Journal.*

Probably the most astonishing letter of all, however, came from Mrs Duncan Carse, of Crowthorne, in Berkshire, England (published by *The Times* on 5 October 1932). This is because her oddly vocal serpent was not some exotic, far-distant species, but was actually a specimen of *Natrix helvetica,* the exceedingly familiar barred grass snake. One hot morning in summer 1932, she and her dog had spied a grass snake lying asleep in her garden. The dog froze:

... and at the same instant the snake 'spotted' us, and let out a clear bird-like call, obviously of alarm, and the next second had disappeared like a flash into the undergrowth. The 'note' of the snake was so loud that my husband, who was working in his studio several yards away, heard it distinctly, and came dashing out to see "what sort of a weird bird" had flown into our garden!

Concluding her grass snake letter, Mrs Carse steadfastly maintained that:

... there is not the slightest doubt that this one screamed: a clear, peculiar, bird-like call, quite as loud as the note of a blackbird.

Barred grass snake *Natrix helvetica* (Benny Trapp, CC BY-A 4.0)

While on the subject of snakes producing distinctive alarm calls, Indian zoologist Dr B.K. Behura published a concise paper in the July 1962 issue of the *Journal of the Utkal University, Bhubaneswar* that was entirely devoted to non-sibilant vocal sounds produced by snakes. Supporting his claim with several cases featuring species

16 | SERPENTINE VOCALISTS

such as pythons, kraits, and rat snakes (see the quote from his paper that opens this present chapter of my book), he concluded:

> Normal healthy snakes can produce sounds other than hissing. When alarmed or under duress, they produce a sound resembling 'Umh' of a man in agony.

Still with snake alarm calls: back in 1933, a Northern Rhodesian correspondent to the periodical *East Africa* reported killing two snakes in his orange-packing warehouse that had emitted sounds described by him as 'hoooh'. Furthermore, they belonged to a species (unnamed by him, unfortunately) that the native people in the area claimed could crow.

All of this may seem quite unbelievable, but as mentioned by veteran Belgian cryptozoologist Dr Bernard Heuvelmans in his book *Les Derniers Dragons d'Afrique* (1978), and also by British zoologist Dr Maurice Burton when considering the matter in his own book *More Animal Legends* (1959), reports describing virtually the same sounds for such snakes have emerged from many different localities, documented by eye-witnesses totally unknown to one another, and in completely separate publications. These reports collectively yield a formidable coincidence to explain away—unless they truly are based upon genuine incidents involving snakes that really do produce these singularly unsnake-like sounds.

Not surprisingly, and in agreement with Heuvelmans's stated sentiments, I feel that the alternative option (i.e. supporting Pitman's 'ventriloquism' hypothesis) would be somewhat rash. This is because the 'explanation' that such snake-emitted sounds are actually due to sightings of snakes containing assorted goats, deer, cows, dogs, cats, and birds, all freshly engulfed and still alive (plus a goodly supply of self-ringing bells!) is, in every sense, extremely difficult to swallow!

Even so, diehard disbelievers have traditionally responded to the claimed ability of snakes to emit sounds other than hisses with two daunting arguments against this (as expressed in a long series of correspondence published by the periodical *East Africa* during 1928). These arguments are as follows:

> Argument #1: *It would be pointless for a snake to have a voice, whether for communication or for any other*

purpose, because snakes are totally deaf, completely unable to detect airborne sounds.

The ear of a snake is very degenerate in comparison to that of other terrestrial reptiles. It has neither an eardrum nor an air-filled middle ear cavity, but it is able to detect ground-borne vibrations, because with snakes the tiny ear bone known as the stapes or stirrup (which conducts airborne sounds to the inner ear in lizards) is connected to the quadrate bone—present at the upper jaw's rear end, attached to the braincase, and articulating with the lower jaw. Thus, when a snake rests its head on the ground, any vibrations passing through the ground will be transmitted via the lower jaw, quadrate, and stapes into the snake's inner ear.

To the great surprise of herpetologists everywhere, however, it has been shown that snakes can actually detect certain airborne sounds too. Indeed, as far back as 1960, researchers Drs E.G. Wever and J.A. Vernon reported in a *Journal of Auditory Research* scientific paper that these supposedly deaf reptiles were really rather sensitive to airborne sounds within a frequency range of 100-500 Hz.

In 1971, these findings were expanded by Dr P.H. Hartline in a *Journal of Experimental Biology* paper. His series of experiments testing the sensitivity of snakes to ground-borne and airborne vibration revealed that in relation to frequencies within the 150-400 Hz range, the snake's auditory system was more sensitive than the system of vibration detectors ('somatic hearing') present in its skin. Moreover, between 200-400 Hz the snake's hearing was more acute than that of a frog (which is very sensitive, although rather less so than that of mammals). In short, snakes are not deaf at all, and the findings of the above researchers and various others lend credence to the possibility that future workers will unfurl evidence for even greater auditory ability among snakes.

Indeed, during the early 1990s I received some remarkable confirmation of snakes' auditory abilities from noted Exmoor-based English naturalist and conservationist Trevor Beer. Recalling to me some incidents from his boyhood nature rambles in the company of Jack, a gentleman poacher very knowledgeable in the ways of wildlife (as described by Trevor in his delightful book *Poachers Days*, 1985), Trevor mentioned that whenever Jack wanted to pick up a snake safely (regardless of whether it was a barred grass snake *Natrix*

16 | SERPENTINE VOCALISTS

helvetica or a European adder *Vipera berus*), he would tell Trevor to click his fingers. This invariably caused the snake to turn its head away from Jack, and towards the direction of the click, whereupon Jack would bend down swiftly and pick up the unsuspecting snake from behind. As far as I am aware, this remarkable ability of grass snakes and adders to detect the sharp sound of clicking fingers has not been previously documented in the herpetological literature, and it greatly deserves formal scientific investigation.

In addition, studies published in the *Journal of Experimental Zoology* by Dr Bruce A. Young of Hollins College, Virginia, in 1991 with king cobras *Ophiophagus hannah* revealed that these snakes were readily able to hear the unusually deep, growl-like hisses that are characteristic of their species and which are believed to be produced via pocket-like structures called tracheal diverticula, evaginating from the windpipe and functioning as low-frequency resonance chambers. Young's researches into the auditory and sound-producing capabilities of snakes subsequently yielded an extremely informative, enlightening survey published in 2003 by the *Quarterly Review of Biology*, in which he confirmed that snakes are actually more sensitive to airborne than to groundborne sounds, thus totally reversing the traditional view concerning snakes' auditory abilities.

> Argument #2: *Snakes cannot possibly produce sounds other than the usual hisses, because they have no vocal cords.*

It is indeed true that although snakes have a voice-box (larynx), it does not contain any vocal cords. However, the same is also true for fishes, yet many species are known that can give voice to loud (sometimes quite stentorian) noises—as discussed long ago by London Zoo naturalist Walter S. Berridge in his book *Animal Curiosities* (1922), and later by Dr Maurice Burton in *More Animal Legends* (1959), among others. And remarkable as it may seem, those most versatile of animal vocalists the song-birds are also without vocal cords inside their larynx. Their varied mellifluous and cacophonous outpourings are due instead to a specialised structure called the syrinx, positioned some distance below the larynx. Clearly, therefore, the possession of vocal cords is not obligatory for a vertebrate to emit loud, distinctive sounds.

Nevertheless, the more recalcitrant sceptics of reports concerning vocalising snakes have continued to regard these reptiles' lack of vocal cords as the last word on the matter, refusing to believe that without such structures snakes could ever crow, bleat, bark, bellow, chime, etc. If only, somehow, a snake could be formally discovered that can utter something more, much more, than a mere hiss (even one of the notable power famously displayed by the previously-mentioned North American bull snake), thereby instantly, and audibly, annihilating for all time this obsolete obstacle to believing that a vocal serpent could truly exist.

It was a long time coming, but eventually such a find was indeed made, one that stupefied zoologists.

In 1980, Philip Chapman from the City Museum in Bristol, southern England, took part in what proved to be a herpetologically historic scientific exploration of the huge Melinau limestone cave system in Sarawak's Gunung Mulu National Park on the large southeast Asian island of Borneo. During the expedition team's penetration of the largely unknown and predominantly lightless world of Clearwater Cave (up to 10,000 ft underground), its members were suddenly confronted by a very loud and extremely eerie yowling sound, evidently coming from some animal just ahead. Very cautiously, almost fearfully, they shone their torches in its direction, to expose the originator of these disturbing noises, and saw to their amazement that they were being made by a snake!

As I learnt from Philip in correspondence with him, the snake in question was coiled up on the cave floor (*not* hanging from the wall, as some reports have erroneously alleged) and was emitting a hoarse, yowling miaow, just like a cat. Very surprisingly, however, this singular serpent did not represent a new species. On the contrary, it belonged to a form already well known—the Bornean cave racer *Orthriophis taeniurus grabowskyi*, This is a slender, blue, non-venomous subspecies known not only from caves but also from above-ground, and from Sumatra as well as Borneo, but of comparable appearance wherever found. Yet somehow its extraordinary vocal capability had never before been documented, or even suspected, by scientists. It was duly reported in a December 1985 article published by the *Sarawak Museum Journal*.

Moreover, the team soon learnt something equally mystifying concerning these strange snakes. Their prey consists of very small but fast-flying, cave-dwelling birds called Bornean swiftlets

Collocalia dodgei—which, astonishingly, they can catch in total darkness, while the birds are still *in flight*. Yet the cave racers cannot see the swiftlets, and without limbs or other tactile organs they cannot make physical contact with them either, except when actually striking. So when the birds are in flight, how can the snakes know where they are, let alone be able to catch them on the wing? It may be fairly easy to snatch a swiftlet flying through a narrow tunnel, but what about in the great open spaces inside the main caves themselves? Perhaps the racers detect the birds by smell, or respond to their wings' vibrations carried through the air—or perhaps there is an even more ingenious method?

As the domain of the cave swiftlets is shrouded in continuous, absolute darkness, they avoid collisions with one another, with the cave walls, and with other objects by carrying out echo-location, just like bats do, emitting shrill cries of extremely high frequency. Is it just a coincidence, therefore, that their serpentine predator, the cave racer, is also able to give voice to a high, yowling cry? Could this be an attempt on the snake's part to mimic the birds' calls, in order to lure them within striking range, or perhaps even an attempt to disrupt their echo-location, in order to throw them off-course, so that they fly towards the cave walls or the ground, and thence to the waiting snakes?

Such suggestions as these, however, require one further assumption. In order for the snakes to mimic the swiftlets' cries, they must be able to detect them. And if this is genuinely the case, then, in addition to the above activities involving its own vocal powers, such a snake could also make use of an approaching swiftlet's vocalisations—by gauging the precise direction and timing of its strike according to the direction and volume of the echo-location cries emitted by the bird (which thus betrays its precise position). I realise that the concept of a snake sensitive to high-frequency airborne sounds must seem extremely radical, but we must never forget that not so long ago no one believed that snakes could detect *any* airborne sounds at all.

Incidentally, although most of the unexpected sounds attributed to snakes in reports presented in this chapter do seem to involve hitherto-unsuspected vocal abilities on the part of these reptiles, there is one such category of sound that may be of a non-vocal nature.

As far back as 27 June 1908, eminent British zoologist Richard Lydekker noted in a report published by *The Field* magazine that during the mating season, the males of some species of American terrapin possess two patches of horny tubercles on their hind legs, which, like crickets, they rub together in order to produce a very loud, musical note, apparently to attract mates. According to Lydekker, similar sounds are also produced by Asia's wonder geckos *Teratoscincus* spp. and Africa's barking geckos *Ptenopus*, via friction on their tails' horny rings. Furthermore, egg-eating snakes *Dasypeltis* spp. and the saw-scaled viper *Echis carinatus* can produce very audible rustling or rasping sounds by rubbing together strongly serrated scales on several lateral scale-rows of writhing coils.

Could such a mechanism also be responsible for those reports of serpents emitting bell-like or other musical sounds? Worth remembering is Captain Ritchie's allegation noted earlier here that puff adders attract their mates by producing such sounds—instantly recalling Lydekker's terrapin disclosure.

Also well worth noting here is that at the beginning of a skin-shedding cycle, snakes will often exhale more heavily than normal, using the pressure of the air expelled from their lungs to assist in loosening and dislodging the old layer of skin inside their nostrils, this forced exhalation creating a whistling sound. Moreover, if such whistling occurs at other, non-shedding times, it can sometimes indicate the presence of a respiratory infection, which is particularly well-documented from pet American corn snakes *Pantherophis* [formerly *Elaphe*] *guttatus*. Incidentally, most snakes only possess a single (right-hand) lung, but certain species have two or even four lungs (the fully-developed right-hand lung, a semi-developed left-hand lung, and two primordial tracheal lungs situated next to the throat). Still with snakes that whistle: in his book *Red Sand, Green Heart: Ecological Adventures in the Outback* (2003), John L. Read documents a traditional aboriginal legend concerning a fabulous whistling snake.

Lastly: although rattlesnakes are famous for the loud sounds produced by their tail's rattles, they are not alone in the serpent world in possessing such abilities. The common American garter snakes *Thamnophis* spp. can produce a very audible, deep-toned, non-vocal hum via the rapid vibration of their tail's tip. Indeed, according to a letter written by F.A.T. Reuss of Berlin, Germany, that was published in 1951 by the journal *Herpetologica*, in a quiet location this sound can be heard at a distance of 2-3 yards.

16 | SERPENTINE VOCALISTS

Teratoscincus microlepis (Kamran Kamali, CC-0)

Corn snake *Pantherophis guttatus* (PD)

In short, not only are the auditory abilities of snakes far more profound than once assumed, so too it would seem is the diversity of their vocal and non-vocal sound-producing capabilities. Neither deaf nor dumb after all, which is certainly something for herpetologists to crow about—even if the mysterious crowing crested cobra itself remains scientifically unconfirmed.

17
KIPLING AND KARAIT—AN OPHIDIAN BUNGLE IN *THE JUNGLE BOOK?*

> . . . when Teddy came running down the path, Rikki-tikki was ready to be petted.
>
> But just as Teddy was stooping, something flinched a little in the dust, and a tiny voice said: "Be careful. I am death!" It was Karait, the dusty brown snakeling that lies for choice on the dusty earth; and his bite is as dangerous as the cobra's. But he is so small that nobody thinks of him, and so he does the more harm to people.
>
> . . . Karait struck out. Rikki jumped sideways and tried to run in, but the wicked little dusty grey head lashed within a fraction of his shoulder, and he had to jump over the body, and the head followed his heels close . . . [but] Karait had lunged out once too far, and Rikki-tikki had sprung, jumped on the snake's back, dropped his head far between his fore-legs, bitten as high up the back as he could get hold, and rolled away. That bite paralysed Karait [killing him].
>
> Rudyard Kipling—'Rikki-Tikki-Tavi', in *The Jungle Book*

Two of my best-loved books as a child (and still today, for that matter) were *The Jungle Book* (1894) and *The Second Jungle Book* (1895), both authored by Rudyard Kipling, which I first read at much the same time that Disney's classic animated movie version was first screened in cinemas (1967), and which I also adored despite its many liberties taken with Kipling's source material. Although most famous for their Mowgli stories, these two books also contain a number of others that do not feature him and are not set in the Indian jungle.

Of these non-Mowgli tales, my own personal favourite is 'Rikki-Tikki-Tavi', which was included in the first of Kipling's two *Jungle Books*. Its eponymous mongoose star (henceforth referred to here simply as RTT for brevity) successfully and successively saved from a series of potentially lethal attacks by Nag and Nagaina—a malign pair of garden-inhabiting Indian (spectacled) cobras *Naja naja*—the human family that he had 'adopted' after their young son Teddy had rescued him from almost drowning in a flood.

INTRODUCING KARAIT—KIPLING'S DIMINUTIVE BUT DEADLY DUST-DWELLING SNAKELING

However, cobras were not the only snakes that RTT dispatched. He also killed a much smaller but seemingly no less deadly serpentine threat to Teddy and family—namely, the "dusty brown snakeling" Karait, whose meagre description provided by Kipling is quoted in full at the beginning of this present chapter. Even as a child (and nascent cryptozoologist), I was fascinated by Karait, for whereas cobras were readily familiar to me, Karait remained mysterious, because no formal identification of his species was provided by Kipling.

So what *was* Karait—possibly an inaccurately-described known living species (i.e. a veritable bungle in *The Jungle Book*), or an entirely fictitious one that Kipling had specifically invented for his RTT story, or conceivably even a real species but one that either was now long-extinct (at least in India, but possibly everywhere else too) or had still to be formally described and named by science? There was only one way to deal with these and other options on offer. So after watching a cartoon version of it and then re-reading the original story a couple of years ago, I conducted some investigations into Kipling's minute but highly mystifying Karait, and here is what I found out.

KARAIT AND THE KRAITS

Naturally, the name 'Karait' instantly calls to mind the very similar name 'krait', applied both colloquially and scientifically to a number of species of venomous elapid snake native to India and elsewhere in Asia, and belonging to the genus *Bungarus*—which is why as a child I had simply assumed from his name that Karait had indeed merely been a krait. However, my fascination with Kipling's diminutive yet deadly dust serpent increased during subsequent years (in tandem with my increasing ophidian knowledge) when I realised that what little morphological and behavioural information concerning Karait *had* been given by Kipling did not accord with any krait species (either in its adult or in its juvenile form) known to exist anywhere within or even beyond the Indian Subcontinent.

The most familiar krait species, and also the most abundant, widely distributed one in India, is the common Indian krait *B. caeruleus*. When adult, however, it can attain a total length of up to

Exquisite illustration of Rikki-Tikki-Tavi the mongoose and an unspecified Indian snake, from a 1924 French edition of *The Jungle Book*

5.75 ft (3 ft on average, but still very much longer than Kipling's Karait), and its body is handsomely marked with a characteristic banded pattern of light and dark stripes (often black and white, but famously black and gold in the closely-related banded krait *B. fasciatus*, also native to India and up to 7 ft long). Moreover, when it is a juvenile and therefore much smaller (hence much more comparable in size to Karait than the adult is), its stripes are even more distinct than they are in the adult snake and its background colouration is bluish, not brown.

Adult specimen of the common Indian krait *Bungarus caeruleus* (Jayendra Chiplunkar, CC BY-SA 3.0)

Most other krait species also exhibit striping, albeit of different degrees of vividness. Needless to say, however, any mention of such markings in Kipling's description of Karait is conspicuous only by its absence, which would be highly unusual for Kipling if he had indeed intended Karait to be a krait, because his knowledge and descriptions of other Indian fauna were always very skilled. True, a few krait species do not possess stripes, but these still tend to have a very bold background body colour, such as shiny brown, glossy black, or even deep blue with a bright red head in one species (*B. flaviceps* from southeast Asia). Once again, therefore, they differ substantially from the decidedly nondescript appearance ascribed by Kipling to Karait.

It is odd, therefore, that prior to that section's en bloc deletion on 27 March 2020 the 'In fiction' section of Wikipedia's entry for the genus *Bungarus* referred to Kipling's Karait as "a small sand-colored krait", apparently unaware of the fundamental morphological flaws in such an identification that I have enumerated above. Similarly unaware, it would seem, is the Kipling Society, because on its official website its brief entry for Karait states: "karait (or krait) A small highly poisonous snake, known to Kipling and common in India". Common in India it may be (and, indeed, is), but small it certainly is not.

No less damaging to a krait identity claim for Karait than incompatible morphology is the notable reluctance of these snakes to bite or strike out at a potential aggressor, preferring to coil up and hide their head within their coils, exposing and lifting up their tail tip instead. This behaviour does not correspond at all with the much more active, antagonistic striking behaviour of Karait, plus their predominantly nocturnal lifestyle means that kraits rarely encounter humans during the daytime anyway, which is when Karait encountered Teddy. Consequently, as the only link between the kraits and Karait is a shared colloquial name, it would seem most parsimonious to assume that Kipling simply selected the name Karait for its sound or familiarity, rather than to indicate any taxonomic affinity between his story's snake and the genuine kraits.

A LOAD OF COBRAS?

The website *Litcharts* offers a very different ophidian identity from a krait for Karait—nothing less, in fact, than an infant cobra. In its list of minor characters that appear in Kipling's story 'Rikki-Tikki-Tavi', it describes Karait as:

> The young cobra hatchling, implied to be a child of Nag and Nagaina, whom Rikki-tikki battles in the garden early in the story. His small size in fact makes him *more* dangerous than the older snakes, as he is quicker and harder to catch, but Rikki-tikki defeats him nonetheless.

This entry's claim baffles me, because nowhere in Kipling's coverage of Karait and his unsuccessful attack upon RTT can I spot any implication that Karait was a young cobra hatchling, other than perhaps the term 'snakeling', which may imply a young snake. Equally, however, it may imply a small adult snake. In any case, even the smallest Indian cobra hatchlings, which still measure a respectable 10 in long, possess their species' characteristic hood—yet which, just like the stripes of kraits, is again conspicuous only by its absence in Kipling's description of Karait. Furthermore, by specifically stating that Karait's bite "is as dangerous as the cobra's", surely Kipling is actually delineating Karait from the cobra, rather than assimilating it with the latter snake? Certainly, that is how this statement reads to me.

A SAW-SCALED IDENTITY?

A third snake identity, and one that I feel has much greater plausibility than either of the previous two discussed here, is a species of saw-scaled viper, belonging to the genus *Echis*, which includes among its number the Indian saw-scaled viper *E. carinatus*, the best-known representative. Just like Karait, these snakes are small, predominantly brown with only faint patterning sometimes, extremely venomous, notoriously irascible, and often found in dry, dusty, arid terrain, where they are very inconspicuous, frequently burying themselves in sand or dirt until only their head is visible, thereby enabling them to ambush unsuspecting approaching prey. Is it just a coincidence, therefore, that Kipling specifically states that Karait "lies for choice on the dusty earth"?

Moreover, these snakes readily strike out aggressively if threatened, just as Karait did, and so potent is their venom (as was Karait's) that saw-scaled vipers are one of the most significant snakebite threats throughout their zoogeographical range, killing many people every year. Yet some such species are no more than 1 ft long even as adults. Clearly, therefore, this type of snake corresponds very closely with Karait across a wide range of different characteristics—morphological, behavioural, and ecological.

Interestingly, as a *ShukerNature* reader pointed out to me on 20 November 2021, the saw-scaled viper is historically viewed in India as a sort of 'profane' snake due to its bad temper and having killed a saintly Indian figure that no other snake would ever bite. So that lends further support to this species being the identity of the small but savage Karait.

Worth a brief mention here is the hump-nosed viper *Hypnale hypnale*, which is native to India, greyish-brown in colour with a double row of large dark spots, and no more than around 2 ft long (averages 12-15 in). However, it generally frequents dense jungles and hilly coffee plantations, rather than the more arid, dusty terrain favoured by *Echis*, and spends the day hidden in thick bushes and leaf litter, all of which readily argues against this species as a plausible Karait candidate.

Saw-scaled viper *Echis carinatus* (Daniel Lajko, CC BY-SA 4.0)

IS THE DEADLY KARAIT MERELY A FALLACY?

The fourth major identity to be considered here is fundamentally different from the others inasmuch as it is based not upon factual similarities but rather upon fallacious ones. Superstitious and non-scientific traditional native lore in many regions of the world often ascribes all manner of fanciful, often highly venomous attributes to various animal species that in reality are entirely harmless.

For instance, there is an Indian lizard known locally as the bis-cobra that for untold ages has been deemed by fearful villagers in rural areas to be totally lethal in every way, yet as confirmed by scientific examination of specimens it is in reality completely innocuous (see my 2014 book *The Menagerie of Marvels* for a detailed account of this unfairly-maligned saurian). Various geckos and chameleons are viewed with comparable yet wholly unwarranted native dread too. Certain equally inoffensive species of worm-like limbless amphibian known as caecilians, various vermiform legless reptiles called amphisbaenians, and some reclusive fossorial snakes like sand boas and blind (thread) snakes have also suffered persecution due to similarly erroneous layman beliefs.

While investigating the possible taxonomic identity of Karait, I communicated with Mark O'Shea, the internationally-renowned snake researcher and handler from the West Midlands Safari Park, based not very far from where I live in England, and Mark echoed my own thoughts regarding this identity option, stating: "People fear what they think are dangerous even if they aren't, i.e. blue-tongued skink or large geckos". Could it be, therefore, that Karait belongs to one such species, i.e. a very small and thoroughly harmless dust-dwelling serpent (or a serpentine herpetological species of some other kind) that has been wrongly deemed to be venomous? But why would Kipling continue to perpetrate such a fallacy? Surely as a keen amateur naturalist he would have preferred to expose it in his story as being nonsensical folklore with no foundation in fact?

AS GENUINE AS CONAN DOYLE'S INDIAN SWAMP ADDER?

Also well worth considering is that Karait may have been a total invention on Kipling's part, created perhaps to add an unexpected, additional element of danger into a plot that already contained the ever-present threat posed by the malevolent pair of cobras Nag and Nagaina (whose evil plan was to kill RTT and the humans, and then move into their house). There is, after all, a notable literary precedent for the incorporation of a deadly but zoologically non-existent Indian snake into a work of fiction—none other than the lethal Indian swamp adder or 'speckled band' that confronted the master detective Sherlock Holmes in a famous short story penned

17 | KIPLING AND KARAIT

Rudyard Kipling

by Holmes's creator, Sir Arthur Conan Doyle (see Chapter 1 of this present book of mine for my comprehensive investigation of this sinister serpent).

'The Adventure of the Speckled Band' was first published in 1892 (by London's *Strand Magazine*), i.e. just a couple of years before Kipling's *Jungle Books* were published. Who knows, might it even have directly inspired Kipling to dream up a fictitious death-dealing snake of his own?

Rather less likely, but by no means impossible, is that Karait represented either a valid species that did exist back in Kipling's time but has since become extinct without ever having been formally named and described, or one that still exists but is so elusive that it has yet to be officially discovered and recognised by science. With no supportive evidence known to me for either of these two options, however, they must remain for now entirely speculative.

GIFTED THE MISSING PIECE IN KARAIT'S PERPLEXING JIGSAW PUZZLE

At this stage in my investigation, therefore, the identity for Karait that I personally deemed to be most tenable was that of a saw-scaled viper, but I always greatly value receiving the thoughts, opinions, and possible additional information offered by other interested parties too. Consequently, on 25 March 2019 I posted the following concise summary of the Karait case on my *Facebook* timeline and also in various snake-relevant FB groups:

> Watching the 1974 Chuck Jones cartoon version of Rudyard Kipling's mongoose-starring story Rikki-Tikki-Tavi recently, I was reminded of a mystery that always puzzled me when reading it as a child. To which species did the extremely venomous but tiny dust-inhabiting, "dusty brown snakeling" Karait belong? As a child, I'd simply assumed that it was a species of krait, on account of the similarity in names and the occurrence of kraits in India. But when I learnt more about such snakes I discovered that young Indian kraits *Bungarus caeruleus* are actually vividly striped and bluish in colour, not unmarked

17 | KIPLING AND KARAIT

and dusty brown. And even young kraits seem bigger than Karait was. I've since read various alternative suggestions, e.g. that Karait was actually a saw-scaled viper, or even an infant cobra. Or could he have been a wholly fictional species, as apparently the Indian swamp adder that confronted Conan Doyle's detective Sherlock Holmes was? There may even be the possibility that it is a real yet totally harmless small species, like one of the Gerrhopilidae blind snakes of India, but which is erroneously deemed in local folklore to be very venomous. There are many such cases on record, from caecilians to an Indian lizard dubbed the bis-cobra, which I have previously documented. Do any of my herpetological friends or those of Indian heritage have any ideas as to Karait's likely identity? If so, I'd love to read your thoughts! Here is Kipling's all-too-brief description of Karait's morphology: [I then quoted the second paragraph of the three-paragraph excerpt from Kipling's book that opens this present chapter.]

I then sat back to await any postings that may be forthcoming. In the event, I received quite a number of comments (including a greatly welcomed, detailed evaluation by American biologist Dr Christopher Mallery that closely echoed my own thought processes regarding the case), which revealed that the overriding opinion concerning Karait's likely identity was the same as mine—a saw-scaled viper.

However, there was one nagging problem with this identity that I could neither resolve nor overlook. If Karait had truly been based upon a saw-scaled viper, why did Kipling, who was so knowledgeable concerning Indian fauna, give to it a name that is applied locally to the krait? This made no sense at all—until, that is, Robert Twombley, a longstanding *Facebook* friend who is passionately interested in both herpetology and cryptozoology, and is also the creator of the reptile/amphibian-specific cryptozoological group Ethnoherpetology, posted a brief but remarkable revelation there on 29 March 2019 that was entirely new to me, but which in my opinion provides the long sought-after missing piece of the perplexing Karait jigsaw puzzle. Here is what he wrote:

Bungarus caeruleus (Schneider, 1801) and *Bungarus fasciatus* (Schneider, 1801), were once placed in the same genus *Pseudoboa* (Schneider, 1801) same with *Echis carinatus* (Schneider, 1801).

In other words, back in 1801 the Indian (as well as the banded) krait and the Indian saw-scaled viper had been taxonomically lumped together by German naturalist Johann G.T. Schneider within the very same genus, *Pseudoboa* (which he had officially coined in his 1801 treatise *Historiae Amphibiorum Naturalis et Literariae Fasciculus Secundus Continens Crocodilos, Scincos, Chamaesauras, Boas, Pseudoboas, Elaps, Angues, Amphisbaenas et Caecilias*), and were therefore viewed scientifically as closely related, similar serpents. (It was only in later years that they were eventually shown to be quite distinct, both anatomically and genetically, so were duly split not only into separate genera but also into separate taxonomic families—Elapidae for the kraits as well as the cobras, and Viperidae for the vipers.)

So it is not unreasonable to assume that back then the colloquial name 'karait' had been more inclusive too, all of which could in turn explain why Kipling had applied the latter name to a snake that was quite evidently not a krait but a saw-scaled viper.

THE PICHU-CUATE—IS KARAIT ALIVE AND WELL AND LIVING IN AMERICA?

Finally: it is nothing if not intriguing that a cryptozoological snake bearing a remarkable resemblance both morphologically and behaviourally to Kipling's Karait has been reported from New Mexico and Arizona in the southwestern USA.

Known as the pichu-cuate—allegedly an Aztec name, in turn suggesting that knowledge of this snake dates back many centuries—it is described as being a tiny species of viper, no bigger or thicker than a normal lead pencil, bearing a pair of small horns above its eyes (supra-ocular), and is a nondescript grey dorsally, rose-pink ventrally, but more venomous than any other North American snake. Extremely rare but also inordinately aggressive, the pichu-cuate supposedly spends its time concealed in sand and dust, sometimes with just its triangular head visible, but will not

17 | KIPLING AND KARAIT

hesitate to bite anything or anyone that touches it, whether deliberately or inadvertently, which almost invariably leads to its victim's exceedingly rapid, agonizing death. There are claims that people who have been bitten on the hand or a finger by a pichu-cuate have swiftly cut off the wounded appendage in the desperate hope of saving their life by preventing this snake's highly virulent venom from travelling further into their body.

The only venomous snakes on record from New Mexico and Arizona are rattlesnakes and coral snakes, which certainly do not resemble the pichu-cuate. Moreover, the morphological and behavioural description presented above for the latter cryptozoological serpent does not match that of any snake species known to exist in these two U.S. states.

This diminutive but highly dangerous Karait-like snakeling was first brought to widespread attention by newspaper writer Charles Fletcher Lummis in his compilation book of traditional New Mexican lore *The King of the Broncos* (1897). Lummis claimed to have encountered a pichu-cuate on three separate occasions, and on the first of these to have even killed it, whose body he then examined in detail. Regrettably, however, he didn't retain it afterwards for scientific scrutiny. Lummis described its colouration as leaden grey dorsally, matching the sand in which it had been hiding, but rosy-red ventrally, like a conch shell's aperture. Its tiny fangs were no more than one eighth of an inch long, but moveable, slotting into grooves in the roof of its mouth when not about to strike.

In his own book *Cryptozoology: Science and Speculation* (2004), American herpetologist/cryptozoologist Chad Arment devoted a chapter to the pichu-cuate, in which he documented Lummis's coverage of it. However, he pointed out that the name 'pichu-cuate' and variations of it are also used in the southwestern USA and Mexico non-specifically, for any snakes deemed by locals to be venomous (regardless of whether they actually are). Hence it is not applied exclusively to this one particular, cryptic serpent.

Equally, however, Lummis's mention of the latter's fangs slotting into grooves in the roof of its mouth when not striking is significant, because in North America the only front-fanged venomous snakes with fangs that can move are viperids, thereby eliminating elapids from consideration, as well as rear-fanged colubrids. Also informative is his mention of the pichu-cuate's supra-ocular horns, because as noted by Chad, only four known Latin American snakes possess them. Moreover, two of these, the sidewinder *Crotalus cerastes* and the eyelash viper *Bothriechis schlegelii,* can be instantly eliminated, because the former was well known to Lummis, and the latter is arboreal and too colourful. This leaves only the Mexican horned pit viper *Ophyracus undulatus* and the montane pit viper *Porthidium melanurum*. Of these two, the former provides the closer match morphologically, but geographically it is not known to exist anywhere near New Mexico or Arizona.

Consequently, Chad concluded his coverage of the pichu-cuate by pondering whether either *O. undulatus* previously exhibited a broader distribution range than it does today, extending into those two U.S. states, or a small, undescribed viper species formerly inhabited them, and may perhaps still do so today? The following details suggest that this might be true.

On 6 May 1984, in his regular 'New Mexican Scrapbook' column published by the *El Paso Times,* Marc Simmons recalled Lummis's documentation of the pichu-cuate almost a century earlier, and then added some very intriguing, modern-day information of his own. During his travels around New Mexico, Simmons had mentioned the pichu-cuate to various old-timers, but the name meant nothing to them. However, they did tell him about an enigmatic snake known to them as the nino de la tierra ('child of the earth') that sounded suspiciously similar to the pichu-cuate. For it is said to be a small but very deadly, vicious snake that buries itself in the sand, and fatally strikes anyone who sits or lies in that place. But that is not all.

A couple of years earlier, Simmons saw a friend who had been hiking in the rocky foothills of central New Mexico's Ortiz Mountains. The friend mentioned that in a dry arroyo (steep-sided gulley) he had encountered a small grey snake with a triangular head, which in spite of its diminutive size had given him such a chill that he'd instinctively backed away straight away. So perhaps the pichu-cuate (aka nino de la tierra?) is more than just a myth after all.

Lastly, there may be some further information concerning the perplexing pichu-cuate hidden away in the collection of photographs and artwork by Lummis that is preserved at the Southwest Museum in Los Angeles, California. Time, therefore, for some enterprising Californian cryptozoologist to seek an opportunity to examine them there?

18
BOUNCING IN THE BALKANS—
THE YUGOSLAVIAN JUMPING SNAKE

> Nothing is too wonderful to be true, if it be consistent with the laws of nature.
>
> Michael Faraday—Diary, entry dated 18 March 1849

Snakes are known to move in a variety of different ways—but propelling themselves rapidly along via a series of high vertical jumps is not one of them, or is it? A very venomous mystery snake reputedly executing a remarkable jumping mode of locomotion has long been claimed to exist in the Balkans region of eastern Europe, inhabiting much of the old, pre-fragmented Yugoslavia, and various identities have been proposed for it—but is it indeed real, or entirely fictitious, or something in between?

This fascinating creature first came to widespread attention via a detailed letter from a Mr M.F. Kerchelich of Sarajevo (in what was, prior to 1992, the Yugoslavian republic of Bosnia and Herzegovina, but which declared independence that year during Yugoslavia's break-up). In his letter, subsequently published by British zoologist Dr Maurice Burton within his book *More Animal Legends* (1959), and which I first read during the late 1980s, Kerchelich stated that a dreaded type of jumping snake known locally as the poskok could be found in Yugoslavia. He claimed that it occurred mainly in the Croatian region of Dalmatia along the east coast of the Adriatic Sea, plus the mountainous regions of Herzegovina and Montenegro. He also noted that there was even an island close to Dubrovnik in Croatia that was called Vipera, due to the fact that it was a well-known breeding ground for the poskok.

According to Kerchelich, the poskok's average length is 24-40 in, but he also noted that considerably larger specimens have been seen. It varies in colour, from granite grey to dark reddish-brown, depending upon the specific terrain that it inhabits. Apparently, the poskok usually conceals itself when humans approach, but is still greatly feared on account of its venom and aggressiveness.

Kerchelich then related three separate personal encounters with this intriguing serpent. The first one took place during a car trip in Montenegro. Stopping the car to take a walk, he spotted a poskok lying in the middle of the road, some 100 yards ahead, sleeping in the sun. Kerchelich watched it for a time, until the snake awoke, whereupon it promptly curled up, jumped at least 5 ft horizontally and 2.5-3 ft vertically into a dry thorn bush at the road kerb, then disappeared from view.

His second encounter occurred while driving a jeep in southern Dalmatia. Coming around the corner of a road, he spied a poskok about to cross it just ahead of him. Possibly frightened by the jeep's sudden approach, the snake leapt at the front mudguard and was killed by the rear wheel. And on the third occasion, Kerchelich had been fishing a small stream in Croatia when, while leaning against a dry tree trunk, he abruptly heard a hissing sound above him. After peering up and carefully scrutinising the branches of the tree overhead (being mindful that snakes existed in this area), he eventually realised that one of them was not a branch at all but was in fact a poskok, which was watching him very intently.

Kerchelich did not give length measurements for any of the poskoks seen by him. However, he did note that none was over 1.5 inches across at its body's thickest point.

What could the poskok be? Bearing in mind its supposedly venomous nature, and noting that the Dubrovnik island where it allegedly breeds is called Vipera, after first reading Kerchelich's letter in Burton's book I naturally favoured a species of viper as the most plausible candidate, especially as at least three such species are already known to occur in the former Yugoslavia. These are the common European viper or adder *Vipera berus*, Orsini's viper *V. ursinii*, and the nose-horned viper *V. ammodytes*.

Nose-horned vipers *Vipera ammodytes* (Holger Krisp, CC BY 3.0)

As a possible means of eliciting further information on Yugoslavia's anomalous jumping snake, I briefly alluded to it in my summary of still-unidentified animals at the end of my book *In Search of Prehistoric Survivors* (1995). And sure enough, in August 1998 I received an email from cryptozoology enthusiast Marko Puljic, who lives in the USA but is of direct Yugoslavian descent, and had read my snippet about the poskok in my prehistoric survivors book. Eager like me to find out what it could be, Marko had subsequently been in communication with Croatian herpetologist Dr Biljana Janev, who replied to his enquiries by stating that the poskok was the nose-horned viper, and that 'poskok' actually translates as 'jumper', because it was widely believed by laymen in Croatia that this species could jump considerable distances.

However, Dr Janev assured Marko that the poskok's reputed jumping prowess was in reality limited to lunging during an attack, which might carry it up to 18 in but no more. Accordingly, she suggested that perhaps the local belief that this species could jump much further and higher stemmed from the fact that, particularly in autumn, it climbs upon shrubs and low trees where it can hunt young birds and that presumably, when it attacks, lunging forth, it may look as if it has jumped quite a distance.

The nose-horned viper is found throughout much of Croatia and also various other portions of the Balkans, is extremely venomous (the most venomous species of snake found anywhere in Europe, in fact), and tends to inhabit rocky terrain. It rarely grows longer than 3 ft, but specimens of almost 3.5 ft have been confirmed (northern individuals tend to be larger than southern ones). Males are smaller and greyer or more yellowish in colour than females, and usually bear a well-defined black zigzag stripe dorsally (although this is not always a continuous stripe, as it can be broken up into segments). Females, conversely, are brown or reddish, and the dorsal zigzag is less well-defined. Both sexes possess a very distinctive nasal horn. Moreover, according to reliable Croatian herpetological sources that I have checked, 'poskok' is indeed the common name given to this species by Croats.

Clearly, therefore, in terms of its name, venom, and zoogeographical range, the nose-horned viper does correspond with the mystifying Yugoslavian jumping snake. However, if these two snakes are indeed one and the same species, it seems strange that no-one encountering the jumping snake (including Kerchelich, who claimed no fewer than three separate sightings) appears to have reported seeing either a nasal horn for it, which is very noticeable in the nose-horned viper (as readily seen in this present chapter's earlier photograph of two specimens), or the latter's eye-catching dorsal zigzag stripe (unless only females have been seen jumping?). Also, the nose-horned viper's body is relatively thick, which one wouldn't expect for a species of snake able to execute sizeable jumps, and behaviourally it is not aggressive (unlike the Yugoslavian jumping snake) and generally very sluggish, not given to fast locomotion at all. So is its alleged ability to leap considerable distances precisely that—an allegation, unconfirmed and implausible scientifically?

In fact, there is some noteworthy evidence to suggest that although far from common, it is certainly not impossible for snakes to behave in this manner. In his afore-mentioned book's coverage of the Yugoslavian jumping snake, Dr Maurice Burton included two separate first-hand experiences of grass snakes *Natrix* sp. performing highly-unexpected but quite spectacular leaps. In the first of

18 | JUMPING SNAKES

these, Burton personally observed a grass snake jump horizontally over a ditch that measured 2 ft across and 1 ft deep, executing a total leap distance estimated by Burton at 5 ft. And in the second, he saw a grass snake leap with lightning speed over the 1.5-ft-high wall of a makeshift vivarium *after* stiffening and holding its body in a vertically-erect position without any external support.

Burton also included the report given to him by eyewitness Mary Lupton, who saw a snake behave in much the same manner as the vivarium grass snake while she and her husband were walking along a mountainous path in Liguria, Italy, during April 1926. Indeed, when they first saw it they initially thought that someone out of sight was repeatedly throwing a vertically-aligned walking stick up into the air as he or she was walking along. Then they obtained a clearer view, and realised to their amazement that it was actually a jumping snake, which was holding its body vertically and entirely stiff as it leapt upwards, then falling back onto the ground in coils before repeating its rigid vertical leap upwards.

Based upon these and several other noteworthy reports chronicled by him, Burton concluded: ". . . the ability [of snakes] to progress in vertical jumps becomes at least feasible. All that is needed is the stimulus". The most likely ones are undoubtedly fear and surprise. Moreover, as Burton also emphasised, grass snakes do travel on occasion over the ground while being supported upon their body's most posterior third, with the two anterior thirds of their body being held erect. Consequently, it would not involve much more than this to effect a jump into the air.

Not everyone has been so convinced, however, that snakes can truly jump. In his book *Wild Life in a Southern County* (1879), the county in question being Wiltshire in southern England, Richard Jefferies suggested that, stimulus or no stimulus, such activity is merely an optical illusion:

> The belief that snakes can jump—or coil themselves up and spring—is, however, very prevalent. They all tell you that a snake can leap across a ditch. This is not true. A snake, if alarmed, will make for the hedge; and he glides much faster than would be supposed. On reaching the 'shore' or edge of the ditch he projects his head over it, and some six or

eight inches of the neck, while the rest of the body slides down the slope. If it happens to be a steep-sided ditch he often loses his balance and rolls to the bottom; and that is what has been mistaken for leaping.

Yet this activity clearly cannot explain those two separate grass snake incidents personally observed by Burton and documented above, in which the modes of leaping—one horizontally, the other vertically— did not involve any sliding by the respective snakes down a slope. Also, Burton was both a qualified zoologist and a very experienced field naturalist, whose accuracy of observations appertaining to wildlife, therefore, surely cannot be doubted.

During the 1990s, I discussed the Yugoslavian jumping snake not only with Marko but also with eminent University of London zoologist Prof. John L. Cloudsley-Thompson, who later referred to it in a paper on reptiles that jump and fly, published in 1996 by the *British Herpetological Society Bulletin*. In that paper, Prof. Cloudsley-Thompson provided some additional, fully-verified examples of jumping snakes.

In particular, he documented the Mexican jumping viper *Metlapilcoatlus* [=*Bothrops*] *nummifer*. A stocky, terrestrial species of pit viper native to Mexico and Central America, it derives its 'jumping' epithet from the ferocity of its strikes, which are so forceful that they can sometimes actually lift this snake off the ground, so that it makes a short jump. And when striking sideways, it may even be able to propel itself over 3 ft, according to Cloudsley-Thompson. Moreover, the large green rat snake *Ptyas nigromarginata* of southern Asia can throw itself through the air for appreciable distances down steep slopes when pursuing prey or escaping from enemies. And southeast Asia's famous so-called flying snakes *Chrysopelea* spp. become airborne by actively jumping from the branches of trees (after which they glide—not fly—through the air by rendering their ventral body surface concave).

As for the Yugoslavian jumping snake, Cloudsley-Thompson offered a thought-provoking alternative suggestion to the nose-horned viper as a possible identity for it. Namely, the western or green whip snake *Hierophis* [formerly *Coluber*] *viridiflavus*.

Unfortunately, this species' distribution only extends into the former Yugoslavia's northwestern section. However, two of its close

18 | JUMPING SNAKES

Western whip snake *Hierophis viridiflavus*
(Bernard Dupont, CC BY-SA 2.0)

Caspian whip snake *Dolichophis caspius*
(Yuriy Kvach, CC BY-SA 3.0)

relatives—the Balkan whip snake *H. gemonensis* (which greatly resembles it) and Dahl's whip snake *Platyceps najadum*—occur more widely in this region. There are also unconfirmed records of a third species, the large or black whip snake *Dolichophis jugularis*, existing in the Balkans.

On 14 February 2019, I received a very interesting email from Danish correspondent Philip H. Jensen, who informed me that Philippe Geniez's book *Snakes of Europe, North Africa and the Middle East* (2018) contains a relevant snippet of information concerning a fourth species of whip snake, the Caspian whip snake *Dolichophis caspius*, which again is native to parts of the Balkans. It states that this species is known in German as Springnatter ('jumping snake'), which is derived from its ability when on the defensive to jump to a height of half its body length, and that its average body length is 4.5-5.5 ft but can exceed 6 ft (individuals of 8 ft have been cited). Moreover, according to Kazakh horsemen, the jumping ability of this species can cause their horses to flee.

Exhibiting quite a range of colours, including those reported for the Yugoslavian jumping snake, these four whip snake species cited above are of similar size to it too; the large (black) and the Caspian whip snakes can also attain the lengthier sizes sometimes claimed for it. Additionally, all are very slender, fast-moving, aggressive when captured, given to biting hard, and lithe enough to offer a much greater likelihood than the thickset nose-horned viper of being able to jump or leap into the air. In stark contrast to claims for the Yugoslavian jumping snake, conversely, none of these whip snakes is more than very faintly (if at all) venomous.

Could it be, therefore, that reports of the nose-horned viper and one or more species of Balkans-inhabiting whip snake have been erroneously combined or confused with one another by eyewitnesses, thereby creating a non-existent composite creature, the Yugoslavian jumping snake, possessing attributes of both snake types, i.e. the viper and the whip snakes?

Several unfeasibly diverse mystery creatures, such as the sea serpents, Nandi bear, and Loch Ness monster, may in reality each stem from sightings of several different types of animal that have been erroneously lumped together in the past by investigators to yield a composite beast that does not exist. Might the Yugoslavian jumping snake be yet another example?

Certainly, unless we discount all such reports as fantasy, and blatantly ignore the first-hand accounts of zoologically-competent reliable eyewitnesses like Dr Maurice Burton, there seems little doubt that some snakes can on occasion perform leaps and jumps of quite prodigious proportions. How else too can we explain the testimony of a relief worker in Metkovic (southern Croatia, on the Bosnian border), speaking to my Yugoslavian correspondent Marko in October 1996, who stated that he always warned the British SFOR (NATO Peacekeeper) soldiers to take care where they trod, as a snake exists here that can jump 6 ft into the air? Folklore, fancy . . . or fact?

Finally, no chapter on jumping and leaping snakes could possibly close without mentioning a truly remarkable somersaulting snake from the Philippines. For I have recently discovered—and watched—a fascinating video produced by a longstanding cryptozoological friend, Tony Gerard, that provides conclusive proof of at least one species of snake's extraordinary ability to make dramatic somersaulting leaps through the air when fleeing a perceived threat.

The species in question is the northern triangle-spotted snake *Cyclocorus lineatus,* a small, non-venomous member of the very

Cyclocorus lineatus (Brown et al. 2013, CC BY 3.0)

diverse, elapid-related taxonomic family Lamprophiidae and endemic to the Philippines. The video (posted on YouTube by American cryptozoologist Chad Arment as StrangeArk on 19 May 2019 at: https://www.youtube.com/watch?v=PWUCPw2x32M) shows Tony with one of these snakes held briefly under a bowl. When Tony lifts up the bowl and gently prods the snake, it rapidly flees via a series of very dramatic somersaulting leaps through the air and across the ground, so that it bears more than a passing resemblance to the fabled hoop snake documented in Chapter 3.

Indeed, the only reason why I am including it here, rather than in Chapter 3, is that whereas the hoop snake was said to turn itself into a hoop by gripping its tail in its mouth and then rolling along like a vertical hoop or wheel, this Philippines snake engenders its superficially hoop-like appearance by way of repeated somersaulting leaps, without ever grasping its tail in its mouth. Nevertheless, the overall visual effect is similar enough to make me wonder if other snakes can also accomplish such somersaults and, in turn, whether the hoop snake tales originated from sightings of snakes performing this acrobatic ability, with the tail-in-mouth detail being subsequently added in elaborated retellings. From such are myths, legends, and folktales born.

19
IN SEARCH OF SERPENT KINGS

> The serpent king was a huge snake as thick as a tree, with a golden crown on his head from which came the light. Round the royal mound, and arching over the golden bowl, were more serpents than it seemed possible for the world to hold—serpents of all sizes and colours, coiling and hissing.
>   The young man dashed forward, dipped his bread in the milk and crammed it into his mouth as he turned and rushed away. A million poisoned fangs flashed out to strike him, and the sound of angry hisses deafened him. But the serpents were packed so closely together that they could not reach the young man when he stooped over the golden bowl; and he was well away before they could untwine and follow him.
>
> Roger Lancelyn Green—'The Curious Young Man', in *Myths From Many Lands*

'The Curious Young Man' is an enthralling but little-known Estonian folktale that I first read as a child. It featured in a wonderful book entitled *Myths From Many Lands* (1965), written by Roger Lancelyn Green, a celebrated chronicler and reteller of fascinating world legends, which my mother Mary Shuker bought me, along with several other Green-authored works too (engendering in me a life-long interest in and love of mythology), all of which I treasure and still re-read to this day. The eponymous character in 'The

Curious Young Man' passionately yearned to see the arcane mysteries of the night hidden from all human sight. In order to do so, however, he had to attend in secret a feast held only one night in every seven years, in the depths of a great forest, attended by the serpent king, and consume some milk from the king's tribute, a huge bowl of goat's milk set before the enormous reptile and his myriad ophidian minions. If he succeeded in accomplishing this exceedingly hazardous task, the young man would at last achieve his long-desired ambition. And indeed he did, but as is so often the case in such tales, his success brought him nothing but anguish, leading narrator Green to warn darkly: "There is a blindness which is man's highest good".

The serpent king in this tale was a single entity, but years later, when researching a most intriguing phenomenon involving rats (and occasionally squirrels too), I realised that 'serpent king' could be utilised as a very apt term for a comparable phenomenon featuring snakes, especially as the latter's essential component, a massive entanglement of serpents, did actually feature in the above-cited folktale. Allow me to explain.

Copper engraving depicting the rat king
of Gross Ballheiser, Germany,
found by a miller on 13 July 1748

19 | SERPENT KINGS

Occasionally, a group of rats is discovered whose members (as many as 32 in one extraordinary case) are closely huddled together and found to be inextricably bound to one another by their hopelessly entangled tails. Such a congregation is known as a rat king, of which there are many records (some dating back centuries) and a few highly prized, painstakingly-preserved specimens in museums. However, the phenomenon remains a source of mystery to zoologists, who still cannot explain satisfactorily how the tails of the rats managed to become inseparably intertwined in this Gordian manner. A smaller number of cases involving squirrels—squirrel kings—are also known, plus at least one fieldmouse king. And if a cat gives birth to a litter of kittens whose umbilical cords are similarly tangled, the litter is termed a cat king. All four of these mammalian phenomena are extensively documented in my book *A Manifestation of Monsters* (2015).

However, there are certain cases of extraordinary intertwined snake masses on record too, which are the subject of this present chapter. Consequently, for the sake of nomenclatural uniformity, it would seem appropriate to refer to these throngs as serpent kings.

Such throngs have been spasmodically reported for a long time, and with a number of different species. Moreover, because of their grotesque appearance they have generally attracted appreciable if cautious attention from their eyewitnesses.

During his expeditions through Guyana during the late 18th Century, explorer, Alexander von Humboldt recorded seeing some piles of entwined serpents, which since then has served as an inspiration to others to make a point of documenting comparable sights. In 1848, for example, an anonymous *Scientific American* account of its author's travels across the Izacubos savannahs in Guyana contained a vivid description of what he called "the most wonderful, and most terrible spectacle that can be seen". He continued:

> We were ten men on horseback, two of whom took the lead, in order to sound the passages, whilst I preferred to skirt the great forests. One of the blacks who formed the vanguard, returned at full gallop, and called to me—'Here, sir, come and see the serpents in a pile'. He pointed out to me something elevated in the middle of the Savannah or swamp, which appeared like a bundle of arms. One of my company

A small serpent king of adders

then said, 'this is certainly one of the assemblages of serpents, which heap themselves on each other after a violent tempest; I have heard of these but have never seen any; let us proceed cautiously and not go too near'. When we were within twenty paces of it, the terror of our horses prevented nearer approach, to which none of us were inclined. On a sudden the pyramid mass became agitated; horrible hissing issued from it, thousands of serpents rolled spirally on each other shot forth out of their circle their hideous heads, presenting their envenomed darts and fiery eyes to us. I own I was one of the first to draw back, but when I saw this formidable phalanx remained at its post, and appeared to be more disposed to defend itself than attack us, I rode around it in order to view its order of battle, which faced the enemy on every side. I then thought what could be the design of this numerous assemblage, and I concluded that this species of serpents dread some collosean enemy, which might be the great serpent or cayman [actually a type of crocodilian], and that they re-unite themselves after having seen this enemy, in order to resist him in a mass.

Reading this graphic account, it occurred to me that an unexpected encounter with such a horde in olden days may well have helped to foster the famous Greek myth of the multi-headed hydra. Assuredly, it would be an almost supernatural spectacle to witness, and one likely to remain in the onlooker's memory for many a long day afterwards. As for the above author's record that these serpent kings were presumed to be formed following a violent storm, and his own notion that they amass as a means of defending themselves against a very much larger enemy, neither proposal is really very plausible. Rather, it is much more likely that what he encountered was a frenzied mating en masse.

After emerging in spring from a winter's hibernation, some snake species congregate in enormous numbers for mating. In the case of the North American garter snake *Thamnophis* [formerly *Eutoenia*] *sirtalis,* for instance, a harmless, handsomely striped species of colubrid, several hundred males will all seek to copulate with a comparatively small number of females. In one closely monitored incident, a pre-copulating serpent king consisted of a solid ball of 15-20 garter snakes, observed by J.B. Gardner on 18 April 1954 at Seymour, Connecticut (*Copeia,* 1955). In April 1955, he saw a second example, again at Seymour (*Copeia,* 1957).

Equally, an early account of a garter snake mass mating was one of two serpent king reports penned by the quasi-anonymous 'E.L.' *(American Naturalist,* 1880). Both encounters had taken place during the early spring, in expanses of Maryland wilderness:

> I first saw such a bundle of snakes in the neighbourhood of Ilchester, Howard Co., Md., on the stony bank of the Patapsco river, heaped together on a rock and between big stones. It was a very warm and sunny location, where a human being would scarcely disturb them. I reasoned that the warmth and silence of that secluded place brought them together. Some hundreds of them could be counted, and all of them I found in a lively state of humor, hissing at me with threatening glances, with combined forces and with such a persistency that stones thrown upon them could not stop them or alter the position of a single animal. They would make the proper movements and the stone would roll off. All the snakes in this lump were common [garter] snakes (*Eutoenia sirtalis* L.). The second time I noticed a ball of black snakes (*Bascanion* [now *Coluber*] *constrictor* L.) rolling slowly down a steep and stony hillside on the bank of the same river, but about two miles above Union Factory, Baltimore county, Md. Some of the snakes were of considerable length and thickness, and, as I noticed clearly, kept together by procreative impulses.

Even today, such immense congregations of garter snakes are far from unknown, and in southern Manitoba, Canada, they have even become a major tourist attraction. Each year here, they come out of hibernation in the form of huge serpent kings or what are called mating balls in this region. Each of these kings or balls contains as many as 20,000 snakes, with 100 or more males for every female.

(Top) A serpent king and (Bottom) close-up of mass aggregation of garter snakes *Thamnophis sirtalis* (Both by Greg Schechter, CC BY 2.0)

In Britain, aggregations of adders (aka common vipers) *Vipera berus* are sometimes met with, newly emerged from hibernation (often communal). Encounters with serpent kings of this type no doubt contributed to a fascinating albeit decidedly odd folk belief known as the adder-stone legend.

Also called the ovum anguinum ('snake egg'), the adder-stone is a stone-like object that supposedly originates as a ball of froth exuded by entwined masses of snakes (but particularly adders) at midsummer—or at least according to an ancient Celtic belief reported by the Druids of Gaul and documented by Roman philosopher and naturalist Pliny the Elder during the 1st Century AD. This was the inspiration for the druid song included by English poet William Mason within his epic poem *Caractacus* (1759):

> From the grot of charms and spells,
> Where our matron sister dwells,
> Brennus, has thy holy hand
> Safely brought the Druid wand,
> And the potent Adder-stone,
> Gender'd 'fore the autumnal moon?
> When in undulating twine
> The foaming snakes prolific join,
> When they hiss, and when they bear
> Their wondrous egg aloft in air;
> Thence, before to earth it fall,
> The Druid in his hallowed pall
> Receives the prize,
> And instant flies
> Followed by the invenom'd brood,
> Till he cross the crystal flood.

The last lines record the belief that the adder-stone can protect anyone who captures it within a cloth, and before it hits the ground, from poison and all manner of other undesirable substances, provided that he can successfully escape the pursuing adders—by crossing a river. According to Welsh naturalist and author Thomas Pennant, writing in 1769:

> Our modern Druidesses give much the same account
> of the ovum anguinum (Glein Neidr, as the Welsh

19 | SERPENT KINGS

Engraving depicting the hazardous procurement of an ovum anguinum

call it; or the adder-gem) as the Roman philosopher [Pliny the Elder] does; but seem not to have so exalted an opinion of its powers, using it only to assist children in cutting their teeth, or to cure the hooping-cough, or drive away an ague.

In reality, it is unlikely even to have achieved these feats. For although specimens of adder-stones or ova anguina do exist, they are merely fossil sea urchins, also known from Cornwall and referred to there as milprev or milpref—as reported by geologist Dr Michael Bassett in his fascinating booklet *'Formed Stones', Folklore and Fossils* (1982).

An engraving from 1487 depicting two
ova anguina—merely fossil sea urchins

Incidentally, a piscean parallel to serpent kings is the occurrence of eel kings—see Christopher Moriarty's book *Eels: A Natural and Unnatural History* (1978). These constitute tightly-entwined balls of pre-migrating eels, occasionally spied floating along streams.

Staying with aquatic creature kings but returning to serpents: as Sherman Minton and Harold Heatwole reported in *Oceans* (April 1978), the yellow-bellied sea-snake *Pelamis platurus* is well known for congregating in immense numbers, often several thousand at a time, passively drifting at the Pacific Ocean's surface, and carried by wind and wave for great distances.

In addition, the above authors commented that groups of several thousand have also been noted in Panama Bay.

19 | SERPENT KINGS

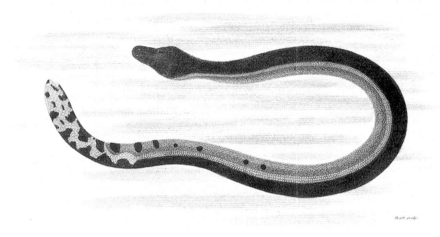

Yellow-bellied sea snake *Hydrophis platurus*

The sea-snake serpent king par excellence, however, was witnessed sometime before 1932 by Willoughby P. Lowe, a collector of natural history specimens for the British Museum, and featured Stokes's sea-snake *Astrotia* [=*Hydrophis*] *stokesii*, the heaviest of all sea-snakes and measuring up to 6 ft long. As recorded in *The Trail That is Always New* (1932), Lowe was aboard a steamer travelling in the Malacca Strait between the Malay Peninsula and the Indonesian island of Sumatra, when:

> After luncheon on 4 May I came on deck and was talking to some passengers, when, looking landward, I saw a long line running parallel with our course. None of us could imagine what it could be. It must have been four or five miles off. We smoked and chatted, had a siesta, and went down to tea. On returning to the deck we still saw the curious line along which we had been steaming for four hours, but now it lay across our course, and we were still very curious as to what it was. As we drew nearer we were amazed to find that it was composed of a solid mass of sea snakes, twisted thickly together. They were orange-red and black, a very poisonous and rare variety known as *Astrotia stokesii* . . . . Along this line there must have been millions; when I say millions I

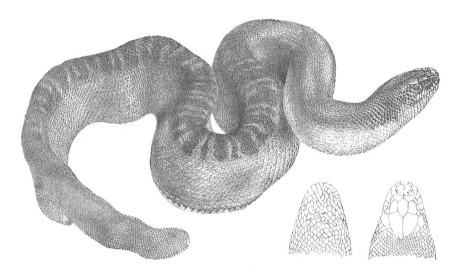

Engraving of a Stokes's sea snake *Astrotia stokesii*

consider it no exaggeration, for the line was quite ten feet wide and we followed its course for some sixty miles. I can only presume it was either a migration or the breeding season . . . it certainly was a wonderful sight.

The spectacle of millions of extremely venomous serpents heaving and writhing in a solid, 60-mile-long mass at the ocean's surface may not be everyone's idea of a wonderful sight, but it definitely merits inclusion in any book dealing with unexpected snakes!

20
A SNAKE WITH A HEAD AT EACH END? THE AMPHISBAENA AWAKES!

Far away in the twilight time
Of every people, in every clime,
Dragons and griffins and monsters dire,
Born of water, and air, and fire,
Or nursed, like the Python, in the mud
And ooze of the old Deucalion flood,
Crawl and wriggle and foam with rage,
Through dusk tradition and ballad age.
So from the childhood of Newbury town
And its time of fable the tale comes down
Of a terror which haunted bush and brake,
The Amphisbaena, the Double Snake! . . .

Whether he lurked in the Oldtown fen
Or the gray earth-flax of the Devil's Den,
Or swam in the wooded Artichoke,
Or coiled by the Northman's Written Rock,
Nothing on record is left to show;
Only the fact that he lived, we know,
And left the cast of a double head
In the scaly mask which he yearly shed.
For he earned a head where his tail should be,
And the two, of course, could never agree,
But wriggled about with main and might,
Now to the left and now to the right;

> Pulling and twisting this way and that,
> Neither knew what the other was at.
>
> John Greenleaf Whittier—'The Double-Headed Snake of Newbury'

As documented in Chapter 7, freak two-headed (aka dicephalous or bicephalic) snakes, although rare, are by no means unknown. In some examples, the two heads each emerge directly from the body; in certain others, they each possess their own neck that emerges independently from the body; and in a few instances, one head emerges directly from the body whereas the other emerges via a neck. However, what they all have in common is that both heads occur at the same end of the body, the front (anterior) end, with a tail at the posterior end.

This is why the freak specimen of rough earth snake *Haldea* [formerly *Virginia*] *striatula* (a small, non-venomous, fossorial colubrid) discovered in early September 2012 by workmen at the home of the Logan family in South Carolina (and cared for by the grandfather of the two Logan children, Preston and Savanna) attracted such interest. For this remarkable little snake's two heads were seemingly located at opposite ends of its body! Instead of possessing a tail, it sported what looked like a head at the posterior end of its body, plus a head at the anterior end as normal. This extraordinary teratological condition is known as amphicephaly, and, as revealed later here, is so rare that the Logans' pet may be the only modern-day example ever confirmed—always assuming, however, that it really was amphicephalous . . .

On 24 September 2012, America's Fox News released a short video of the snake as part of an interview with the Logan family concerning it (viewable for a while online at https://www.youtube.com/watch?v=aP2gPbY72kU), and their report claimed that the snake definitely had two heads, each with its own pair of eyes, a mouth, and a tongue, but that one head was more dominant than the other, although each head would take control of the body's movements. The snake was less than 1 ft long and very slender, smoky grey dorsally, slightly paler ventrally. It was a local biology teacher who identified this specimen as a rough earth snake, which is native to the southeastern USA, and after observing it in the video I entirely agree with this identification.

Having said that, I was unable to spot a tongue emerging from the mouth of the subordinate head, in contrast to the constant tongue-flicking behaviour of the dominant head. However, the subordinate head did appear to possess a pair of eyes (or eye-like markings?). So, could the Logans' snake truly be amphicephalous, and, if so, are there any verified precedents? Or is there some other, more orthodox, conservative explanation?

A normal rough earth snake *Haldea striatula* (Jscottkelley, CC BY 3.0)

Quite a number of snake species (especially fossorial ones) and also lizard species (ditto) have a tail that closely resembles their head both in shape and in colouration, and they often move their tail in a manner that deftly mimics the head's movements. The purpose of this deceptive duplication is to confuse predators, so that if they do attack, they seize the least important body end (the tail, which can often be regenerated later), rather than the head. This condition thereby constitutes 'pseudo-amphicephaly'. Such species include southeast Asia's red-tailed pipe snake *Cylindrophis ruffus*, the Indian sand boa *Eryx johnii*, the Australian stump-tailed lizard *Tiliqua rugosa* (=*Trachydosaurus rugosus*), and in particular the so-called worm-lizards or amphisbaenians.

In contrast, genuine amphicephalous individuals are rarely if ever recorded (until now?). Probably the best modern-day review of

Two Iberian amphisbaenians or worm-lizards
Blanus cinereus (Richard Avery, CC BY-SA 3.0)

such animals was a paper by Prof. Bert Cunningham of Duke University in North Carolina, published by *Scientific Monthly* in 1933. His paper considered a selection of potentially genuine reptilian amphicephali. However, these were mostly collected from medieval bestiaries and other antiquarian writings, which tend not to be the most reliable or scientifically accurate of sources. And certainly, the vast majority of those examples seemed to be either misidentifications of pseudo-amphicephalous species or deliberate fakes. Two, conversely, may well have been genuine.

One of these was a supposed amphicephalous snake specimen catalogued in 1679 within the famous natural history collection of the eminent Dutch biologist Jan Swammerdam (1637-1680). Moreover, it was personally observed a year later by another prominent scientist, Dutch physician/entomologist Steven Blankaart (1650-1704)—all of which lends a degree of veracity to this specimen's authenticity.

The second example was a lizard with a head at each end, represented by an illustration in *Historia Serpentum et Draconum* by Italian naturalist Ulisse Aldrovandi (1522-1605), published posthumously in 1640. Aldrovandi is said to have made his drawing

20 | THE AMPHISBAENA

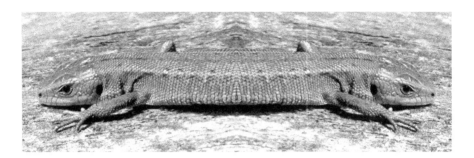

What an amphicephalous lizard might well look like if such a creature could truly exist (© Dr Karl Shuker)

Jan Swammerdam's reputed amphicephalous snake, drawn by Blankaart and published in 1680

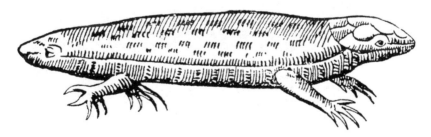

Aldrovandi's drawing of an alleged amphicephalous lizard

from the *living* animal, which, if true, increases the likelihood of this specimen having been truly amphicephalous.

Also worth recording here is a pair of conjoined (i.e. 'Siamese') terrapin twins reported in 1928 by C.H. Townsend. For whereas conjoined terrapins (a fair number of which have been documented down through the years) are generally linked to one another laterally (i.e. side by side) or ventrally (belly to belly), these two individuals were joined to each other posteriorly (rear to rear). This yielded a double animal that approached the genuine amphicephalous state. Other, more recent examples of this semi-amphicephalous version of conjoined terrapins are also known.

Moreover, the subject of the poem opening this present chapter really did exist, although whether it was a bona fide amphisbaena has never been scientifically confirmed. Newbury is a town in Massachusetts, and when, during the early 1700s, news of the recent discovery there of a supposed amphisbaena—the 'double-headed snake of Newbury'—reached the ears of theologian Cotton Mather, known for his keen interest in the supernatural, Mather lost no time in contacting a local minister, the Reverend Christopher Toppan, requesting details concerning this ostensibly fabulous beast. Rev. Toppan in turn made some enquiries among the inhabitants of Newbury, and in a letter of reply to Mather he stated the following:

> Concerning the amphisbena, as soon as I received your commands I made diligent enquiry of several persons who saw it after it was dead, but they could give me no assurance of its having two heads.

However, Toppan subsequently did find someone who vouched for the creature's amphicephalous form. So he added the following comment to his letter:

> This person is so credible that I can as much believe him as if I had seen it myself. He tells me of another man that examined it as he did, but I cannot meet him.

All of which only makes it all the more regrettable that the fate of this potentially significant snake's remains is apparently unrecorded. Most probably, once its novelty had worn off, the dead specimen was simply discarded, with only Whittier's poem, inspired by it, remaining as testimony to its erstwhile existence.

20 | THE AMPHISBAENA

Returning to the medieval bestiary sources consulted by Prof. Cunningham, these would certainly have referred to the most famous amphicephalous beast of all, albeit one that is entirely mythical—the amphisbaena. Generally categorised as a serpent dragon, i.e. limbless like a snake but dragon-headed (although occasionally portrayed as legged), the amphisbaena had a head at each end of its body, and could therefore move in either direction—sometimes accomplished by grasping one head in the jaws of the other so that its body became a hoop that could roll rapidly over the ground.

An amphisbaena was almost impossible to approach unseen, because only one head slept at a time, the other one staying awake, particularly when this creature was laying eggs. And if an amphisbaena were cut in half, the two segments would promptly rejoin.

According to Greek mythology, the amphisbaena was spontaneously generated from drops of blood falling onto the desert sands from the severed head of the gorgon Medusa when her slayer, the hero Perseus, flew over Libya with it on his journey back home to the Greek island of Seriphos. Recalling this legend, in his famous painting 'The Head of Medusa', dating from c.1617-1618 and portraying Medusa's decapitated head, the highly-acclaimed Flemish artist Peter Paul Rubens included an amphisbaena among the various serpents breaking free from her hair following her death.

Rubens's painting 'The Head of Medusa', in which an amphisbaena can be seen (below Medusa's head mid-centre of painting) among the diversity of snakes breaking free from Medusa's hair

Although the amphisbaena's principal diet was ants, it was claimed by some writers to be extremely venomous, and one was blamed for the subsequent death of Mopsus. He was a seer, and also one of the famed Argonauts that accompanied the legendary Greek hero Jason on his quest for the Golden Fleece.

Amphisbaena reported from Mexico, depicted in Johannes Faber's *Thesaurus* (1651)

Yet despite its deadly nature, the dual-headed amphisbaena was often cited by early scholars for its medicinal qualities. Sometimes a living specimen was needed, otherwise the skin of one was sufficient. Among the assorted ailments that it reputedly eased were arthritis, chilblains, and the common cold, as well as assuring a safe pregnancy, and keeping warm during the winter if working outside. Eating the meat of an amphisbaena could even attract lovers, and killing one during a full moon would imbue its slayer with great power provided that he was pure of heart and mind.

Amphisbaenas often featured in Mesoamerican and Inca cultures too, frequently depicted with a vertically undulating body, and symbolised eternity. Some of the most spectacular renditions are composed of Spanish cedar wood overlain with turquoise mosaic, a stone believed by the Aztecs to emit smoke, and therefore a very fitting mineral for portraying a dragon, especially in versions representing Xiuhcoatl—known variously as the fire serpent or the turquoise serpent. In these New World versions, one head was sometimes much larger than the other, rather than always being identical as in the original Old World amphisbaena.

20 | THE AMPHISBAENA

An Aztec double-headed serpent in the form of an amphisbaena, sculpted from Spanish cedar wood, overlain with turquoise, 15th-16th-Century, Mexico, housed at the British Museum (Geni, CC BY-SA 4.0)

In Chile, the oral traditions of the Elqui villagers tell of a 6-ft-long spotted amphisbaena known as the culebrón. During the day, it crawled very slowly upon the ground, but at night it took flight, because, uniquely among amphisbaenas, this version sported a pair of wings.

Perhaps the strangest South American amphisbaena, however, was the manora, whose basic form resembled a giant earthworm. Its head and tail ends were indistinguishable from one another, but its body was covered all over with sharp feather-like quills.

Today, the legendary amphisbaena gives its name to a group of real-life reptiles, the amphisbaenians, which are also known as worm-lizards. Their heads are so similar in appearance to their tails that it can be difficult to distinguish which end is which, thus recalling the amphicephalous amphisbaena.

Having said that, the legendary amphisbaena underwent a profound transformation during medieval times. It gained not only a pair of legs but also a pair of wings, as well as a clearly-delineated tail—at the end of which was its second head. It also acquired the literally petrifying, gorgonesque ability to turn anyone who looked at it to stone with just a single glance. This advanced version of the amphisbaena is known as the amphisien, and commonly occurs in heraldry.

The amphisien version of the amphisbaena, as depicted in the *Aberdeen Bestiary* (Aberdeen University Library MS 24)

In modern-day fiction, the most famous amphicephalous creature must surely be the pushmi-pullyu, featuring in Hugh Lofting's beloved series of 'Doctor Dolittle' novels for children (and the subject of a detailed coverage by me in *ShukerNature 2*, 2020). In reality, however, no such animal could exist, because as mammals have a head at one end of their body and an anus at the other, an amphicephalous mammal would lack an anus and therefore be unable to defaecate—a condition that would rapidly prove fatal.

Indeed, this has even been confirmed occasionally with reptiles too. In October 2001, for instance, *Fortean Times* included a full-page colour photograph of an amphisbaena-like baby crocodile that had hatched on 23 June 2001 at a private crocodile farm in Samut Prakern, just south of Bangkok, Thailand. It consisted of two conjoined specimens that each possessed a head, upper and mid torso, two pairs of legs, and even a tail, but were joined at the stomach, with neither of them sporting an anus. Both heads took in food, but they died just a week later—from severe constipation, a tragic but inevitable fate.

Surely, therefore, this same argument negates the plausibility of the Logan family's alleged amphicephalous snake too? Not necessarily—because in snakes, being limbless and proportionately very long and slender, the end of the abdominal body region merges entirely into the tail (in mammals, conversely, outwardly the tail appears merely as a slender offshoot from the much broader, limbed abdominal body region). Consequently, the external excretory orifice in snakes (which is actually a cloaca, as it also functions as a genital orifice) is situated not at their posterior pole but about a quarter of the way up from this. Theoretically, therefore, an amphicephalous snake could have two cloacae, each positioned some distance away from the opposite head.

But how might an amphicephalous snake arise in the first place? If due to some developmental malfunction an early snake embryo were to split laterally from the head downwards to nearly the end of the tail, this would yield two almost completely separate snakes. However, they would remain permanently attached to one another because of their undivided (and hence shared) terminal tail portion. Nevertheless, each snake would possess its own fully-formed cloaca-containing abdominal body section. Consequently, this would then be an amphicephalus, and possibly even a viable one (always assuming, of course, that such a specimen survived up to birth/hatching).

No mention of any cloacal presence was reported for the Logans' snake, and, as far as I am aware, no further reports, containing additional details or confirmation of its dual anatomy, subsequently emerged. This is very regrettable, because, after all, it's not every day that a veritable resurrected beast of classical mythology hits the news headlines around the world.

The amphisbaena awakes? Let's wait and see . . .

A ceramic ornament portraying the amphisbaena of classical mythology (Dr Karl Shuker)

21
SEEKING GLYCON—THE ROMAN EMPIRE'S BLOND-HAIRED (AND HUMAN-EARED!) OPHIDIAN ORACLE-UTTERER

> Reading Lucian's account [re Alexander of Abonoteichus and his supposed talking snake deity Glycon] in full, one's often reminded of contemporary sceptics and professional magicians. Lucian knows how an effect *could* be produced—therefore that's how it *must* be produced. Take the speaking tube of crane's windpipes, for example. This is certainly possible, and the Christian writer Hippolytus (c.170-c.236) mentions similar speaking tubes used to make skulls appear to speak. However, this doesn't *prove* that's how Alexander made Glycon 'talk'. An early form of ventriloquism would explain the effect much more elegantly, in the same way that some form of glove-puppet would provide a simpler answer than a linen head manipulated by horsehair; and no one at the shrine would have been likely to reveal the secret of either of these to Lucian. In boasting that he knows how the trick was done, Lucian is plainly covering up the fact that this can only be a matter of conjecture. These conjectures *may* be very close to the truth; but they remain conjectures, not proof. . . . Besides, you've just got to love a man with a talking snake. If there were a TV show called *Paphlagonia's Got Talent*, he'd win it hands down.
>
> Steve Moore—'The Fake, the Snake, and the Sceptic', *Fortean Times*, June 2011

A snake with a blond head of hair and human ears would certainly be a marvel—but how much more so if it could also speak, and even foretell the futures of those who sought an audience with this wondrous ophidian oracle? All of this and much more—or, quite probably, a great deal less—was Glycon, the Roman Empire's incredible serpentine soothsayer.

In c.105 AD, a very controversial, enigmatic figure was born who would in time come to be known far and wide as Alexander of Abonoteichus, after the small fishing village on the Black Sea's southern coast that was his birthplace. Back in Alexander's time, Abonoteichus was located within the Roman province of Bithynia-Pontus (specifically within Paphlagonia, which was sandwiched between Bithynia and Pontus), but today it is contained within the Asian Turkish province of Kastamonu, and is now named Inebolu.

Apparently very handsome and tall with an extremely charismatic personality, Alexander was originally apprenticed to a physician/magician, but after his mentor died Alexander met up with a Byzantine chorus-writer nicknamed Cocconas, and the two spent some time thereafter travelling around together, earning their living as fake magicians, quack doctors, and via other chicanery. Eventually, they reached Pella in Macedonia, and it was here that Glycon was born, so to speak, because this is where they purchased for just a paltry sum of money an extremely large and impressive-looking yet very tame snake (such serpents being commonly for sale in this locality at that time).

It was probably an African rock python *Python sebae*, as specimens of this very sizeable species (averaging 15.75 ft long but sometimes exceeding 20 ft) were apparently brought back to Rome, because it is depicted in Roman mosaics. Also, fertility-related snake cults had long existed in Macedonia, stretching back at least as far as the 4th Century BC.

Alexander and Cocconas then journeyed to Chalcedon, a maritime town in Bithyna, where they lost no time in concealing inside its temple to the god Apollo a series of bronze tablets proclaiming that both Apollo and his serpent-associated son Asclepius, the Greek god of medicine and healing, would soon be appearing in Alexander's home village of Abonoteichus. They then contrived for these 'hidden' tablets to be found, and news of the tablets' sensational proclamations swiftly travelled widely, eventually reaching Abonoteichus itself, whose inhabitants promptly began building a

21 | GLYCON

The statue of Glycon unearthed at Tomis, Romania, in 1962

African rock python *Python sebae natalensis*
(USGS / Graham J. Alexander)

Apollo after slaying the serpent dragon Python, in an engraving by William Grainger, late 1700s

21 | GLYCON

temple dedicated to Apollo and Asclepius. It was then, in or around 150 AD, that the partnership of Alexander and Cocconas broke up, with Cocconas electing to stay in Chalcedon and continue producing phoney oracles, whereas Alexander was keen to put the next stage of their original plan into action, and so he duly set off back to Abonoteichus.

Using more fake oracles to proclaim himself as a prophet and healer, Alexander also claimed that his father was none other than Podaleirius, son of Asclepius himself and a legendary healer in his own right. Moreover, as signal proof of this, he arranged for a goose egg that he had 'discovered' inside Abonoteichus's newly-built temple to be publicly opened by him at noon on the following day in the village's marketplace before a crowd of curious but credulous onlookers, promising that a wonder would be revealed that would confirm all that he had alleged. And sure enough, when he opened the egg, a tiny snake emerged (one that supposedly he had subtly inserted inside before overtly 'discovering' the egg in the temple). As snakes were sacred to Asclepius (one common European species, the Aesculapian snake *Zamenis longissimus*, is actually named after Asclepius's Roman counterpart, Aesculapius), Alexander's grandiose claims were readily accepted by Abonoteichus's simple, unworldly villagers.

As an interesting aside here: Chickens are often infected with parasitic gut-inhabiting worms, including the ascarid roundworm *Ascaris lineata*, a nematode species that can grow to a few inches in length (a related giant species in humans can grow to over 1 ft in length!). They are often passed out of the bird's gut when it defaecates. Unlike in mammals, however, the bird's gut and its reproductive system share a common external passageway and opening—the cloaca. Sometimes, therefore, an ascarid worm ejected from the gut finds its way into the bird's reproductive system rather than being excreted into the outside world, and moves into the oviduct. Once here, however, it becomes incorporated into the albumen of an egg, inside which it remains alive yet trapped when the egg is laid. But as soon as the egg is broken open to eat by some unsuspecting diner, the worm wriggles its way out of it and inevitably scares the diner, who frequently but mistakenly assumes that this unexpected creature is actually a tiny snake.

I wonder if such a scenario explained the above 'snake-inside-egg' incident involving Alexander? Or could the egg have actually

Statue of Asclepius, 2nd Century AD,
found on the Greek island of Rhodes

been a genuine snake egg, but passed off to the ingenuous crowd by Alexander as an unshelled, undersized goose egg, perhaps?

But that was not all. Alexander also stated that the baby snake was itself a deity, and that he would therefore be caring for it. After a few days had elapsed with the villagers not setting eyes upon this infant reptilian god, Alexander reappeared, once again thronged by awed spectators, but now only briefly and ensconced within a small dimly-lit shrine inside the temple where viewing conditions were

21 | GLYCON

far from ideal. Moreover, this time his huge, fully-grown pet snake from Pella was wrapped around his body, and he glibly announced that the baby serpent deity had miraculously matured into adulthood.

Yet even that incredible high-speed transformation was not the most surprising facet of Alexander's outrageous revelation. Instead of possessing a typical snake's head, the head of this remarkable creature apparently resembled that of a man, and sported an abundance of long blond hair sprouting liberally from it, as well as a pair of human ears! Moreover, it could even speak, and in the future would directly voice certain oracles or autophones to temples worshippers seeking guidance. Alexander announced that this astonishing entity was called Glycon, and constituted a new, living, physical manifestation or incarnation of Asclepius.

Henceforth, Alexander's reputation, wealth, prestige, influence, and power, derived from his status as a celebrated prophecy-spouting soothsayer and in turn a highly-esteemed personage attracting acclaim and attention from all strata of Roman society, knew no bounds. In particular, the temple that he had established at Abonoteichus (by now a prosperous town) became a focus for fertility-

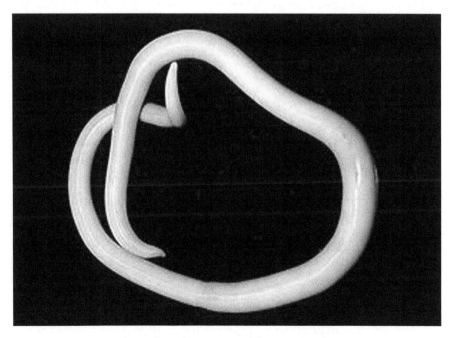

Ascaris, a large parasitic nematode

themed worship and offerings by barren women wishing to become pregnant; and also for the very lucrative provision of oracles (always requiring prior receipt of payment). Moreover, Alexander was frequently consulted by public figures of high political standing anxious to solicit his ostensibly Heaven-sent advice regarding significant matters of state. The fact that sometimes his advice was by no means reliable seemed to be conveniently overlooked.

Thus it was, for example, that in 161 AD, Alexander provided a very favourable oracle to Marcus Sedatius Severianus, the Gaul-originating Roman governor of Cappadocia, on the basis of which Severianus put into action his plan to invade Armenia—only for his invasion force, including himself, to be slaughtered by the Parthians. Allegedly, Alexander soon afterwards replaced the official temple record of his oracle with a revised one that was much less favourable.

In 166 AD, Alexander provided an oracle verse that was utilised as an amulet and inscribed above the doors of numerous houses throughout the Roman Empire in the hope of warding off the devastating Antonine Plague that had been introduced into the Empire

Two Romanian postage stamps, issued in 1974 *(l)* and 1994 *(r)*, depicting the famous statue of Glycon unearthed in 1962

by troops returning home from campaigns in the Near East, and which killed thousands of people every day. Not surprisingly, the amulets had no effect (indeed, it was actually claimed by critics of this futile course of action that households bearing an amulet suffered more plague-induced deaths than those not bearing it!), but Alexander was too powerful by then for his standing to be affected by any such dissension.

Not long after that debacle, the Roman emperor himself, Marcus Aurelius, requested Alexander to send an oracle to his troops on the Danube River during ongoing warfare (168-174 AD) with a Germanic tribe called the Marcomanni. The oracle that Alexander duly sent declared that victory would be achieved if two lions were thrown alive into the Danube. Once again, however, the stark fact that after obeying this unusual command the emperor's army was annihilated there (20,000 Roman soldiers killed, and even the hapless lions clubbed to death) failed to elicit any censure for the unperturbed Alexander, who coolly pointed out that the oracle had not specified *which* side in the war would achieve success!

Of course, Alexander was far from being entirely unsuccessful as a prophet, but reputedly his triumphs often involved the use of spies, thugs, and blackmailers to obtain the necessary information upon which to base his oracles. In addition, there were claims that sealed scrolls containing requests for oracles that acolytes presented to him were secretly opened by him using hot needles in order to discover what information they contained and thus devise an oracle in accordance with it. He also benefited from making friends in (extremely) high places, one of the most significant of whom was Publius Mummius Sisenna Rutilianus, a former Roman consul and provincial Roman governor in Asia and Upper Moesia, who declared himself protector of the Glycon oracle. He also provided Alexander with some very high-ranking contacts in Roman society, and he even married Alexander's own daughter.

Not content with merely being an exceptionally famous mystic, meanwhile, Alexander utilised Rutilianus's own eminence to help launch a very spectacular annual three-day festival replete with processions, ceremonies, and re-enactments of various mystical rituals, all held at the temple in Abonoteichus. These were devoted to the celebration of Apollo's birth and that of his son Asclepius, the appearance of Glycon, Alexander's own mother's supposed marriage to Asclepius's son Podaleirius, and even an alleged romance between

Alexander himself and the Greek moon goddess Selene that purportedly led to the birth of Alexander's daughter, now the wife of Rutilianus.

Alexander even persuaded the Roman emperor Antoninus Pius to change Abonoteichus's name to the much grander-sounding Ionopolis ('Greek city'). In addition, this same emperor and also his successors Lucius Verus and Marcus Aurelius all issued coinage depicting Glycon. Yet despite achieving such successes as these, with savage irony a prediction that he made about himself proved to be singularly inaccurate—just like many that he had predicted for others had been. He prophesied that he would live to the age of 150, but died at only 70 in or around 170 AD, caused by a gangrenous limb. Yet although the cult's leader was no more, the cult itself, and its veneration of Glycon, persisted for at least a further century—having occupied a vast area at its peak of popularity, stretching from the Danube in the west to the Euphrates in the east—before eventually petering out. Having said that, it is nothing if not interesting to note that as recently as the 1970s, belief in a "magical snake" still existed among Turkish locals living in the vicinity of Inebolu (formerly Ionopolis/Abonoteichus).

But how do we know about Alexander and Glycon, almost two millennia after their demise? In fact, only a single primary source for the extraordinary history of the reputedly phoney prophet and his talkative hairy-headed human-eared snake god is known, and it just so happens to be an exceedingly acerbic, hostile account written by an infamously vituperative satirist with a very specific reason for hating Alexander and all that he represented. Naturally, therefore, one may well be forgiven for wondering whether the entire saga was totally fictitious.

Happily, however, independent corroboration for the reality of the Glycon cult also exists. This includes not only the survival of some of the afore-mentioned Roman coinage bearing the image (and even the name) of this very singular deified serpent, but also a magnificent marble statue of Glycon, dating from the Severan dynasty (193-235 AD), standing almost 3 ft tall, and in excellent condition. It had been excavated in April 1962 along with various other statuary under the site of a former railway station in Constanta, Romania, formerly the ancient city of Tomis.

So spectacular and unexpected was this ornate Glycon sculpture, now housed at Constanta's Museum of National History and

21 | GLYCON

Archaeology, that it featured on a Romanian postage stamp issued in 1974 (which is what first brought Glycon to my attention, as an enthusiastic stamp collector during my childhood), as well as on a second one in 1994, and also on a Romanian 10,000 lei bank note in 1994.

Moreover, smaller Glycon statuettes in bronze have been found in Athens too, confirming the cult's spread into and across southwestern Europe. And according to the 2nd-Century-AD Christian philosopher Athenagoras of Athens, writing in his *Apology* (c.176/177 AD), a statue of Alexander once stood in the forum of Parium, which was a Greek city in Mysia on the Hellespont (now called the Dardanelles).

Consequently, as there can be no doubt that Glycon, regardless of its true nature, really did exist, should we look more favourably upon its sole primary literary source, even though said source originated from the pen of an inimical satirist? This is where it all becomes much more complex, as now shown.

The source in question is a concise but coruscating essay tersely entitled *Alexander the False Prophet*, written in Ancient Greek by Lucian of Samosata (Samosata being an ancient Syrian city on the west bank of the Euphrates river). A popular Greek satirist and rhetorician, Lucian was a contemporary of Alexander, and was particularly noted for the scoffing, sarcastic nature of many of his writings. His essay contained the history of Alexander and Glycon that I have summarised here in this present chapter, but also included many additional claims and suppositions of fraud, lewd behaviour, and other undesirable activities relative to its human and serpentine subjects.

For instance, Lucian confidently asserted that the talking head of Glycon was not this snake's real head (which, he claimed, was kept well hidden under Alexander's armpit), but was instead an artificial construction made from linen and skilfully manipulated by Alexander using a lengthy internal tube composed of conjoined bird windpipes that led out from the false head into a hidden chamber where an assistant spoke words into the tube, thus making it seem as if Glycon were speaking. Lucian further alleged that a series of very fine, attached horse-hairs acted as internal pulleys to make the false head open and close its mouth, and extend and retract its tongue.

Lucian also 'explained' how various of Alexander's correct predictions had been achieved via fraudulent activity. He even alleged

Steve Moore (© Etienne Gilfillan)

that shortly after a somewhat acrimonious meeting with Alexander (in c.162 AD) during which he, Lucian, had tried to trick Alexander and had even attempted (albeit unsuccessfully) to dissuade Rutilianus from marrying the latter's daughter, he had narrowly avoided death during a boat trip when Alexander had supposedly paid the vessel's crew to murder him, only being saved when the captain prevented them from carrying out the heinous deed.

Traditionally, this vicious character assassination of Alexander by Lucian in literary form has tended to be viewed uncritically by those modern-day scholars actually aware of it (with Glycon in particular being among the Roman Empire's least-known figures of interest nowadays). However, all of that changed dramatically in June 2011, with the publication of a fascinating, eye-opening article presenting a very erudite reappraisal of Alexander, Glycon, and their portrayal by their longstanding nemesis Lucian. Published in the British monthly periodical *Fortean Times* (which is devoted to the serious investigation and chronicling of unexplained and controversial phenomena of every conceivable—and inconceivable!—kind), the article was authored by Steve Moore, a highly-respected veteran researcher of ancient Asian and European mysteries, and it directly challenged many of Lucian's long-accepted claims.

For example, Steve questioned how Lucian could have known any specific details about Alexander's early years, especially those shared with Cocconas, bearing in mind that he, Lucian, had not spent any time alongside the pair to witness anything at first hand, and that Cocconas and Alexander were hardly likely to have informed him (or anyone else, for that matter) what they had been doing if they had truly been engaged in fraudulent activity during that time period, as vehemently asserted by Lucian in his account. Indeed, Steve went even further, by questioning whether Cocconas even existed—after all, there is no mention of him outside Lucian's poisonous diatribe. Might he therefore have been a wholly fictitious character, invented specifically by Lucian in order to cast Alexander's early years in as bad a light as possible?

No less circumspect are Lucian's wholly unsubstantiated claims of spying, thuggery, blackmail, furtively opening sealed scrolls, and a varied assortment of other equally unpleasant activities attributed by him to Alexander. As for Lucian's once again unconfirmed allegation of almost being murdered by henchmen of Alexander while taking a boat ride, this just so happens to have been a very popular storyline in romantic works of fiction from that time period (and of which Lucian would certainly have been well aware). So it should clearly be viewed with great caution as a supposed statement of fact.

Equally, Steve pointed out that Lucian's bold statements regarding the nature of Glycon's head and speech were mere supposition too. True, the notions that Lucian had put forward regarding the mechanisms by which a fake head could have been secretly operated by Alexander were nothing if not ingenious, but that is all that they were—notions, not facts. No physical evidence or direct eyewitness observations confirming them were presented by Lucian in support of his accusations; it was all speculation (and spiteful speculation at that) on his part, nothing more. Other, much less controversial options also existed but which Lucian never mentioned, such as ventriloquism to make Glycon speak, and a simple glove or sock puppet-like creation to make its fake head move and open its mouth (always assuming of course that a fake head really was present).

Moreover, we only have Lucian's very questionable testimony that Glycon actually talked at all! In fact, it is even possible that Lucian never actually saw Glycon or spoke to anyone who had done so, because, amazingly, his essay makes no mention whatsoever of Glycon's two most remarkable physical features—its human ears and blond hair. Conversely, whereas Lucian claimed that it possessed a human-like head, most of the physical depictions of Glycon currently known (i.e. the various coins and statues noted earlier by me in this chapter) actually portray it with a long-snouted head that is certainly more pythonesque than humanoid in appearance. If for no other reason than this, therefore, the authentic nature of the content of Lucian's essay clearly should not—can not—be taken in any way for granted.

Returning to the matter of the mobility and loquacity of Glycon's head, it would be very prudent here to quote Steve's take on Lucian's assertions regarding this:

> In boasting that he knows how the trick was done, Lucian is plainly covering up the fact that this can only be a matter of conjecture. These conjectures *may* be very close to the truth; but they remain conjectures, not proof.

Steve also applied this same line of sound reasoning very successfully and convincingly to many other of Lucian's scathing claims masquerading as facts against Alexander. In addition, certain of Alexander's activities that Lucian deemed to be evidence of his fakery—most notably his retreating overnight into an inner, subterranean sanctuary called the adyton, in order to receive his oracles in peaceful solitude via dreams, and then reveal them publicly the following morning—were shown by Steve to be no different from those performed by various soothsayers and oracle-givers who had *not* been accused of or linked to fraud, such as the very famous, much-revered Oracle of Apollo at Claros, on the coast of Ionia in present-day Anatolia, Turkey.

Indeed, there is even a very relevant, present-day parallel, as Steve tellingly revealed in his own article:

> The adyton is an underground chamber, and it's now known that withdrawal to a cave or subterranean chamber to obtain visions and mystic revelations was a common practice among Greek seers, being used similarly to a modern sensory deprivation tank.

As for charges made by Lucian against Alexander of lewd behaviour and even male prostitution: such activities were by no means uncommon back in their day, and some of the ceremonies and rituals performed during the kinds of celebration that Alexander had modelled his own annual three-day festival upon were notoriously liberal to say the least! Once again, therefore, why was Lucian singling out Alexander, this time for indulging in behaviour that was no different—or worse—than that of many others in his role?

The answer would seem to be quite simple, but hitherto ignored by those who have supported Lucian's writings unquestioningly. Lucian was an Epicurean (a follower of the teachings of the ancient Greek philosopher Epicurus), whereas Alexander was no fan of Epicureans, or Christians either, for that matter, banning both groups from his annual festivities. His reasons for doing so are that Epicureans were known for their fervent scepticism of superstition and claimed cases of divine intervention, and Christians would certainly not have tolerated any snake-worshipping cult derived from the Greek deity Asclepius (or indeed any other such cult).

Consequently, the activities of Alexander would have made him a prime focus for disdain by Lucian. And when this was coupled with Alexander's dislike of Epicureans, as well as his immense success and fame, overshadowing Lucian's own accomplishments at that time, it was inevitable that literary sparks would fly when Lucian chose to write about him.

Certainly, there was never any hope for an unbiased, objective account from Lucian, who definitely did not disappoint on that score—the result being a destructive, cynical, hyper-sceptical, and uber-vitriolic outpouring of verbal venom specifically designed to diminish, denigrate, and entirely discredit the reputation of the subject of his enmity.

And for many centuries, this is exactly what Lucian's vindictive essay achieved, abetted by Christian scholars and scientists alike (for whom stories of snake deities and diviners of the future were anathema). Then Steve Moore's much-needed objective perspicacity opened readers' eyes to what may well have been the greatest of all trickeries associated with Alexander and Glycon—one which,

Astronomically, Asclepius is immortalised as the constellation Ophiuchus, the snake-bearer, as depicted here in *Urania's Mirror*—a set of constellation cards published in London in c.1825

ironically, was none of their own doing either, but was instead the ostensibly accurate yet substantially inaccurate account of their lives penned by Lucian.

In short, the true nature of this toxic treatise had been hidden in plain sight for a very long time indeed, shielded from any penetrating analysis by Lucian's name and by generations of readers with their own compatible agenda, until the coming of Steve's diligent, iconoclastic detective work.

Obviously, there is no doubt that hoaxing did play some part in certain of Alexander's activities, most notably in relation to the physical serpent Glycon. Equally, however, as Steve so forensically revealed, it is likely that he was nowhere near as villainous as Lucian would have everyone believe—more sinned against than sinning, in fact. It is often said that the pen is mightier than the sword, but never more so than when that pen has been liberally dipped in the lethal venom of hatred and jealousy.

My sincere thanks to Steve Moore (1949-2014) for encouraging my writings and researches throughout my career, and whose revelatory *Fortean Times* article on Glycon so enthralled me that it inspired me to conduct my own researches, resulting in this present chapter.

22
REMEMBERING THE BEAST OF BODALOG —WALES'S MYSTERY WATER SNAKE... OR A WATER VAMPIRE?

> Centuries ago, people local to the River Wye believed that the river was home to something terrifying that required a human sacrifice once a year, as a form of appeasement and to ensure that the beast did not launch an all-out, murderous rampage around the area. Based on what happened in Rhayader in late 1988, perhaps the old legends had a basis in terrifying, savage fact.
>
> Nick Redfern—'A 30th Anniversary of Monstrous Terror', *Mysteriousuniverse.org,* 3 December 2018

Just over 30 years ago, one of the strangest, eeriest cryptozoological cases ever reported from the British Isles was making headlines nationally and even internationally, and in 1997 I became the first cryptozoologist to document it in book form when I devoted a chapter to it (based upon an earlier article of mine published in *Fate Magazine*) within my book *From Flying Toads To Snakes With Wings*. Three decades later, conversely, this perplexing riddle is all but forgotten, yet it remains unsolved.

To describe one of Britain's most bizarre mystery beasts as a water vampire may not be as melodramatic as one would first suppose—especially after considering its unique characteristics.

According to media reports, during September to December 1988 this cryptic entity's home was seemingly a lengthy river, the River Wye, situated close to the town of Rhayader in mid-Wales, from which it apparently emerged at night to kill sheep on a nearby 2000-acre farm called Bodalog, owned by the Pugh family.

Unlike those of foxes and dogs, however, its victims' carcasses were not ripped or torn in any way. Instead, the only sign of their mystifying marauder's attack was a small but deep, penetrating bite just below the neck, close to the sternum or breast-bone (and which duly earned it the memorable moniker of water vampire in some media accounts). No evidence of the creature feeding upon the carcasses was found either, thus making its predatory behaviour even more weird and difficult to understand.

Nevertheless, by the middle of October 1988 this mysterious beast had killed at least 35 sheep. Its scent had been trailed back and forth to the river by foxhounds, but it was never seen or identified, and no recognisable paw prints were found either. However, the presence of very visible flattening of the grass around the carcases indicated that whatever it was, this uncanny creature had initially circled round its prey before moving in for the kill.

As noted by London's *Daily Mail* newspaper on 10 October 1988, many suggestions regarding its possible identity had been offered, ranging from otter and dog, to mink and even some form of snake. University scientists had examined the carcasses and admitted to being thoroughly perplexed.

Their bewilderment is not surprising, as the Bodalog Beast clearly poses some singular problems, with none of the more conservative explanations satisfying the facts available.

Its aquatic habitat immediately rules out a fox, cat (even an escapee big cat), or stray dog as the culprit—as well as a human hunter using a crossbow, which had also been suggested by some authorities. European otters *Lutra lutra* are relatively large creatures, but are certainly not sheep killers. They are known to take small mammals in their diet from time to time, but nothing approaching the size of a sheep. In any event, their principal sources of food are fishes and aquatic crustaceans—and, needless to say, they do eat prey killed by them and they do leave tell-tale spoor behind.

Mink, although much smaller than otters, are far more bloodthirsty by nature. Not native to the British Isles, they now exist

Could the Bodalog Beast have been a large species of snake living in Britain and readily able to swim, such as a species of grass snake (some examples of which are depicted here in a beautiful illustration by Heinrich Harder from 1912)?

Could it have been a native European otter?
(Peter Trimming, CC BY 2.0)

in a naturalised state in many parts of the U.K.—descendants of fur-farm escapees belonging to the American species, *Neovison vison*. Mink have wide tastes, ranging from fishes to birds as large as moorhens, and mammals as large as young rabbits (reports even exist of mink having killed pet cats and dogs!). Nevertheless, sheep would surely be far too large for any mink to tackle successfully.

One suggestion, from an unnamed 'expert', was that some form of giant mink was responsible! Mink, however, do not normally attain a total length greater than about 26 inches in the wild, and there is no evidence whatsoever that mink of a size commensurate for sheep killing have ever existed in Britain.

Or could it have been a naturalised American mink?
(© Cephas, CC BY-SA 3.0)

A little-known species called the sea mink *N. macrodon* once inhabited the coastal waters of New England and the Canadian maritime provinces, and was indeed somewhat larger than other mink species. However, it became extinct in the early 1880s, and is totally unknown either in living or in fossil form within the Old World.

Britain only has three native species of snake [NB—herpetological researchers revealed in 2017 that there were actually two taxonomically distinct species of grass snake living here, not just one, but only one of them is native, namely the barred grass snake *Natrix helvetica*; unfortunately, various media reports confusingly and erroneously claimed at the time that both of them were native and that there were therefore four native snake species existing here]. The sole venomous species is the European viper or adder *Vipera berus*, which is predominantly ground-living, diurnal, and feeds on nothing larger than lizards and small mammals.

Relatively more aquatic by nature are the non-venomous and diurnal eastern grass snake *Natrix natrix* (represented in Britain via various small, introduced, non-native populations) and its close relative the western or barred grass snake *N. helvetica* (the new name for Britain's native grass snake species). The preferred prey of these two species are amphibians and fishes, although nestling birds and small mammals are also occasionally taken.

In addition, Britain has a small number of the smooth snake *Coronella austriaca*, again native but confined to southern England. This is another non-venomous, diurnal species whose diet consists mainly of lizards and small mammals.

Also worthy of note is the Aesculapian snake *Zamenis longissimus*, which is a mainland European species that has established a couple of small but seemingly thriving naturalised population in Great Britain—one in central London, England, and the other in

Aesculapian snake *Zamenis longissimus*
(Felix Reimann, CC BY-SA 3.0)

Colwyn Bay, Wales. Both populations originally arose from escapee/released specimens surviving and mating in the wild in these locations. So might the Beast of Bodalog have been an Aesculapian snake, derived from the Welsh contingent? At up to 7 ft long, this species is certainly lengthier than any of Britain's native species, but just like all of them it is diurnal, and it is not venomous. Clearly, therefore, none of these five species constitutes a very convincing candidate for the Welsh sheep killer.

It has never been formally ascertained whether the Pughs' sheep were actually poisoned by their attacker, but if tests were to reveal that this did occur, it is possible that a non-native and evidently sizeable, aquatic venomous snake was on the loose at that time. It might have been a pet that either escaped or was released, as in the above-noted London and Welsh instances featuring the Aesculapian snake. Yet if this were true, it could have potentially posed a very real, severe dilemma—because there are few animals on Earth as elusive as snakes, especially those species that are adept at travelling not only across the land but also through the water.

Perhaps, therefore, it is not too surprising that the sinister 'water vampire' of Wales was never seen, let alone tracked down. Even noted British cryptozoologist Nick Redfern (now based in Texas) was unable to spy it, despite spending three days and nights on site searching for this elusive enigma. Its killing spree abruptly ended in early December 1988, and nothing like it has ever been reported since from Bodalog (or anywhere else, for that matter, at least as far as I am aware), so presumably it simply died (see below)—always assuming, of course, that it didn't simply move elsewhere.

Interestingly, there is already on file at least one possible historical precedent for a large, dangerous, non-native snake existing for a while in the wilds of Great Britain. A 10-ft-long serpent dragon was reported from St Leonard's Forest, near Horsham in West Sussex, southern England, during August 1614. According to a pamphlet circulated at that time (which is the original source of this report and was subsequently republished in the *Harleian Miscellany*, 1744-1753), it killed two people, two dogs, and several cattle by spitting venom at them, but (echoing the Bodalog Beast's own odd behaviour) it did not try to devour them. A spitting cobra (ringhals) brought to England during the early 1600s as an exotic pet or exhibit that later escaped or was deliberately released into the countryside could provide a plausible identity for this venom-projecting serpent dragon. Science recognises several species of such snake, which incapacitate their prey or potential aggressors by spitting accurately, and from some distance away, a stream of venom into their eyes.

Yet if the Bodalog Beast had indeed been some form of very large, powerful (and possibly even highly venomous) snake, why did it kill so many sheep but never make any attempt to feed upon their carcasses afterwards? And how can the circles of flattened grass present around the dead sheep be explained as serpentine in origin, bearing in mind that such behaviour is not typical for snakes?

Moreover, how could such a creature as a sizeable non-native snake have survived for at least two months amid the distinctly chilly climate present in mid-Wales during late autumn/early winter? After all, snakes are poikilothermic (cold-blooded) and therefore rely upon warm external, environmental temperatures to maintain their own body heat. Like all others associated with this decidedly strange saga, these questions are likely to remain unanswered indefinitely.

23
VANQUISHING *BOTHRODON*—
HOW A GIANT SNAKE WAS
TRANSFORMED INTO A SEASHELL!

> It was during the preparation of this manuscript that the author received the greatest surprise in the many years he has studied the serpent clan—and it related to a rear-fanged snake. It was in the form of a booklet, printed as an author's extra, and came from Professor J. Graham Kerr, of the University of Glasgow, in Scotland. Its title was "*Bothrodon pridii*, an Extinct Serpent of Gigantic Dimensions." The article contained a photograph of a poison fang as long as the claw of a tiger. As the poison-conducting teeth of the rear-fanged snakes are short in proportion to the body length, the size of this monster is open to thrilling conjecture. Speaking in gross terms, the fang is approximately nine times larger than that of a six-foot boomslang. Theorizing from such a comparison we have indicated a poisonous snake nearly sixty feet long, or twice the size of the largest pythons existing today.
>
> Raymond L. Ditmars—*Snakes of the World*

In contrast to insidious and infamous zoological frauds such as Piltdown Man and the stuffed 'Feejee Mermaids' of Oriental origin, many cases of confused taxonomic classification have occurred not through deliberate, predetermined intentions to deceive by creating non-existent creatures or by luring scientists along false trails, but instead via simple misidentifications. Nevertheless, the results have often been both unexpected and spectacular, but few more so than in the case of the giant venomous serpent of South America's Gran Chaco (a vast, semi-arid region overlapping northwestern Bolivia,

One of several artworks by Swiss painter Henry Fuseli (1741-1825) with a cryptozoological connection— *Reiter Von Riesenschlange Überfallen* ('Horseman Attacked by a Giant Snake'); watercolour, painted in c.1800

western Paraguay, northern Argentina, and a small portion of southwestern Brazil). After all, how *can* such an ostensibly monstrous reptile be transformed into a spiky seashell of far more modest proportions and far less dangerous attributes?

As I now reveal, the story of this astonishing metamorphosis, although largely forgotten today, must surely rate as one of the most extraordinary (and embarrassing) incidents in the entire history of 20th-Century zoology.

Deep within the most secluded realms of the mystery beast investigator's mind lies a dark and mournful cemetery, whose gates are for the most part firmly chained and heavily barred. Whenever his speculations and theories aspire to the grandiose and gothic, however, he is forced to tread the shadowy pathway leading to this most dreaded and dreadful of destinations—the mausoleum of monsters.

In this forsaken spot—within this cryptic catacomb of mythological mammalia, apocalyptic archosauria, and other fabulous fauna of every type—no ordinary assemblage of skeletons is ensconced. No, indeed. Here, amongst shattered dreams and mocking illusions, lie the hastily-jettisoned remains of those great zoological discoveries that were subsequently exposed as sorry misidentifications. A faux-pas phantasmagoria, whose forbidding presence within the annals of zoology serves as a stern warning to all cryptozoologists of the perils of premature pronouncement or imprudent identification. Let us tarry a while here, and examine one of its most (melo)dramatic examples.

In 1926, the *Proceedings of the Royal Society of Edinburgh* published a paper by Prof. Sir John Graham Kerr, at that time Regius Professor of Zoology at the University of Glasgow, Scotland, in which he described a huge, curved poison fang belonging to a hitherto unknown genus and species of giant snake—which he formally named *Bothrodon pridii* (with *Bothrodon* translating as 'furrow-tooth'). Approximately 2.5 in long as measured along the outside of the curve, this fang was truly enormous.

Indeed, as noted by mollusc expert David Heppell (1937-2004), formerly of the Royal Museum of Scotland, who documented this specimen in *The Conchologist's Newsletter* (March 1966), it was roughly nine times longer than that of a 6-ft-long boomslang *Dispholidus typus*—one of the world's deadliest snakes.

Moreover, it even dwarfed the fangs of the Gaboon viper *Bitis gabonica*. Native to much of sub-Saharan Africa, this formidable serpent not only is the largest member of the genus *Bitis* and the world's heaviest species of any type of viperid, but also holds the record for the longest fangs of any known species of snake alive today—up to 2 in long.

Accordingly, judging from the relative size of the fang, Prof. Kerr estimated that the total length of its venomous owner, *Bothrodon pridii*, could have approached 60 ft or so. Truly a monster, in every sense of the word!

The poison fang had been obtained by one of Kerr's friends, missionary Andrew Pride (after whom Kerr had named this outsized ophidian) from the Gran Chaco's silt-like deposits, which dated back no further than the Pleistocene epoch (2.5 million to 11,700 years ago). Despite a prolonged, thorough search of this locality by Pride for this mega-snake's skeletal remains, however, none were found.

In his paper, Kerr concisely described the fang's appearance, including the prominent poison groove running all along its apparent external face, as well as the two narrow parallel stripes, dark-brown in colour, that lay along the distal (terminal) portion of its length. He also discussed the possible phylogenetic relationships of *Bothrodon pridii* itself, by comparing its fang's morphology with that of contemporary snake species.

From these studies, Kerr concluded that the fang most closely resembled those of the opisthoglyphans. This is a group of rear-fanged colubrid snakes that include the boomslang, and which point the way towards the more highly-evolved present-day venomous snakes. In addition, Kerr deduced from the fang's peculiar hook-like shape that, rather than functioning as a striking fang, it most probably served to hold the prey stationary whilst its poison entered the wounds produced by the snake's other teeth in the prey's flesh.

Sherlock Holmes would certainly have approved—because Kerr's paper demonstrated most effectively the considerable amount of information concerning an entire organism (be it serpent or sapient!) that could be deduced by meticulous analysis of only a single component of that organism. Or so it seemed . . .

Kerr duly presented this unique fang to the Hunterian Museum of the University of Glasgow, and in 1933 a cast of it was displayed alongside a label stating that *Bothrodon* may have fed upon cumbersome plains-dwelling creatures such as the now-extinct giant ground sloth *Megatherium*.

Bothrodon pridii 'fang', pictured in 1926

Prof. Sir John Graham Kerr (T & R Annan & Sons Ltd, CC BY 4.0)

Conversely, noted herpetologist Raymond Ditmars suggested small mammals as likely prey in his classic book *Snakes of the World* (1931). Nevertheless, he was palpably impressed by Kerr's discovery and documentation of *Bothrodon*, exclaiming in his book:

> It was during the preparation of this manuscript that the author received the greatest surprise in the many years he has studied the serpent clan—and it related to a rear-fanged snake.

The possible stature of *Bothrodon* also excited him:

> As the poison-conducting teeth of the rear-fanged snakes are short in proportion to the body length, the size of this monster is open to thrilling conjecture. . . . Indeed the thought it inspires rather dulls the conjectural image of that dinosaurian star, *Tyrannosaurus*, whose races passed away ages before this mammoth *Bothrodon* prowled the soil.

I'm not quite sure how a limbless creature can be said to prowl; but in any event, as a serpent of substance *Bothrodon* remained unchallenged—until 1939. That was when it was unceremoniously dethroned, disgraced, and, worst of all, exposed as nothing more than a snail in snake's similitude!

For German palaeontologist Dr Werner Quenstedt, after closely examining a coloured cast of the fang sent to the University of Berlin's Paleontological Museum by Prof. Kerr, recognised the specimen's true identity. It was one of those six curved projections, long and groove-bearing, that fringe the large aperture of the distinctive shell belonging to *Lambis* [now *Harpago*] *chiragra*, the Chiragra spider conch—a large and ornate, modern-day species of Indo-Pacific gastropod mollusc! Every feature of the 'fang' confirmed this identity—its size, shape, long groove, brown stripes. There could be no mistake—*Bothrodon pridii* was no more.

To be fair, however, Kerr's misidentification is not as surprising as it may seem on first sight. After all, he could hardly have been expected to anticipate the discovery within the deposits of Paraguay's Gran Chaco of a shell fragment from a gastropod normally inhabiting the Indo-Pacific oceans.

23 | BOTHRODON

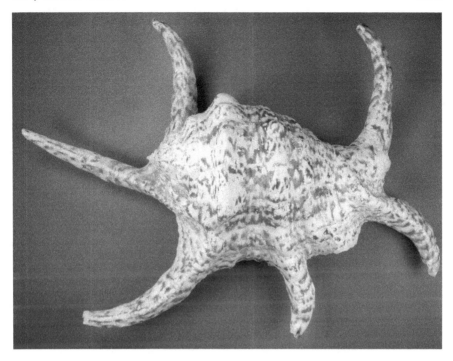

Chiragra spider conch's shell, upper side (James St John, CC BY 2.0)

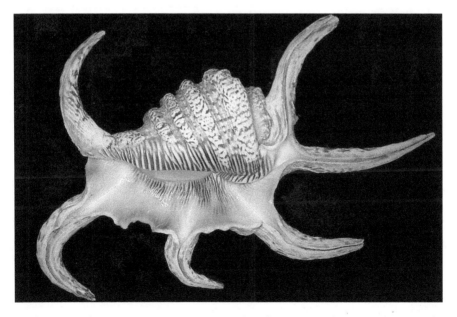

Chiragra spider conch's shell, underside (Udo Schmidt, CC BY-SA 2.0)

Indeed, this one aspect of *Bothrodon*'s bizarre history remains totally unexplained and seemingly inexplicable even today. How *could* a section of shell from a modern-day Indo-Pacific mollusc have been obtained in Gran Chaco? David Heppell noted that there is no doubt about Gran Chaco being the correct locality involved. Thus, as he also remarked, the discovery can be explained only by way of some human introduction.

Notwithstanding this, the survival of *Bothrodon pridii* within the zoological literature on taxonomic synonyms serves as a stark reminder of just how easily and how far one can travel along the wrong track after having once set foot upon it. Certainly, as noted earlier, although many weird metamorphoses have been documented from the animal kingdom, few can compare with a giant snake's transformation into a spiky seashell!

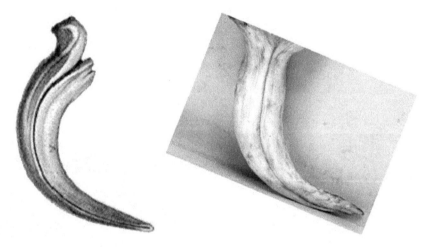

Bothrodon fang and Chiragra spider conch shell projection

Incidentally: this tragic taxonomic tale has a curious if little-known footnote (assuming, of course, that anything concerning snakes can possess a foot!). For even though the re-identification of the *Bothrodon* 'fang' as a prong from the shell of a Chiragra spider conch was swiftly and fully accepted by the herpetological community following Quenstedt's dramatic denouement in 1939, it is possible that Kerr himself was not so quick to accept this embarrassing revelation.

The reason why I suggest this is that while browsing through Kerr's book *A Naturalist in Gran Chaco*, first published in 1950 and chronicling the zoological expedition that he mounted during the late 1890s to this region of southern South America, I was very surprised to find that although he included just over a page devoted to the *Bothrodon* specimen's discovery and his studies of it, he made no mention whatsoever of its molluscan re-identification. Equally, I can find no mention anywhere else either of his ever having publicly discounted or disputed this latter taxonomic reassignment of it.

So how can we explain such a very curious, and conspicuous, absence in Kerr's book, which was first published more than a decade *after* Quenstedt's own fateful, published declaration? Did Kerr refuse to countenance Quenstedt's re-identification of his once-celebrated specimen, or is it conceivable that he wasn't even aware of this? As Kerr died just seven years later, in 1957, it is likely that we shall never be able to answer this highly intriguing question with any degree of certainty.

No less perplexing, however, is that in 1958, shortly after Kerr's death, his successor at Glasgow University, Prof. Edward Hindle (also related to Kerr by marriage), perpetuated Kerr's erroneous identification of *Bothrodon* as a snake fang in a biography of him. Yet even if Kerr had genuinely been unaware of the truth, surely it is too implausible to assume that Hindle had been too? All very strange.

Taxonomically speaking, therefore, *Bothrodon pridii* may indeed be long dead and buried within the mausoleum of monsters, but perhaps its mystery is not entirely extinguished after all.

Finally: this was not the first time that a supposed fossil snake had featured in a notable palaeontological misidentification. During early 1851, publicity broadsides were being posted on walls around the Welsh town of Neath to draw public attention (and attendance) to an eye-catching object currently being exhibited in the town hall during three consecutive days (30 and 31 January and 1 February). For according to the broadside, the object was none other than a very sizeable fossil serpent, 8 ft 3 in long and 7 in across.

As revealed by F.J. North in the second edition of his book *Coal, and the Coalfields in Wales* (1931), however, it was actually the trunk of an enormous, superficially tree-like, but long-extinct relative of club mosses and (especially) quillworts, known as *Lepidodendron*, which thrived during the Carboniferous Period around 360 million years ago, and attained a height of up to 180 ft. Its fossils are found preserved in coal deposits, and it is characterised by its trunk's noticeably scaly outer surface (*Lepidodendron* actually translates as 'scale tree'), although its 'scales' are actually leaf scars, created when its leaves fell off.

Moreover, its fossils' true botanical identity had been known to scientists for several years before this exhibition. So one can only assume that the latter's organiser did not intend to let a mere technicality like the truth stand in the way of making some easy money from scientifically-naive visitors anxious to see the mortal remains of an alleged prehistoric serpent! Indeed, amateur exhibitions at sideshows and fairs of similar *Lepidodendron* specimens masquerading in best Barnumesque fashion as giant fossil snakes or even lizards were by no means uncommon back then.

Giant tree-like *Lepidodendron* plants thriving during the Carboniferous Period

24
IN PURSUIT OF IMPOSSIBLE SNAKES— A FURTHER COLLECTION OF PSEUDO-SERPENTS

> One thing I've come particularly to admire about Karl over the years is his dogged persistence in following up a promising cryptozoological tid-bit or intriguing clue in the hopes that it will yield up something more substantial farther down the line. Even when the trail goes cold, Karl will wait until a new lead emerges—whether from a fresh piece of witness testimony, a letter from one of his many correspondents or a bit of evidence turned up in a forgotten book or archive. As Karl—like a true Fortean—writes: "Some of the most interesting cryptozoological discoveries initially take place not in the field but in the library".
>
> David Sutton—foreword, *Karl Shuker's Alien Zoo*

In Chapter 3, I documented two of North America's most famous pseudo-serpents (i.e. false snakes once deemed to be genuine species but ultimately exposed as imaginative folktales, monstrous misidentifications, or deceiving hoaxes). Those were the horn snake and the hoop snake. Now I have pleasure in presenting a second, extremely diverse but this time much less famous, far more obscure selection of pseudo-serpents, their hitherto scarcely-documented sources spanning the globe and featuring all manner of truly fascinating examples.

FAWCETT'S TELESCOPIC SNAKE

One anomalous snake that is unquestionably a pseudo-serpent, originating in local folklore or even as a complete invention with which to bemuse or alarm gullible western explorers, is the Bolivian telescopic snake. During an exploration of Bolivia in 1907 (prior to vanishing in 1925 during an expedition to Brazil, never to be seen again), the famous British explorer Lieutenant-Colonel Percy H. Fawcett had reached San Ignacio, capital of Bolivia's Chiquitos Province. This is an area that he referred to as being possibly the worst terrain for venomous snakes and snake-perpetrated human fatalities in the whole of South America.

Moreover, several of the locals whom he encountered there also assured him that this dreadful region was home to a most extraordinary serpent, roughly 3 ft long, that possessed the astonishing ability to telescope into itself before striking. Happily, it was not very venomous.

Unsurprisingly, Fawcett considered this feat to be an anatomical impossibility. Equally unsurprisingly, he never saw one of these telescopic snakes either.

Although certain animals possess retractable jaws (perhaps most famously the goblin shark *Mitsukurina owstoni*), there is no vertebrate that can perform telescopic behaviour of its body. So unless this was merely an exaggerated description of a snake that possibly recoiled its body quite significantly before striking forward, we can definitely file the Bolivian telescope snake within cryptozoology's bulging folder of pseudo-serpent reports.

THE CONGOLESE JIBATE—
A MISSILE-SPITTING MYSTERY

From 1908 to 1923, American missionary Everard R. Moon lived in what was then the Belgian Congo (later Zaire, now the Democratic Republic of the Congo). In his book *I Saw Congo* (1952), recounting his life there, he included the following details of what would be a truly remarkable snake if this information, supplied to him by the native people, is true:

24 | IMPOSSIBLE SNAKES

Lieutenant-Colonel Percy H. Fawcett

Ringhals or rinkhals, a spitting cobra,
Hemachatus haemachatus
(Lee Berger, CC BY-SA 2.5)

24 | IMPOSSIBLE SNAKES

All over the Central Congo Basin the natives told me of a snake they call *"jibate,"* that "throws poisonous missiles," hurling them with deadly accuracy fifteen or twenty feet. One man told me that they would always throw at some bright object. He said, "if you are carrying a gun with bright metal parts, just hold the gun off to one side and you can hear the missiles strike the metal, one at a time. When the snake has hurled all its missiles it is harmless, but if you do not kill it after you are gone it will gather them up to use again." I never put any stock in the story for I soon found that while the children of the jungle have wonderful general knowledge of animal life, their observations are made with far from scientific accuracy.

It is well known that, as a defence mechanism against a would-be attacker, several species of ringhals or spitting cobra will shoot out streams of venom from their mouth by the muscular squeezing of their venom glands, which sprays forth the venom through a tiny hole near the top of each fang.

Conversely, if the native' testimony is true, the jibate must actually pick up small pebbles or similar objects off the ground with its mouth (inside which they duly become coated with its fangs' venom), and then spit them back out both at speed and with not inconsiderable force at an antagonist or a prey victim. This would undoubtedly be a novel tactic, and although it is not so unlikely as to be impossible, I agree with Moon that it is certainly not very believable.

NEVER A NEITHER

In England, the two most common species of snake are the barred grass or ringed snake *Natrix helvetica* (often referred to in southern England simply as the snake) and the European viper or common adder *Vipera berus*. Belonging as they do to two entirely separate, only distantly related taxonomic families (Colubridae and Viperidae respectively), it is hardly likely that these two snakes would ever come together even to mate, let alone produce viable hybrid offspring. Yet there is a longstanding belief emanating from southern England's very sizeable New Forest that such crossbreeds can and do occur. According to H.M. Livens's book *Nomansland: A Village History* (1910), for instance:

> It is affirmed throughout the [New] Forest that there is a casual hybrid between the [grass] snake and the adder, which, in consequence of being neither adder nor [grass] snake, is known as a *Neither* (pronounced nither). In colour it varies between those of its parents, sometimes showing a greater leaning to the one side, and sometimes to the other. In its proportions it runs closer to the adder than to the [grass] snake, being about 18 inches long; that is, rather longer than an adder but not quite so stout. The Neither is usually found on or near damp ground about the head of a bog. When attacked it will bite the stick as an adder does. A [grass] snake will not do this. Its bite is said to be venomous. It is not known to breed.

Is the implausible neither in reality the highly elusive, mysterious smooth snake? (Piet Spaans, CC BY 2.5)

The New Forest is also home to Britain's third, rarest, and least-known native species of snake, the smooth snake *Coronella austriaca*. Yet, oddly, it is mentioned only very briefly, in passing, by Livens, claiming that it is rare here, when in reality it is found throughout the New Forest's extent. Moreover, its barred markings are reminiscent of both the grass snake's and the adder's, but it is so shy as to be seldom seen and remains very much a mysterious, enigmatic serpent here.

Consequently, I think it highly likely that the smooth snake is the true identity of Livens's alleged grass snake x adder hybrid, the neither. Even its favoured habitat of damp heath and bog compares well with that of the neither, as does its well-known predilection for biting if antagonised or captured. True, the smooth snake is not venomous, but many non-venomous animal species are wrongly deemed to be through local superstition or ignorance, especially if, like the smooth snake, they are rarely-seen, elusive creatures—which would also explain why the neither is not known to breed.

All in all, therefore, it would seem that the neither is an impossible snake rendered possible after all.

LOST IN TRANSLATION—THE PARAGUAYAN BARKING SNAKE

Some non-existent mystery beasts owe their temporary reality not to tall tales or native folklore but merely to imperfect translations of reports from one language to another. A prime example of this is the mboi-yagua or Paraguayan barking snake, whose exposure I documented in my book *From Flying Toads To Snakes With Wings* (1997).

During the early 1970s, America's scientific circles and general public alike were besieged by incredible stories of a large snake known locally as the mboi-yagua that was on display in Paraguay's principal zoo—the Jardin Botanico, Museo y Zoologico, in Asuncion. According to these stories, it had hooks on its tail, a notably swollen abdomen, and—most startling of all—the ability to bark like a dog! As it appeared to be something totally new, everyone was very eager to learn more about this singular serpent. In the USA, its talents were first reported by a Seattle newspaper, which had relied upon a translation from an original Spanish-language story published earlier in Paraguay.

The story created such a storm that eventually zoo officials in Asuncion called a press conference in order to reveal their most famous inmate's true nature. For it turned out that their miraculous mboi-yagua was nothing more than an ordinary green anaconda *Eunectes murinus*, whose remarkable vocal powers were due not to Nature but instead to a mistranslation of its name by whoever was responsible for dubbing it 'the barking snake'.

The correct translation of 'mboi-yagua' was not 'dog-snake' or 'snake-dog', as had been claimed, but was actually 'tiger-snake', because the green anaconda is spotted like South America's famous (if inappropriately named) 'tigre'—the jaguar. Thus the barking snake's bark was no more. Equally quick to vanish was its swollen abdomen—when it gave birth to 61 live young on 20 May 1972. As for its tail hooks—these were nothing more than a gross exaggeration of the fact that the anaconda tends to anchor itself to a tree or some other solid object by 'hooking' its tail around it!

So ended the Paraguayan barking snake—stripped of a series of spectacular features that it had never possessed anyway, except in the words of an article based upon an inaccurately-translated local name.

Green anaconda *Eunectes murinus* (Tserres34, CC BY-SA 4.0)

24 | IMPOSSIBLE SNAKES

HAMMERING HOME THE STORY OF OREGON'S HAMMERHEAD SNAKE

Due no doubt to their potential danger and phobia-inducing qualities, snakes appear to have inspired a disproportionately large number of journalistic yarns and spoof articles—a genre of reportage that seemed particularly common in 19th-Century and early 20th-Century American newspapers. The following account may well be one such example, although it is remotely conceivable that a genuine freak, teratological specimen was its basis. It appeared on 13 August 1916 in *The Oregonian*, an Oregon newspaper, and features a bizarre serpent called the hammerhead snake, but as far as I am aware it has not been documented before in a cryptozoology book.

According to that newspaper account, the snake was originally discovered by a prospector on South Sixes River in Oregon's Curry County, but has since been seen there occasionally by other miners too. Rock-grey in colour and about 2 ft long, it is known locally as the hammerhead snake, due to its head's peculiar shape and alignment. The head is much broader than its length, with an eye at each end, widely separated from one another, and the head itself is set at right angles to the neck, so that it resembles a tack hammer on a handle.

As noted earlier, although on first sight such a strange appearance seems implausible, it is possible that this snake is a teratological anomaly. Perhaps it is an incompletely-formed two-headed (dicephalous) specimen, in which during embryogeny the snake's head widened to an abnormal degree, but did not actually divide and duplicate into two fully-formed heads. However, this would not explain why its head is placed at right angles to its neck, unless it had suffered a vertebral injury at some stage after its birth or hatching, or some developmental defect during its neck's embryogeny.

THE BLOW SNAKE OR SPREADING ADDER

These are names given to a supposedly malevolent serpent frequenting the USA that in the words of Clifford B. Moore, then director of the Trailside Museum in Springfield, Massachusetts, documenting a wide range of American mythical snakes in a *Scientific Monthly* article of January 1949:

> ... blows its poisonous breath or spits venom from a distance into the innocent observer's face, thereby producing burns, blindness, infection, or convulsions. Even though the majority of these stories are related secondhand, there seems to be no dearth of actual eyewitness "evidence" of such personal encounters, with consequent poisonings.

In reality, however, as Moore goes on to explain, the serpent in question is nothing more than the entirely harmless hog-nosed snake, of which there are three closely-related species, belonging to the colubrid genus *Heterodon*. They are famous for their remarkable performances of thanatosis—playing dead—when threatened to a potential aggressor. In such a situation, a hog-nosed snake will violently contort its body and throw itself on its back, with mouth hanging limply open and tongue lolling out, then lie perfectly still as if it has fatally expired from some dreadful disease or poison, thus appearing sufficiently alarming to ward off its would-be predator. (Sometimes, however, just like all of the worst human ham actors, a hog-nosed snake in the inert throes of thanatosis will

Hog-nosed snake *Heterodon platirhinos,* playing dead (USFWS)

over-act its part—for if this seemingly dead snake is picked up and placed right-side up, it will immediately flop back onto its back, thereby comically betraying itself!)

However, playing dead is this shamming serpent's last line of defence. Before it resorts to thanatosis, the hog-nosed snake will attempt to bluff its way out of trouble, via pseudo-aggression. So it raises its head and up to a third of its total body length off the ground, flattens its neck like a cobra, hisses very loudly in a highly intimidating, threatening manner, and sometimes even makes a few feigned strikes, but very seldom actually bites. It is this faux ferocity that has earned the hog-nosed snake its 'blow snake' and 'spreading adder' soubriquets—yet another of numerous examples recorded from around the globe of a non-venomous creature wrongly being assumed to be venomous.

HORNING IN ON THE UNICORN SNAKE

Whereas the hammerhead snake, although undeniably weird, is not necessarily fraudulent, and the blow snake is certainly not, both the unicorn snake and the American snow snake are unequivocal hoaxes—pseudo-serpents in every sense.

During the Middle Ages and even several centuries later, explorers and travellers to exotic far-flung localities around the globe would often return home to Europe with unusual animal specimens as interesting souvenirs. Sadly, however, some of these items were outright fakes (such as the infamous 'Feejee mermaids', which were composite creations deftly manufactured from preserved monkeys and large fishes) or deliberately misidentified objects (such as ibex or antelope horns masquerading as griffin or dragon claws) that had been sold to the unsuspecting voyagers at exorbitant prices by unscrupulous indigenous vendors.

An ophidian representative from these shaming cabinets of credulities was the unicorn snake. This usually took the form of a dried, preserved serpent of fairly sizeable proportions but sporting as its most eye-catching characteristic a long spine protruding from the centre of its brow like a veritable herpetological unicorn.

Needless to say, however, an examination of such a specimen by an experienced naturalist invariably revealed that its 'horn' was merely the quill of a porcupine or a spine from a long-spined species of hedgehog that had been carefully inserted and glued inside the serpent's head. I have also read of living specimens of supposed unicorn snakes, although I can't imagine that any snake would live very long if they had been subjected to such a barbaric treatment, because the inserted spine or quill would probably pierce their brain.

Worth noting is that there is a real species of snake that is sometimes dubbed the green unicorn. More commonly termed the rhinoceros rat snake *Rhynchophis boulengeri*, however, this green-scaled non-venomous colubrid from Vietnam and China earns its unicorn and rhino epithets from the very prominent, pointed, scaly protrusion borne upon the front of its snout like a small horn.

JOINT AND BRIMSTONE SNAKES

In his afore-mentioned *Scientific Monthly* article of January 1949 dealing with a wide range of American mythical snakes, Clifford B. Moore included a brief mention of the joint snake:

> In the case of the "glass," or "joint," snake we have, in the popular mind, a serpent which, like no other animal, has the ability to break up its body into small pieces, reassemble itself at its convenience, and resume a normal existence.
>
> From a colonial traveller and writer we learn that the brimstone snakes of North Carolina, being brittle as glass, were easily broken; but, according to a North Carolina doctor, "several in these parts confidently affirm, that if they remain in the same place untouch'd, they will joyn [sic] together again."

As noted by Moore, however, this fable no doubt stems from observations of *Ophisaurus ventralis*, the real American glass snake. In reality, however, this species is not a snake at all but instead a very serpentine legless lizard, which when attacked or threatened by a predator will often shed its tail.

Moreover, the shed tail can in turn break into several sections, and all of these will move and flex independently of one another for a while, due to their internal muscles. While the predator is bemused by these animated segments, the glass snake can make its

24 | IMPOSSIBLE SNAKES

Unicorn snake—a digital recreation (© Dr Karl Shuker)

Rhinoceros rat snake *Rhynchophis boulengeri*, showing its distinctive snout horn

American glass snake *Ophisaurus ventralis*, with broken tail (Semiv87, CC BY-SA 4.0)

escape and will subsequently regenerate its tail, although the new one tends to be shorter than the original, and different in colour too.

THE SNOW SNAKE—A COLD-BLOODED DECEPTION IN EVERY SENSE!

Much more modern but no less a hoax is the North American snow snake. The lumberjacks, hillbillies, cowboys, and other frontier folk of the early American West created a fascinating, entirely original world of folklore, inhabited by all manner of extraordinary creatures. Many of these were potentially very dangerous, and were known collectively as 'fearsome critters'. Happily, however, they were also entirely imaginary, and in 1939 their tall tales were collated by Henry H. Tryon into a delightful compendium duly entitled *Fearsome Critters*.

One of the most ingenious members of this fictitious fauna was the snow snake—a very singular species that, uniquely among snakes, had evolved to withstand with ease even the coldest of environmental temperatures. According to frontier folklore, it had originated in Siberia, but crossed into Alaska many moons ago when the Bering Strait was frozen over during an exceptionally severe winter. Since then, this white-scaled serpentine invader, measuring 3-6 ft long, with eyes that are typically transparent like shards of ice but can glow pinkish-red when irritated, has spread south and now exists in a number of other US states too, including Michigan, Pennsylvania, and Ohio, as well as Manitoba in Canada.

During the summer months, the snow snake remains hidden underground in a state of dormancy or hibernation known as brumation. Once winter begins, however, it emerges onto the surface and remains concealed in low-lying snow drifts, coiled and waiting for prey victims to walk by—whereupon it lunges at them with jaws open. A single bite will inflict sufficient venom to kill even sizeable animals as well as humans (such as unsuspecting skiers and snowboarders), by rapidly freezing their blood and reducing their body temperature until they succumb to hypothermia. However, tanglefoot oil is reputedly effective as a remedy—or at least it may well be if it actually existed, but of course it doesn't, being just as fictitious as the deadly snow snake itself.

During 2014 a short report of unknown origin and authorship circulated widely online, imploring its readers to beware of emerging snow snakes, even claiming that three (unnamed) people had already been bitten by these devastating reptiles. Moreover, the report included a good-quality colour photograph of one such snake—such good quality, in fact, that close examination of it swiftly revealed that the depicted snake was not real but rubber. It was some child's rubber toy snake!

Needless to say, all of the claims made for the snow snake are total nonsense. Yes, there are white snakes, and even (among albino specimens) white individuals with pinkish-red eyes. Due to their poikilothermic ('cold-blooded') physiology, however, no species of snake (whether in Siberia, North America, or anywhere else for that matter) could be exclusively active in cold, snowy conditions, because they require external heat to maintain their normal body temperature as they are incapable of maintaining it endothermically. [NB—A few atypical cases of snakes active in snow are on file, including an illustrated article in *The Field* for 6 October 1945, in which Bernard Gooch recalled photographing common adders *Vipera berus* basking in the sun amid snow on Dartmoor in southwestern England, but the prevailing temperature of 49°F (9.5°C) as measured by Gooch was clearly well above freezing point.] No species of snake (or any other animal), moreover, possesses venom that freezes its victim's blood and lowers their body temperature to a hypothermic level if bitten by this snake.

Although undoubtedly novel, the snow snake is also unquestionably a hoax, yet another pseudo-serpent—and one whose contemporary presence online clearly indicates that the human imagination is still very much intrigued (if not mesmerised) by the concept of impossible snakes.

The rubber snow snake (USC Title 17 § 107)

ANTS THAT SNARE AND FEED— THEN FEED UPON—SNAKES?

The final case reported here is one that provides a major twist on the subject of impossible snakes, inasmuch as in this instance it's not the snakes that are seemingly impossible, but rather the bizarre scenario in which they find themselves.

While perusing online some 19th-Century back-numbers of the *Antananarivo Annual and Madagascar Magazine* (a yearly periodical that has proved very fruitful in providing me with fascinating but hitherto obscure, cryptozoologically-unreported material concerning Madagascan mystery beasts), I chanced upon a truly weird report regarding ants and snakes. Appearing in this periodical's Christmas

1875 issue, it consisted of the following account, from an article written by Madagascan traveller/clergyman Rev. H.W. Grainge and entitled 'Journal of a visit to Mojanga and the north-west coast':

> We also noticed about this part a large number of earthen mounds, varying from one to two and a half feet in height; these were the nest of a large ant credited by the men with uncommon sagacity. We were told that they make regular snake traps in the lower part of these nests; easy enough for the snake to enter, but impossible for it to get out of. When one is caught the ants are said to treat it with great care, bringing it an abundant and regular supply of food, until it becomes fat enough for their purpose; and then, according to native belief, it is killed and eaten by them.

(Mojanga is nowadays known as Mahajanga, or Majunga in French—Madagascar is a former French colony; these names are applied to both a city and an administrative district on Madagascar's northwest coast.)

Rev. Grainge's macabre little vignette attracted the attention of a reader named R. Toy, who duly quoted it exactly a year later, in the Christmas 1876 issue of the *Antananarivo Annual and Madagascar Magazine* (incidentally, despite checking through every succeeding volume of this periodical, and widely elsewhere online too, I have not uncovered any additional reports). He then appended his own equally interesting first-hand experiences concerning this very curious affair:

> It would be interesting if some missionary living in the country would test the reality of this reputed fact by digging open a few of these nests. There is no doubt but that the belief is most universal among the natives. I have been assured most confidently over and over again that it is a fact that snakes are kept and fattened by the ants as above described; and knowing the sagacity of ants, and the care they take in feeding the aphides for the sake of their honey, one would not hastily set aside the statement, so generally accepted by the natives, as devoid of truth.

Needless to say, just because a belief is widespread does not necessarily make it true, as the exceedingly widespread yet wholly fallacious belief in hoop snakes, for instance, readily demonstrates (see Chapter 3). Equally, however, as noted by Toy, the farming and milking of aphids by ants for their secretions is well documented.

So too is their rearing within their nests the caterpillars of the large blue *Phengaris arion*, a Eurasian species of lycaenid butterfly. (Although in this instance, the ants are the unsuspecting victims of a lepidopteran version of brood parasitism, with the large blue's caterpillars actually acting as predators after having tricked the ants via morphological and pheromonal mimicry tactics into carrying them inside their nests, then feeding them there; the caterpillars also take the opportunity to prey upon the ants' own pupae).

Even so, it is an immense step up, behaviourally speaking, from ants feeding 'cuckoo' caterpillars that they have been tricked into bringing inside their nests to ants purposefully trapping snakes inside their nests, then fattening them up, before killing them specifically to devour them. Such a highly advanced strategy has no readily apparent, direct parallels elsewhere in the ant, or indeed in the entire insect, world—or does it? Read on.

In August 2019, a trio of Japanese researchers who included Teppei Jono published a fascinating *Royal Society Open Science* paper revealing two very different but closely interacting relationships between a species of Madagascan myrmicine ant *Aphaenogaster swammerdami* and two species of snake, all of which was hitherto unsuspected by science and unequivocally novel. The snakes are a large ant-eating blindsnake called Mocquard's worm snake *Madatyphlops decorsei*, and an even larger snake-eating (ophiophagous) lampropheid called the Malagasy cat-eyed snake *Madagascarophis colubrinus* (also known locally as the ant mother—see later). According to a publicity release issued on *Scimex* when this paper was published:

> A Madagascan ant species can tell whether marauding snakes are friend or foe. When ant-eating blind snakes approach an ant nest, the worker ants run back to evacuate their young, leaving a few behind to mount a biting attack on the intruder. But they also have a second line of defence. The ants allow one of the few known predators of the blindsnake—a

snake-eating snake—into their nest, in what the authors say is a symbiotic relationship where the ants get protection and the snake gets a cosy place to hide. Instead of biting the snake-eating snake when it approaches, the ants touch them with their antenna—a well-known form of communication between ants.

In the past, differences in reactions by ants to other species had only occurred relative to different insect predators or aggressors. Consequently, as noted by York University researcher Dr Eleanor Drinkwater in a *Naked Scientists* website interview on 20 August 2019, this study by Jono *et al.* might be the first to show that ants react differently to different vertebrate predators too. When the researchers conducted experiments to determine the ants' reactions to these snakes, presenting to various nests of this ant species a specimen of each of the two snakes plus one of a third, control snake species, the ants ignored the ant mother snake, but attacked the blindsnake and also the control snake. However, the only snake that sent the ants fleeing back inside their nest to evacuate it was the blindsnake.

Ant mother *Madagascarophis colubrinus*
(Dawson, CC BY-SA 2.5)

Reading this remarkable discovery has made me wonder whether it may have influenced the native Madagascan belief in ants trapping, fattening up, and then killing snakes. After all, the reason why the local tribespeople refer to *M. colubrinus* as the ant mother is that they are well aware of its frequent presence around the nests of this particular species of ant, and that it preys upon the blindsnakes preying upon the ants, thereby indirectly protecting the ants. Also, the nests of some *Aphaenogaster* ants are funnel-shaped and deep, conceivably giving a false impression that they have been specially created as inescapable traps for snaring creatures. (It is possible that in certain Australian *Aphaenogaster* species, their nests' funnel-shaped entrances do act as traps for surface foraging arthropods.)

Could it be, therefore, that the locals knew of the ants' different specific reactions to these two snakes too, long before the researchers scientifically revealed them recently, but that down through many generations of verbal retellings the true nature of these reactions and also of their nests had become distorted and elaborated upon, eventually yielding an imaginative but wholly incorrect scenario whereby the ants do not merely attack the blindsnakes but actually trap, feed, and then feed upon them?

After all, it wouldn't be the first time that garbled, orally-transmitted recollections of elusive animals and unusual animal behaviour by non-scientific observers has resulted in the evolution of memorable yet entirely erroneous folk beliefs—which in turn is as fitting a way as any to bring to a close not just this chapter but also this entire book, devoted as it is to secret snakes and serpent surprises.

25
VENOMOUS VERSES—
A SELECTION OF MY
SERPENT-INSPIRED POETRY

> Gazing through unblinking incarnadine eyes
> And intimately ensheathed in cerulean scales,
> The blue serpent watches long, and waits longer,
> For of what little concern to it is time,
> When the azure sky and the glaucous sea
> Are its infinite dominions to rule through all eternity?
>
> Karl Shuker—'Blue Serpent', in *More Star Steeds and Other Dreams*

Running parallel with my lifelong passion for cryptozoological research and documentation has been an equally longstanding enthusiasm for writing poetry. Its inspiration has been as varied as its output, which includes a number of serpent-themed compositions, some of which have appeared in two published volumes of my poetry—*Star Steeds and Other Dreams* (2009), and *More Star Steeds and Other Dreams* (2015).

Consequently, no comprehensive compilation of my ophidian offerings, whose contents are drawn from the entire spectrum of my published writings down through the past four decades, could be complete without containing at least a few of my snake poems—so here they are.

Our innermost emotions can assume many forms, but, hopefully, none as tangibly malevolent as the version described here—ophiophobes, look away now!

GREEN SNAKE

Well I know you, gleaming Green Snake,
Brightly wrapped in shining mail.
Well I know your silent movement,
Gliding forth on glinting scales,

To your unsuspecting victim
Sleeping peacefully in bed,
As your forked tongue whispers softly
Through the dreams that fill his head.

Now your coils enfold him tightly
In a feverish embrace,
And a potent stream of venom
Drips like fire upon his face

As your toxic tongue still murmurs
Like a wind through silent leaves,
Infiltrating his subconscious,
Till inside his mind it weaves

Webs of Doubt and Greed and Envy,
Soon eclipsing Love and Bliss,
Turning Beauty into Hatred—
Strong and deadly is your kiss.

And when morning comes, your victim
Rises full of Rage and Spite,
Hurting others with his cruelty,
Setting Love and Peace alight

By the flame of Hate inside him
That one day, his heart, will take.
Yes, I know you well of old—for
You are Jealousy, Green Snake.

The concept of Quetzalcoatl—an Aztec serpent god adorned with feathers rather than scales, and gifted with the ability to soar majestically through the heavens without needing wings—is one that has long fascinated me, so it was inevitable that sooner or later I would attempt to capture the wonder of this spectacular ophidian deity in verse.

QUETZALCOATL

Green feathered serpent like Heaven's liana,
Plumes of bright malachite, jasper, and jade,
Furled in bright flourishes, dazzling in glory,
Verdurous rays borne on emerald blades.

And, as you gleam in your jewel-clustered temple,
Coils gliding over your tributes of gold,
Ruby eyes glow with the flames of the cosmos,
Deadly yet passionate, blazing but cold.

Now, as your lightning-forked tongue flickers brightly,
Sibilant breath hissing softly and long,
Bowing before you in rapt veneration
Kneel your disciples in reverent throngs.

Yet, do you laugh at these weak, puny mortals,
Scuttling like ants in the fire of your gaze,
Shielding their eyes in the depths of your shadow—
Turquoise and terrible, willing their praise?

Quetzalcoatl—reptilian idol,
Soaring through Space like a radiant stream.
Aztec divinity, ageless, eternal—
Incarnate god, or a deified dream?

As a child, one of my favourite stories in Rudyard Kipling's Second Jungle Book *was 'The King's Ankus', featuring an agèd white cobra guarding a priceless but long-abandoned treasure trove of untold riches concealed amid the depths of the jungle. Here is my tribute to that still-proud yet etiolated ophidian warden.*

THE WHITE COBRA

Here, 'midst the heat and the steam of the jungle,
I see you, white worm, embittered by hate.
Ruby-fire eyes glowing brightly as embers,
Deep in the darkness, they watch and they wait.

So you persist, poisoned guardian of treasures
Hidden below in your caverns of gloom,
Vaults long abandoned, avoided, forgotten.
Now your pale presence embodies their doom.

No-one dares venture to pillage or plunder,
Still are the caskets encrusted with gold,
Scattered the gemstones like stars cast from Heaven—
Gifts for the gods that no mortal shall hold.

Yet should men find you, encoiled in the silence,
Then would they see that your power long has gone—
Empty the sockets where fangs once bled venom,
Withered by age, only pride lingers on.

Older than time are you, impotent serpent,
Spanning the ages no others shall see,
White as the sun that has bleached you forever,
Ivory sentinel, ever to be

Hooded and poised, though the world has passed by
   you,
Dust and decay wait upon you in thrall.
Yet you live on, with that chill heart still beating.
Life holds scant terror; and death, none at all.

SELECT BIBLIOGRAPHY

Anon., 'Serpents in a Pile in South America' (*Scientific American*, vol. 3, 1848), p.147.
Anon., [Algerian hairy viper] (*The Observer*, London, January 1852).
Anon., [Cefn winged snake] (*Worcester Chronicle*, Worcester, 23 June 1858).
Anon., 'A Pretty Fair Snake Story' (*Maitland Mercury and Hunter River General Advertiser*, Maitland, 8 November 1884).
Anon. [Lummis, C.F.], 'A Tiny Terror—America's Deadliest Snake is the Pichu-Cuate' (*Scottish Chief*, Maxton, NC, 27 June 1894).
Anon., 'Freak Serpent Specimen Found Near Lawton Mystifies Most Credulous' (*Daily News-Republican*, Lawton, OK, 12 September 1908).
Anon., 'Snakes–Snakes and No Jag [Lawton hairy snake]' (*Constitution-Democrat*, Lawton, OK, 17 September 1908).
Anon., '[Lawton hairy snake.]' (*Weekly Examiner*, Bartlesville, OK, 18 September 1908).
Anon., [Giant hairy Javan mystery snake] (*Kalamazoo Gazette*, Kalamazoo, MI, 5 August 1911).
Anon., 'Strange Kind of Snake is Cephalic Marvel' (*The Oregonian*, Portland, 13 August 1916).
Anon., 'The Flying Snake of Asia [including details of Mexican version]' (*The Oregonian*, Portland, 15 March 1942).
Anon., [Cobra playmate] (*Loris*, vol. 11, December 1967), pp.123-124.
Anon., 'Adder for a Playmate' (*Loris*, vol. 11, December 1967), p.124.
Anon., 'The Paraguayan "Barking Snake"' (*Pursuit*, vol. 6, January 1973), p.14.

Anon., *The Animals Who's Who* (Golden Hands Books, London, 1973).

Anon., *Serpent Worship* (Reprinted by Tutor [not Tudor] Press, Toronto, 1980).

Anon., [Hatfield and McCoy, two-headed snake] (*Santa Cruz Sentinel*, Santa Cruz, CA, 13 September 1983), p.27.

Anon., 'Yowling Sid [miaowing cave racer]' (*BBC Wildlife*, vol. 2, April 1984), p.173.

Anon., 'Fiery 2-Headed Snake Upsets Behavior Theory' (*Washington Post*, Washington, 6 February 1989).

Anon., '2-Headed Snake Tries to Share' (*Columbus Dispatch*, Columbus, OH, 21 February 1989).

Anon., 'Conjoined Crocodiles' (*Fortean Times*, no. 151, October 2001), p.11.

Anon., 'Mysterious Bogs Pose Lethal Danger to Russian Mushroom-Pickers [Russian flying snakes]' (*Pravda*, http://English.pravda.ru/science/19/94/378/16500_snake.html 21 November 2005).

Anon., 'Snakes and Serpents [misidentification of fossil *Lepidodendron* trunk as fossil snake at Neath exhibition, 1851]' (*Natural History Museum* (London), https://web.archive.org/web/20120816212754/http://www.nhm.ac.uk/nature-online/earth/fossils/fossil-folklore/themes/myths04.htm accessed 12 August 2012).

Anon., '"They Both Seem to Control It": Family Finds Snake with TWO HEADS—One on Each End of Its Body' (*Daily Mail*, London, https://www.dailymail.co.uk/news/article-2207659/Family-finds-snake-heads--EACH-END-body.html 24 September 2012).

Anon., 'Rikki-Tikki-Tavi Characters' (*Litcharts*, https://www.litcharts.com/lit/rikki-tikki-tavi/characters accessed 24 March 2019).

Anon., 'Unholy Snake-Ant Alliance Keeps Ants Safe from Predators' (*Scimex*, https://www.scimex.org/newsfeed/unholy-snake-ant-alliance-keeps-ants-safe-from-predators 20 August 2019).

Abdulali, H., 'Can Snakes Produce Vocal Sounds?' (*Journal of the Bombay Natural History Society*, vol. 55, no. 3, 1959), pp.578-579.

Abdulali, H., 'Can Snakes Produce Vocal Sounds?' (*Journal of the Bombay Natural History Society*, vol. 57, no. 1, 1960), pp.225-226.

Aflalo, F.G., *A Sketch of the Natural History (Vertebrates) of the British Islands* (William Blackwood and Sons, London, 1892).

Aldrovandi, U., *Historia Serpentum et Draconum* (Bologna, 1640).

Allen, A., "You Spotted Snakes with Double Tongue" (*The Countryman*, no. 3, autumn 1979), pp.80-83.

BIBLIOGRAPHY

Allen, A., 'The Case of the Two-Headed Snake' (*The Countryman*, vol. 84, October-November 1990), pp.116-118.

Andersson, C.J., *Lake Ngami* (Hurst and Blackett, London, 1856).

Andrews, R.C., *On the Trail of Ancient Man* (G.P. Putnam's Sons, London, 1926).

Arment, C., *Cryptozoology: Science and Speculation* (Coachwhip Publications, Landisville, 2004).

Arment, C., 'Mystery Reptiles of the Samoan Islands' (*BioFortean Review*, http://www.strangeark.com/bfr-articles-2007 May 2007).

Arment, C., *Boss Snakes: Stories and Sightings of Giant Snakes in North America* (Coachwhip Publications, Landisville, 2008).

Arment, C., 'The Mystery of the Maltese Viper' (*ZooCreation*, http://www.zoocreation.com/the-maltese-viper 31 October 2021)

Aymar, B. (ed.), *Treasury of Snake Lore: From the Garden of Eden to Snakes of Today in Mythology, Fable, Stories, Essays, Poetry, Drama, Religion, and Personal Adventures* (Greenberg, New York, 1956).

Ayre, James, 'Snow Snake in Michigan, Ohio, & Pennsylvania—Is Deadly Snow-Living Snake Real? (+Ice Worms)' (*PlanetSave*, https://planetsave.com/2015/02/03/snow-snake-michigan-ohio-pennsylvania-deadly-snow-living-snake-real-ice-worms/ 3 February 2015).

Bankes, E.R., 'Small Red Viper' (*Dorset Natural History and Archaeological Society Proceedings*, vol. 27, 1906), pp.262-263.

Bankes, E.R., 'Small Red Viper' (*Dorset Natural History and Archaeological Society Proceedings*, vol. 29, 1908), p.284.

Beck, Daniel B., *Biology of Gila Monsters and Beaded Lizards* (University of California Press, Berkeley, 2005).

Beer, T., *Poachers Days* (Countryside Publications, Barnstaple, 1985).

Behrens, G.H., *Hercynia Curiosa oder Curiöser Hartz-Wald* (Neuenhahn, Nordhausen, 1703).

Behura, B.K., 'On the Vocal Sounds of Snakes' (*Journal of the Utkal University, Bhubaneswar*, vol. 2, no. 1, July 1962), pp.40-42.

Belfrage, J.H., 'Robin Fascinated by a Snake' (*The Zoologist*, vol. 19, 1861), p.7382.

Bennetts, J.A.W., 'The King of the Mambas' (*African Wild Life*, vol. 10, 1956), pp.335-336.

Berridge, W.S., *Animal Curiosities* (Thornton Butterworth, London, 1922).

Beverley, R., *History and Present State of Virginia* (Rev. Edit.) (London, 1722).

Bogert, C.M. and Martin Del Campo, R., 'The Gila Monster and Its Allies: The Relationships, Habits, and Behavior of the Lizards of the Family Helodermatidae' (*Bulletin of the American Museum of Natural History*, vol. 109, no. 1, 1956), pp.1-238.

Bond, H., 'Hedgesparrow Fascinated by a Snake' (*The Zoologist*, vol. 18, 1860), p.7273.

Bougon, ?., 'Les Serpents de Cent Vingt Pieds' (*Le Naturaliste, Séries 2*, vol. 23, 1901), pp.56-57.

Boulay, R.A., *Flying Serpents and Dragons: The Story of Mankind's Reptilian Past* (Rev. Edit.) (The Book Tree, Escondido, 1997).

Boulenger, E.G., *Animal Mysteries* (Duckworth, London, 1927).

Boulenger, G.A., 'An Investigation into the Variations of the Viper in Great Britain' (*The Zoologist, Third Series*, vol. 16, no. 183, March 1892), pp.87-93.

Broadley, D.G., 'The Black Mamba (*Dendroaspis polylepis polylepis*)' (*African Wild Life*, vol. 15, December 1961), pp.299-302.

Broadley, D.G., et al., *Snakes of Zambia* (Edition Chimaira, Frankfurt, 2003).

Brock, S.E., *More About Leemo* (Robert Hale, London, 1967).

Brockie, W., *Legends and Superstitions of the County of Durham* (B. Williams, Sunderland, 1886).

Brook, S., 'Rainbow Serpent Myth Comes to Life' (*The Australian*, Surry Hills, 27 January 2000).

Brown, R, et al., 'The amphibians and reptiles of Luzon Island, Philippines, VIII: The herpetofauna of Cagayan and Isabela Provinces, northern Sierra Madre Mountain Range' (*ZooKeys*, vol. 266, no. 1, 2013).

Browne, J., *An Affecting Narrative of the Extraordinary Adventures and Sufferings of Six Deserters from the Artillery of the Garrison of St. Helena, in the Year 1799. Delivered on Oath, Before a Court of Enquiry, Held at St. Helena, on the 12th of December, 1801* (J. Smeeton, London, 1802).

Buckland, F.T., *Curiosities of Natural History* (Richard Bentley, London, 1857).

Buckland, F.T., *Curiosities of Natural History* (3rd Edit.) (Richard Bentley, London, 1858).

Buckland F.[T.], *Log-Book of a Fisherman and Zoologist* (Chapman and Hall, London, 1875).

Burton, M., *More Animal Legends* (Frederick Muller, London, 1959).

Calvin, J., *Commentaries on the First Book of Moses Called Genesis* (Reprinted by William B. Eerdmans, Grand Rapids, 1948).

Capstick, P.H., *The African Adventurers* (St Martin's Press: New York, 1992).
Caras, R.A., *Dangerous to Man* (Holt, Rinehart and Winston, New York, 1964 and 1975).
Carse, D., 'A Snake's Call' (*The Times*, London, 5 October 1932).
Carter, C.W. and Earle, R., *The Acts of the Apostles* (Zondervan Publishing House, Grand Rapids, 1959).
Carwardine, M., *Natural History Museum Animal Records* (Natural History Museum, London, 2007).
Catesby, M., *The Natural History of Carolina, Florida and the Bahama Islands, Vol. 1* (Privately published, London, 1731).
Chapman, J., 'Snakes with Legs that May Have Walked in the Garden of Eden' (*Daily Mail*, London, 17 March 2000), p.37.
Chapman, P., 'Cave-frequenting Vertebrates in the Gunung Mulu National Park, Sarawak' (*Sarawak Museum Journal, New Series*, vol. 34, December 1985), pp.101-113.
Charlie, 'Rare and Cryptid Snakes, #21' (*Aussie Pythons & Snakes*, https://www.aussiepythons.com/threads/rare-and-cryptid-snakes.73814/page-2#post-1058858 24 January 2008).
Chippaux, J.P., et al., 'Study of the Efficacy of the Black Stone on Envenomation by Snake Bite in the Murine Model' (*Toxicon*, vol. 49, no. 5, April 2007) pp.717-720.
Clark, L., *The Rivers Ran East* (Hutchinson, London, 1954).
Cloudsley-Thompson, J.L., 'Reptiles that Jump and Fly' (*British Herpetological Society Bulletin*, no. 55, 1996), pp.35-39.
Cohen, J., *Human Robots in Myth and Science* (George Allen and Unwin, London, 1966).
Conan Doyle, A., 'Adventures of Sherlock Holmes. VIII—The Adventure of the Speckled Band' (*Strand Magazine*, vol. 3, February 1892), pp.142-157.
Cordier, C., 'Animaux Inconnus du Congo' (*Zoo*, vol. 38, April 1973), pp.185-191.
Corkill, N.L., 'Vocal Sounds from Snakes' (*Journal of the Bombay Natural History Society*, vol. 56, no. 2, 1959), p.350.
Corliss, W.R., *Strange Life* (The Sourcebook Project, Glen Arm MD, 1975).
Corliss, W.R., *Incredible Life: A Handbook of Biological Mysteries* (The Sourcebook Project, Glen Arm, MD, 1981).
Coudray, P., *Guide des Animaux Cachés* (Éditions Du Mont, Trace, 2009).
CSIRO, 'Ants Down Under: *Aphaenogaster* Mayr, 1853' (*CSIRO*, https://web.archive.org/web/20091009202418/http://anic.ento.csiro.au/ants/biota_details.aspx?BiotaID=38379 accessed 11 October 2021).

Cunningham, B., 'Two-Headed Snakes' (*Scientific Monthly*, vol. 25, 1927), pp.559-562.

Cunningham, B., 'Amphicephalous Reptiles. Animals Reputed to Have a Head at Each End of the Body' (*Scientific Monthly*, vol. 37, 1933), pp.511-521.

Curran, B., *Man-Made Monsters: A Field Guide to Golems, Patchwork Soldiers, Homunculi, and Other Created Creatures* (New Page Books, Pompton Plains, 2011).

Davies, G.E., 'Purring Snakes' (*The Times*, London, 2 September 1929).

Davy, J., *An Account of the Interior of Ceylon, and of Its Inhabitants* (Longman, Hurst, Rees, Orme, and Brown, London, 1821).

De Sarre, F., 'Are There Still Dragons in Central France?' (*INFO Journal*, no. 71, autumn 1994), pp.44-45.

Denis, A., *On Safari* [book] (Collins, London, 1963).

Denis, A., and Denis, M., *On Safari* [LP] (Pye Records, London, 1962).

Dethier, M. and Dethier-Sakamoto, A., 'The *Tzuchinoko*, an Unidentified Snake from Japan' (*Cryptozoology*, vol. 6, 1987), pp.40-48.

Dickinson, P., 'Snakes Alive [naturalised Aesculapian snakes in UK]' (*BBC Wildlife*, vol. 2, no. 9, September 1984), p.430.

Dinsdale, T., *The Leviathans* (Routledge and Kegan Paul, London, 1966; 2nd Edit., Futura, London, 1976).

Ditmars, R.L., *Snakes of the World* (Macmillan, New York, 1931).

Downes, J., 'A Study in Scarlet' (*Still On The Track*, http://forteanzoology.blogspot.com/2009/02/study-in-scarlet.html 12 February 2009).

Drinkwater, E., 'Ants Befriend Snakes to Fight Foes' (*The Naked Scientists*, https://www.thenakedscientists.com/articles/interviews/ants-befriend-snakes-fight-foes 20 August 2019).

Duff, H.L., *Nyasaland Under the Foreign Office* (George Bell and Sons, London, 1903).

Duff, H.[L.], 'Purring Snakes' (*The Times*, London, 27 August 1929).

Duncan, P.M. (ed.), *Cassell's Natural History*, 6 vols (Cassell, Petter, and Galpin, London, 1883-1889).

Eberhart, G.M., *Mysterious Creatures: A Guide to Cryptozoology*, 2 vols (ABC-Clio, Santa Barbara, 2002; Rev. Edit., CFZ Press, Bideford, 2013).

EsoterX, 'Muppet Theology: It's Not Easy Being Glycon' (*EsoterX*, 1 March 2015).

Falsani, C., 'Genesis of This Serpent's Tale is Unbelievable [Eden Serpent skin]' (*Chicago Sun-Times*, 10 October 2003).

Fawcett, P.H., *Exploration Fawcett* (Hutchinson, London, 1953).

Fink, H.M., *Verzaubertes Land: Volkskult und Ahnenbrauch in Südtirol* (Tyrolia Verlag, Innsbruck, 1969).

Fitzsimons, F.W., *Snakes* (Hutchinson, London, 1932).

Fitzsimons, V.F.M., *Snakes of Southern Africa* (Purnell and Sons, Cape Town/Johannesburg, 1962).

Frazer, D., *Reptiles and Amphibians in Britain* (Collins, London, 1983).

Freeman, D., '"Belling Snakes"' (*The Times*, London, 27 September 1932).

Freeman, R., 'In the Coils of the Naga' (*Fortean Times*, no. 166, January 2003), pp.30-35.

Gaebelein, F.E. (ed.), *The Expositor's Bible Commentary* (Zondervan, Grand Rapids, 1990).

Gardner, J.B., 'A Ball of Gartersnakes' (*Copeia*, 1955), p.310.

Gardner, J.B., 'A Garter Snake "Ball"' (*Copeia*, 1957), p.48.

Gemmill, J.F., *The Teratology of Fishes* (James Maclehose and Sons, Glasgow, 1912).

Geniez, P., *Snakes of Europe, North Africa and the Middle East* (Princeton University Press, Princeton, 2018).

Göksu, I., 'Flying Snakes of Bulgaria' (*Fortean Times*, no. 78, December 1994/January 1995), p.57.

Gooch, B., 'Adders in the Snow' (*The Field*, 6 October 1945), pp.343-344.

Gorman, P., 'Charmed I'm Sure' (*Mail on Sunday—YOU Magazine*, London, 11 June 1989), pp.24-26.

Goss, M., 'Flying Snakes and Winged Serpents' (*The Unknown*, no. 18, December 1986), pp.10-15.

Gosse, P.H., *The Romance of Natural History, Second Series* (Nisbet and Co., London, 1867).

Grainge, H.W., 'Journal of a Visit to Mojanga and the North-West Coast' (*Antananarivo Annual and Madagascar Magazine*, no. 1, Christmas 1875), pp. 12-35.

Green, R.L., *Myths from Many Lands* (Purnell, London, 1965).

Hadfield, P., 'Is It a Bird? Is It a Plane? No One Knows [*tzuchinoko*]' (*South China Morning Post*, Hong Kong, 6 September 2000).

Hardy, R.W.H., *Travels in the Interior of Mexico, in 1825, 1826, 1827, & 1828* (Henry Colburn and Richard Bentley, London, 1829).

Hartline, P.H., 'Physiological Basis for Detection of Sound and Vibration in Snakes' (*Journal of Experimental Biology*, vol. 54, 1971), pp.349-372.

Head, J.J., et al., 'Giant Boid Snake from the Palaeocene Neotropics Reveals Hotter Past Equatorial Temperatures [*Titanoboa*]' (*Nature*, vol. 457, 5 February 2009), pp.715-717.

Henry, M., *Complete Commentary on the Whole Bible, Vol. 1* (Fleming H. Revell, New York, 1708).

Heppell, D., 'Gigantic Serpent Really a Gastropod!' (*The Conchologists' Newsletter*, no. 16, March 1966), pp.108-109.

Hervey, D., '"Plotosus canius" and the "Snake-stone"' (*Nature*, vol. 62, 24 May 1900), p.79.

Heuvelmans, B., *On the Track of Unknown Animals* (Rupert Hart-Davis, London, 1958).

Heuvelmans, B., *Les Derniers Dragons d'Afrique* (Plon, Paris, 1978).

Heuvelmans, B., 'Annotated Checklist of Apparently Unknown Animals with which Cryptozoology is Concerned' (*Cryptozoology*, vol. 5, 1986), pp.1-26.

Hichens, W., 'African Mystery Beasts' (*Discovery*, vol. 18, December 1937), pp.369-373.

Hindle, E., 'John Graham Kerr, 1869-1957' (*Biographical Memoirs of Fellows of the Royal Society*, vol. 4, 1958), pp.155-166.

Hopley, C.C., *Snakes: Curiosities and Wonders of Serpent Life* (Griffith and Farran, London, 1882).

Hudson, W.H., *Far Away and Long Ago* (J.M. Dent and Sons, London, 1918).

Hutchinson, R.W., 'The Flying Snakes of Arabia' (*The Classical Quarterly*, vol. 8, 1958), pp.100-101.

Hyde, B.T.B., 'Two-Headed Snakes' (*Natural History*, vol. 25, March/April 1925), pp.185-187.

Idemizu, N., 'Bounty Put on Mythical Reptile (*Mainichi Shimbun*, 27 August 2000).

James, C. and Downes, J. (eds), *CFZ Expedition Report 2006 Gambia* (CFZ Press, Bideford, 2006).

James, G.P.L., 'Purring Snakes' (*The Times*, London, 31 August 1929), p.6.

Jefferies, R., *Wild Life in a Southern County* (Smith, Elder and Co, London, 1879).

Jeffreys, M.D.W., 'Snake Stones' (*Journal of the Royal African Society*, no. 41, October 1942), pp.250-253.

Jenkins, A.C. (ed.), *Animal Stories* (Blackie, London, 1967).

Jones, T.R., *A General Outline of the Animal Kingdom and Manual of Comparative Anatomy* (John Van Voorst, London, 1841).

Jono, T., et al., 'Novel Cooperative Antipredator Tactics of an Ant Specialized Against a Snake' (*Royal Society Open Science*, https://royalsocietypublishing.org/doi/10.1098/rsos.190283 14 August 2019).

Joth, G., 'The Word on That Tsuchinoko Specimen' (*cz@egroups.com*, 12 September 2000).

Kappeler, M., 'Der Haselwurm' (*Markus Keppeler*, https://web.archive.org/web/20190826023646/http://www.markuskappeler.ch/taz/frataz.html 26 August 2019).

Keil, C.F. and Delitzsch, F., *Biblical Commentary on the Old Testament, Vol. 1: The Pentaeuch* (William B. Eerdmans, Grand Rapids, 1866).

Kerr, J.G., '*Bothrodon pridii*, An Extinct Serpent of Gigantic Dimensions' (*Proceedings of the Royal Society of Edinburgh*, vol. 46, 1926), pp.314-315.

Kerr, J.G., *A Naturalist in Gran Chaco* (Cambridge University Press, Cambridge, 1950).

King, P.P., *Narrative of a Survey of the Intertropical and Western Coasts of Australia Between the Years 1818 and 1822* (Murray, London, 1827).

Kipling, R., *The Jungle Book* (Macmillan, London, 1894).

Klauber, L.M., 'The Truth about the Speckled Band' (*Baker Street Journal*, vol. 3, no, 2, 1948), pp.149-157.

Klinger, L.S. (ed.), *The New Annotated Sherlock Holmes*, 3 vols (W.W. Norton, New York, 2004-2005).

Knight, C., *Pictorial Museum of Animated Nature*, 2 vols (London Printing and Publishing Company, London, 1856-1858).

Knott, J., '"Crowing Snake"' (*African Wild Life*, vol. 16, September 1962), p.170.

Koens, J.H., 'Purring Snakes' (*The Times,* London, 26 August 1929).

Kuzmin, S.L. (ed.), *The Amphibians of Mongolia* (KMK Scientific Press, Moscow, 2017).

Kv, R., '5 Headed Snake Photoshop in 2 Minutes [video]' (*YouTube*, https://www.youtube.com/watch?v=_czlKY0jDK4 posted 20 June 2011).

'L., E.', 'Bundles of Snakes' (*American Naturalist,* vol. 14, 1880), pp.206-207.

Lawson, J., *A New Voyage to Carolina* (Privately published, London, 1709).

Lazell, J.D., '*Cryptophidion* is Not *Xenopeltis*' (*Cryptozoology*, vol. 12, 1993-1996), pp.101-102.

Leechman, A., 'A Purring Snake' (*The Times*, London, 24 August 1929).

Leighton, G.R., *The Life-History of British Serpents and Their Local Distribution in the British Isles* (William Blackwood and Sons: London, 1901).

Lhote, H. and Weyer, H., *Sahara* (Vilo, Paris, 1980).

Liath, C., *Der Grüne Hain* (Books on Demand, Norderstedt, 2012).

Livens, H.M., *Nomansland: A Village History* (*Salisbury Times and South Wilts Gazette*, Salisbury, 1910).

Lowe, W.P., *The Trail That is Always New* (Gurney and Jackson, London, 1932).

Lum, P., *Fabulous Beasts* (Thames and Hudson, London, 1951).

Lummis, C.F., *The King of the Broncos, and Other Stories of New Mexico* (C. Scribner's Sons, New York, 1897).

Lydekker, R., 'Musical Notes in Tortoises' (*The Field*, vol. 111, 27 June 1908), p.1117.

Lydekker, R. (ed.), *The Royal Natural History*, 6 vols (Frederick Warne, London, 1894—1896).

Mackal, R.P., *Searching for Hidden Animals: An Enquiry into Zoological Mysteries* (Doubleday, Garden City, 1980).

Mackerle, I., 'In Search of the Killer Worm of Mongolia' (*World Explorer*, vol. 1, no. 4, 1994), pp.62-65.

Mackerle, I., 'In Search of the Killer Worm' (*Fate*, vol. 49, June 1996), pp.22-27.

Macpherson, H.A., *A Vertebrate Fauna of Lakeland* (David Douglas, Edinburgh, 1892).

Maruna, S., 'The American Sârâph: An Unnatural History of Winged Snakes in North America', in: Heinselman, C. (ed.), *Elementum Bestia* (Lulu, 2007).

May, J. and Marten, M., *Animal Oddities* [aka *The Book of Beasts*] (Hamlyn Publishing Group, London, 1982).

Michell, J. and Rickard, R.J.M., *Living Wonders* (Thames and Hudson, London, 1982).

Miller, H., 'The Cobra, India's "Good Snake"' (*National Geographic*, vol. 138, no. 3, September 1970), pp.392-409.

Minton, S.A. and Heatwole, H., 'Snakes and the Sea' (*Oceans*, vol. 11, April 1978), pp.53-56.

Minton, S.A. and Minton, M.R., *Venomous Reptiles* (George Allen and Unwin, London, 1971).

Mitchill, S.L., [two-headed snakes] (*American Journal of Science, Series 1*, vol, 10, 1826), pp.48-53.

Moon, E.R., *I Saw Congo* (United Christian Missionary Society, Indianapolis, 1952).

Moore, C.B., 'America's Mythical Snakes' (*Scientific Monthly*, vol. 68, pt 1, January 1949), pp,52-58.

Moore, S., 'The Fake, the Snake, and the Sceptic [Glycon]' (*Fortean Times*, no. 276, June 2011), pp.46-51.

Moriarty, C., *Eels: A Natural and Unnatural History* (David and Charles, Newton Abbot, 1978).

Morris, H.M., *The Genesis Record: A Scientific and Devotional Commentary on the Book of Beginnings* (Baker Books, Ada, MI, 1976).

Morris, R., and Morris, D., *Men and Snakes* (Hutchinson, London, 1965).

Mudie, J., *Early Years: The Childhood of Famous People* (Purnell, London, 1966).

Muirhead, R., 'The Flying Snake of Namibia: An Investigation', in: Downes, J. (ed.), *CFZ Yearbook 1996* (CFZ, Exeter, 1995), pp.112-123.

Mulligan, J.H., 'Samoa: Government, Commerce, Products, and People' (Consular Reports, May 1896).

Murphy, J.C. and Henderson, R.W., *Tales of Giant Snakes: Historical Natural History of Anacondas and Pythons* (Krieger Publishing Company, Malabar, 1997).

Nakamura, K., 'Studies on Some Specimens of Double Monsters of Snakes and Tortoises' (*Memoirs of the College of Science, Kyoto Imperial University, Series B*, vol. 14, no, 2, 7 April 1938), pp.171-191.

Napier, E., *Scenes and Sports in Foreign Lands, Vol. 2* (Henry Colburn, London, 1840).

Netting, M.G. and Wilkes, D., 'Scorpion Stone—A Reputed Cure for Scorpion Sting and Snake Bite' (*Bulletin of the Antivenom Institute of America*, vol. 2, 1929), p.99.

Newton, M., *Encyclopedia of Cryptozoology: A Global Guide* (McFarland and Co, Jefferson, 2005).

Newton, M., *Giant Snakes: Unwravelling* [sic] *the Coils of Mystery* (CFZ Press, Bideford, 2009).

North, F.J., *Coal, and the Coalfields in Wales*, 2nd Edit. (National Museum of Wales, Cardiff, 1931).

O'Mannin, C., 'I Went Hunting for the Legendary Snakes of the West Coast Bush' (*The Spinoff*, https://thespinoff.co.nz/society/03-09-2020/i-went-hunting-for-the-legendary-snakes-of-the-west-coast-bush/ 3 September 2020).

O'Shea, M., *A Guide to the Snakes of Papua New Guinea* (Independent Publishing, Port Moresby, 1996).

Parker, F., *The Snakes of Western Province* (PNG Department of Lands & Environment, Port Moresby, 1982).

Pauwels, O. and Meirte, D., 'The Status of *Cryptophidion annamense*' (*Cryptozoology*, vol. 12, 1993-1996), pp.95-100.

Peaker, M., 'Not a Giant Snake—Just a Broken Mollusc Shell. Sir John Graham Kerr's Howler: How was the Misidentification Perpetuated?' (*Zoology Jottings*, https://zoologyweblog.blogspot.com/2018/03/not-giant-snake-just-broken-mollusc.html 27 March 2018).

Pearse, R., '[Transcription of A.M. Harmon's published translation and notes from 1936 of:] 'Alexander the False Prophet' by Lucian of Samosata' (*Tertullian*, https://www.tertullian.org/rpearse/lucian/lucian_alexander.htm 31 August 2001).

Pennant, T., *British Zoology, Vol. 3* (Benjamin White, London. 1769).

Petzoldt, L., *Kleines Lexikon der Dämonen und Elementargeister* (C.H. Beck, Munich, 2003).

Philipps, T., 'A Purring Snake' (*The Times,* London, 22 August 1929).

Philipps, T., 'A Purring Snake' (*The Times,* London, 30 December 1929).

Philipps, T., '"Belling" Snakes—the Puff Adder's Call to Its Mate' (*The Times*, London, 7 September 1932).

Pitman, C.R.S., *Report on a Faunal Survey of Northern Rhodesia* (Crown Agents, London, 1934).

Pitman, C.R.S., *A Game Warden Takes Stock* (James Nisbet, London, 1942).

Powney, N., 'Giant Caterpillar' (*Fortean Times*, no. 225, special issue 2007), p.72.

Pymm, R., 'Snakestone Bead Folklore' (*Folklore*, vol. 129, no. 4, https://www.tandfonline.com/doi/full/10.1080/0015587x.2018.1515171 21 December 2018).

Quenstedt, W., [Footnote, re *Bothrodon*, to p.28 of Ophidia, in:], Kuhn, O., 'Squamata, Lacertilia et Ophidia', in: Quenstedt, W. (ed.), *Fossilium Catalogus, vol. 1: Animalia* (W. Junk, 's-Gravenhage, 1939).

Rabanser, H., *Hexenwahn: Schicksale und Hintergründe. Die Tiroler Hexenprozesse* (Haymon Verlag, Innsbruck, 2018).

Rabinowitz, A., *Beyond the Last Village: A Journey of Discovery in Asia's Forbidden Wilderness* (Island Press, Washington D.C., 2001).
Radcliffe, J., [Definition of Karait] (*The Kipling Society*, https://www.kiplingsociety.co.uk/readers-guide/rg_braz4.htm 2009).
Radner, K., 'The Winged Snakes of Arabia and the Fossil Site of Makhtesh Ramon in the Negev' (*Wiener Zeitschrift für die Kunde des Morgenlandes*, vol. 97, 2007), pp.353-365.
Randolph, V., *We Always Lie to Strangers* (Columbia University Press, New York, 1951).
Read, J.L., *Red Sand, Green Heart: Ecological Adventures in the Outback* (Lothian, South Melbourne, 2003).
Redfern, N., 'The Beast of Bodalog Remembered' (*There's Something in the Woods . . .*, http://monsterusa.blogspot.com/2010/05/beast-of-bodalog-remembered.html 29 May 2010).
Reuss, F.A.T., 'Humming Snakes of North America' (*Herpetologica*, vol. 7, 1951), p.144.
Russell, T.O., 'Like a Cow's Tail' (*Nature's Realm*, vol. 2, February 1891), p.74.

Scanlon, J.D. and Lee, M.S.Y., 'The Pleistocene Serpent *Wonambi* and the Early Evolution of Snakes' (*Nature*, vol. 403, 27 January 2000), pp.416-420.
Schmidt, K.P., 'The Hoop Snake Story' (*Natural History*, vol. 25, 1925), pp.76-80.
Schneider, J.G.T., *Historiae Amphibiorum Naturalis et Literariae Fasciculus Secundus Continens Crocodilos, Scincos, Chamaesauras, Boas, Pseudoboas, Elaps, Angues, Amphisbaenas et Caecilias*) (F. Frommanni, Jena, 1801).
Scott, M., 'Tradescant and Ashmole' (*Strange Science—Goof Gallery*, http://www.strangescience.net/tradash.htm 14 June 2015).
Shircore, J.O., 'Two Notes on the Crowing Crested Cobra' (*African Affairs*, vol. 43, 1944), pp.183-186.
Shuker, K.P.N., 'Mongolian Death Worm—A Shocking Secret Beneath The Gobi Sands?' (*Strange Magazine*, no. 16, fall 1995), pp.31-32, 48.
Shuker, K.P.N., *Dragons: A Natural History* (Aurum Press, London, 1995).
Shuker, K.P.N., 'A Flight of Fancy? [Namibian flying snake]' (*Wild About Animals*, vol. 8, January 1996), p.13.
Shuker, K.P.N., 'Do Nomads Dream of Electric Worms?', in: McNally, J. and Wallis, J. (eds), *Fortean Times Weird Year 1996* (John Brown Publishing, London, 1996), pp.46-47.
Shuker, K.P.N., 'Mongolia's Death Worm: The Shocking Saga' (*Uri Geller's Encounters*, no. 4, February 1997), pp.42-46.

Shuker, K.P.N., 'Meet Mongolia's Death Worm: The Shock of the New' (*Fortean Studies*, vol. 4, 1997), pp.190-218.

Shuker, K.P.N., *From Flying Toads to Snakes with Wings: From the Pages of Fate Magazine* (Llewellyn Press: St Paul, 1997).

Shuker, K.P.N., 'Sarajevo's Jumping Snake' (*Fortean Times*, no. 123, June 1999), p.46.

Shuker, K.P.N., 'Death Worms of the Desert' (*The X Factor*, no. 87, 2000), pp.2431-2435.

Shuker, K.P.N., 'Loco for a Tzuchinoko' (*Fortean Times*, no. 142, February 2001), p.45.

Shuker, K.P.N., *The Hidden Powers of Animals* (Marshall Editions, London, 2001).

Shuker, K.P.N., *The Beasts that Hide from Man: Seeking the World's Last Undiscovered Animals* (Paraview, New York, 2003).

Shuker, K.P.N., *Dr Shuker's Casebook: In Pursuit of Marvels and Mysteries* (CFZ Press, Bideford, 2008).

Shuker, K.P.N., *Karl Shuker's Alien Zoo: From the Pages of Fortean Times* (CFZ Press, Bideford, 2010).

Shuker, K.P.N., *Dragons in Zoology, Cryptozoology, and Culture* (Coachwhip Publications, Greenville, 2013).

Shuker, K.P.N., *The Menagerie of Marvels. A Third Compendium of Extraordinary Animals* (CFZ Press: Bideford, 2014).

Shuker, K.P.N., *A Manifestation of Monsters: Examining the (Un)Usual Subjects* (Anomalist Books: San Antonio, 2015).

Shuker, K.P.N., *More Star Steeds and Other Dreams: The Collected Poems—2015 Expanded Edition* (Fortean Words, Bideford, 2015).

Simmons, M., 'Deadly Pichu-Cuate Stalks NM Folklore' (*El Paso Times*, El Paso, 6 May 1984).

Smith, A., *Illustrations of the Zoology of South Africa, Vol. I* (Smith, Elder, and Co., London, 1838).

Smyth, J.F.D., *Tour in the United States of America, Vol. 1* (Privately published, London, 1784).

Snopes Staff, 'Is This a 'Snow Snake'?' (*Snopes*, https://www.snopes.com/fact-check/snow-snake/ 3 March 2014).

Steinberger, A.B., *Report on Samoa* (GPO, Washington D.C., 1874).

Stewart, C.M.D., 'The Ndhlondhlo' (*The Zoologist*, 4th Series, vol. 11, May 1907), pp.183-187.

Stoneham, C.T., *Hunting Wild Beasts with Rifle and Camera* (Hutchinson, London, 1933).

StrangeArk, 'StrangeArk Field Notes: The Somersaulting Snake' *(YouTube,* https://www.youtube.com/watch?v=PWUCPw2x32M uploaded 15 May 2019).

Strickland, H.E., 'A Notice Concerning the Red Viper (*Cóluber chersèa* Lin.)' (*Magazine of Natural History*, vol. 6, 1833), pp.399-400.

Strohl, J., 'Les Serpents a Deux Têtes et les Serpents Doubles' (*Annales des Sciences Naturelles Zoologie, Série 10*, vol. 8, 1925), pp.105-132.

Sucik, N., 'Exploring the Prospect of an Unidentified Species of Reptile within Navajo and Hopi Lands' (*Yumpu*, https://www.yumpu.com/en/document/read/377836/exploring-the-prospect-of-an-unidentified-species-of-reptile-within- written April 2004).

Sutherland, J., *The Adventures of an Elephant Hunter* (Macmillan, London, 1912).

Swain, G., 'Riddle of Killer in the River [beast of Bodalog]' (*Daily Mail*, London, 10 October 1988).

Taffs, A. (ed.), *The World of Wonders: A Record of Things Wonderful in Nature, Science, and Art* (Cassell, Petter, and Galpin, London, 1881-1882).

Tennent, J.E., *Sketches of the Natural History of Ceylon* (Longman, Green, Longman, and Roberts, London, 1861).

Tissot, C., *Exploration Scientifique de la Tunisie*, 2 vols (Imprimerie Nationale, Paris, 1884, 1888).

Topham, I., 'The Double-Headed Snake of Newbury' (*Mysterious Britain & Ireland*, https://www.mysteriousbritain.co.uk/cryptozoology/the-double-headed-snake-of-newbury/ 2 October 2008, updated 17 November 2018).

Toy, R., 'Ants and Serpents' (*Antananarivo Annual and Madagascar Magazine*, Christmas no. 2, 1876), p.125.

Trevelyan, M., *Folk-Lore and Folk Stories of Wales* (Elliot Stock, London, 1909).

Tryon, H.H., *Fearsome Critters* (The Idlewild Press, Cornwall, NY, 1939).

Twigger, R., *Big Snake: The Hunt for The World's Longest Python* (Victor Gollancz, London, 1999).

Underwood, A., 'The Snakes of Marcopoulo' (*Fortean Times*, no. 94, January 1997), p.51.

Vonstille, W.T. and Stille III, W.T., 'Electrostatic Sense in Rattlesnakes' (*Nature*, vol. 370, 1994), p.184.

Wachter, D., 'SC Family Finds Two-Headed Snake' (*Fox Carolina 21*, 24 September 2012).

Wade, J., 'Snakes alive!' (*Fortean Times*, no. 197, April 1997), pp.34-37.

Wallach, V., 'Axial Bifurcation and Duplication in Snakes. Part I. A Synopsis of Authentic and Anecdotal Cases' (*Bulletin of the Maryland Herpetological Society*, vol. 43, no. 2, 2007), pp.57-95.

Wallach, V., 'Axial Bifurcation and Duplication in Snakes. Part VI. A 10-Year Update on Authentic Cases' (*Bulletin of the Chicago Herpetological Society*, vol. 53, no. 1, 2018), pp.1-20.

Wallach, V. and Jones, G.S., '*Cryptophidion annamense*, a New Genus and Species of Cryptozoic Snake from Vietnam (Reptilia: Serpentes)' (*Cryptozoology*, vol. 11, 1992), pp.1-37.

Wallach, V. and Jones, G.S., '*Cryptophidion* is a Valid Taxon' (*Cryptozoology*, vol. 12, 1993-1996), pp.102-113.

Waller, H., *The Last Journals of David Livingstone, in Central Africa, Vol. II* (John Murray, London, 1874).

Welfare, S. and Fairley, J., *Arthur C. Clarke's Mysterious World* (Collins, London, 1980).

Wetzel, G., 'Drei Abnorm Gebildete Eier Von *Tropidonotus natrix*' (*Anatomischer Anzeiger*, vol. 18, 1900), pp.425-440.

Wever, E.G. and Vernon, J.A., 'The Problem of Hearing in Snakes' (*Journal of Auditory Research*, vol. 1, 1960), pp.77-83.

Whitty, A. (dir.), *In Search of the Giant Flying Snake of Namibia* [TV documentary] (NNTV, Johannesburg, 1995).

Wils, K., 'Is the Snow Snake Out There?' (*Daily Press*, Escanaba, MI, 3 March 2006).

Wolhuter, H., *Memories of a Game-Ranger* (Wild Life Protection Society of South Africa, Johannesburg, 1948).

Wood, G.L., *The Guinness Book of Animal Facts and Feats,* 3rd Edit. (Guinness Books, London, 1982).

Wood, J.G., *Illustrated Natural History*, 3 vols (Routledge, Warne, and Routledge, London, 1859-1863).

Wood, P., 'Ancient Skepticism and the Snake God Glycon' (*Irregular Times*, 20 August 2014) [archived at https://web.archive.org/web/20180107122136/http://irregulartimes.com/2014/08/20/ancient-skepticism-the-snake-god-fraud-of-glycon/].

Woodruff, S., 'The Rattle Snake Disarmed by the Leaves of the White Ash' (*American Journal of Science, Series 1*, vol. 23, 1823), pp.337-339.

Young, B.A., 'Morphological Basis of "Growling" in the King Cobra, *Ophiophagus hannah*' (*Journal of Experimental Zoology*, vol. 260, 1991), pp.275-287.

Young, B.A., 'Snake Bioacoustics: Toward a Richer Understanding of the Behavioral Ecology of Snakes' (*Quarterly Review of Biology*, vol. 78, 2003), pp.303-325.

INDEX OF ANIMAL NAMES

Abraxas grossulariata, 218
Acanthophis spp., 3, 172-173
Adder (=European common viper), 81-82, 90, 92, 94-97, 267, 289, 304, 343, 361, 371
    black, 81-82
    copper (=scarlet viper), 96
    death, 3, 172-173
    hell, 95
    puff, 25-26, 44, 138, 206, 263
    rhombic night, 258
    spreading, 365-367
    swamp, 19-34, 280-283
Agkistrodon contortrix, 110
    piscivorus, 48
Ajolote, 75-76
Amphisbaena, 309, 314-319
Amphisbaenian (=Worm-lizard), 32, 75-76, 170-172, 280, 311-312, 317
Amphisien, 317-318
Anaconda, 15, 145, 155, 163-164, 364
    black, 155
    common (=green), 151, 364
    giant, 15, 151-156
Anguis fragilis, 226
Annelid worm, 109

Ant, funnel, 376
Ant mother, 374-376
Aphaenogaster swammerdami, 374, 376
Arctia caja, 226
Ascaris lineata, 325, 327
Aspidites melanocephalus, 108
    ramsayi, 108
Astrotia [=*Hydrophis*] *stokesii*, 307-308
Atheris hispida, 220
    squamigera, 92
Austrelaps labialis, 110
    ramsayi, 110
    superbus, 110

Banakon, 75
Bis-cobra, 32, 34, 280, 283
Bitis arietans, 25-26, 44, 138, 206, 263
    gabonica, 61, 349-350
    nasicornis, 25-26
Boa, Indian sand, 311
    Tartar sand, 173
Boa constrictor (=*Boa constrictor*), 27-28, 101, 144, 204
Boas (mythological Italian giant snake), 144

Bodalog Beast, 339-345
Boodon [=*Boaedon*] *lineatus*, 257
Boomslang, 347, 349-350
Bothriechis schlegelii, 286
Bothrodon pridii, 347-355
Bu-rin, 104
Bubu, 58, 62
Bug, electric, 175
Bungarus, 28-29, 275-277
    caeruleus, 276, 282, 284
    fasciatus, 28, 276, 284
Bushmaster, 261-262

Caecilian, 170-171, 280, 283
Cat king, 299
Caterpillar, denkimushi, 175
    giant hairy mystery, 217-222
    gooseberry, 217-220
Causus rhombeatus, 258
Centipede, electric, 175
Cerastes cerastes, 44
Cerberus rynchops, 107
Chalcides chalcides, 30
Chlamydosaurus kingii, 68
Chrysopelea ornata, 79, 177, 182, 292
Coachwhip, 53-54
Cobra, black-necked spitting, 138
    crowing crested, 15, 57-70, 73, 77-80, 258, 272
    Egyptian, 207
    giant spitting, 15
    Indian (=spectacled), 26-27, 127, 202, 207, 274
    king (=hamadryad), 58, 196, 198, 204, 267
    São Tomé, 15
    spitting (ringhals), 344, 360-361
    white, 382-383
Colovia, 39-41
Coluber constrictor, 53-54, 302
Conch, Chiragra spider, 352-354

Copperhead, American, 110
    highland (=Ramsay's), 110
    lowland, 110
    pygmy, 110
Coronella austriaca, 343, 363
Crocodile, conjoined, 318
Crotalus adamanteus, 158
    cerastes, 286
    horridus, 201
    sp., 200
Crowing mystery snake, African, 15, 57-70, 73, 78-80, 258, 272
    Caribbean, 70-73
    Indian, 77
    Palau, 75
    Philippines, 75-77
    Samoan, 74-75
Cryptophidion annamense, 101-103
Culebrón, 317
Cyclocorus lineatus, 295
Cylindrophis ruffus, 311

Daboia russelii, 23-24
Damselfly, 190
Dasypeltis spp., 270
Deilephila elpenor, 190
Dendrelaphis punctulatus, 108
Dendroaspis polylepis, 61-62, 260
Denkimushi, 175
Dispholidus typus, 349-350
Dog, rabid, 135
Dolichophis caspius, 293-294
    jugularis, 294
Draconopides, 241-245, 248
Dragon, serpent, 144-148, 164, 315, 324, 344-345
    St Leonard's Forest, 344
Dudley-Duplex, 116-118

Earthworm, squirter, 169
Echis carinatus, 23-24, 270, 278-279, 284
    ocellatus, 138

INDEX

Eel, sky, 183
Eel king, 306
Elaphe quatuorlineata, 42
Eryx johnii, 311
    tartaricus, 173
Eunectes murinus, 151, 364

Farancia abacura, 52
    erytrogramma, 53
Fearsome critters, 370
Fieldmouse king, 299
Fish, sembilang, 135-136
Fly, robber, 190
Furina diadema, 108

Gecko, barking, 270
    wonder, 270
Gigantophis garstini, 164
Gila monster, 32-33
Gila monster x cobra hybrid, 32, 34
Gloydius [=*Agkistrodon*] *blomhoffii*, 101
Glycon, 16, 321-337
Gnat, fungus, 218, 229-230
Gooseberry wife, 217-219
Gorgon, 315

Hairy Hubert, 225
Haldea [=*Virginia*] *striatula*, 310-311
Hangara, 260
Hazelworm (=war worm, white worm), 226-231
Heloderma alvarezi, 33
    horridum, 32-33
    suspectum, 32-33
Heterodon platirhinos, 366
    spp., 366
Hierophis [=*Coluber*] *gemonensis*, 294
    viridiflavus, 292-293
Hongo, 58

Hydra, 301
Hypnale hypnale, 279

Ibibaboka, 163
Inkhomi, 58, 69

Jibate, 358, 361

Karait, 17, 273-284
Kovoko, 58
Krait, 23, 28, 265, 275-278, 282-284
    banded, 28, 265, 276, 284
    Indian, 275-276, 282, 284

Lachesis muta, 261-262
Lambis [=*Harpago*] *chiragra*, 352
Lampropeltis getulus, 117
    triangulum, 115
Lepidodendron, 355-356
Lepidotes (=*Lepidotus*) sp., 136
Lizard, amphicephalous, 312-313
    Australian legless, 108-109
    Australian stump-tailed, 311
    beaded, 32-33
    frilled, 68
    legless, 29-31, 170, 172, 226, 368, 370
Lutra lutra, 340-341

Madagascarophis colubrinus, 374-376
Madatyphlops decorsei, 374
Madtsoiid, 106, 160
Malpolon monspessulanus, 38-40
Mamba, black, 61-62, 260
Manora, 317
Masticophis flagellum, 53-54
Mbobo, 58
Mboi-yagua, 363-364
Metlapilcoatlus [=*Bothrops*] *nummifer*, 292
Micropechis ikaheka, 108

Mink, American, 342
  sea, 342
Mitsukurina owstoni, 358
Monema flavescens, 175
Mongolian death worm (=Allghoi khorkhoi, Allergorhai horhai), 31-34, 165-176
Morelia [=*Liasis*] *oenpelliensis*, 159
  spilota, 161-162
Moth, cup, 175
  garden tiger, 226
  large elephant hawk, 190
  magpie (currant), 218
  pine processionary, 218-219, 229
Muhlambela, 60, 62, 66

N'gok-wiki, 58
Naga, 105-106, 123-125, 161, 195, 202, 204, 237
  Mekong, 104-107, 161
Naja ashei, 15
  haje, 207
  naja, 26-27, 127, 202, 207, 274
  nigricollis, 138
  peroescobari, 15
Natrix, 15, 290
  helvetica, 40-41, 118, 263-264, 266, 342-343, 361
  natrix, 15, 123, 343
Ndhlondhlo, 66-67
Neither, 361-363
Nematode, 325, 327
Nematus ribesii, 220
Neovison macrodon, 342
  vison, 342
Nerodia sipedon, 116
Ngoshe, 58
Ninki-nanka, 58
Nino de la tierra, 286
Nkweta, 260, 263
Nogo putsane, 260

Ophidiomyces ophiodiicola, 225
Ophiophagus hannah, 58, 196, 198, 204, 267
Ophisaurus ventralis, 368, 370
Ophyracus undulatus, 286
Orthriophis taeniurus grabowskyi, 268
Otter, European, 340-341
Ouroboros, 48-49
Oxyuranus scutellatus, 28

Pantherophis alleghaniensis, 118
  guttatus, 270-271
Pelamis platurus, 306
Phasianus colchicus, 187-188
Pheasant, ring-necked, 187-188
Philodryas schotti (=*patagoniensis*), 254-256
Pichu-cuate, 284-286
Pituophis catenifer sayi, 158, 258-9
  melanoleucus, 116
Planarian, 109
Platyceps najadum, 294
Plotosus canius, 135
Porthidium melanurum, 286
Poskok, 288-290
Psammophis sp., 118
Pseudechis australis, 107-108
Pseudo-serpent, 45-55, 357-376
Pseudonaja nuchalis, 108
Ptenopus spp., 270
Ptyas mucosus, 257
  nigromarginatus, 292
Pumina, 150
Pushmi-pullyu, 318
Python (Greek serpent dragon), 15, 28, 141, 143-145, 148, 324, 347
Python, 260, 265, 309
  amethystine, 160, 162
  black-headed, 108
  Burmese, 104, 159
  carpet (=diamond), 161-162

INDEX

giant, 141-150, 159-161
hairy-necked, 58
Indian, 257
Oenpelli, 159
reticulated, 14, 151
rock, 29. 143-144, 148, 205, 322, 324
woma, 108
Python bivittatus, 104, 159
molurus molurus, 257
reticulatus, 14, 151
sebae, 29. 143-144, 148, 205, 322, 324

Quetzalcoatl, 188, 380-381

Racer, blue, 53
eastern, 53-54, 302
Bornean cave, 268-269
Rail, pygmy, 62
Ramonellus longispinus, 193
Rat king, 298-299
Rattlesnake, 47, 132, 200-201, 212, 270, 285
eastern diamondback, 158
timber, 201
Rhabdophis tigrinus, 101
Rhynchophis boulengeri, 368-369
Roundworm, ascarid, 325, 327

Sampoderma allergorhaihorhai, 32
Saprolegnia, 225
Sarothrura elegans, 62
Sawfly, gooseberry, 220
Sciara [=*Lycoria*] *militaris*, 218, 229
Scolopendra electrica (=*Geophilus electricus*), 175
Scorpion, 131, 134-135, 206
Serpent, Eden (=pre-cursed), 16, 226, 233-249
rainbow, 160
sky, 183

Serpent king, 16, 297-308
Shark, goblin, 358
Shushupe, 261
Sidewinder, 286
Simalia amethistina [=*Liasis amethystinus*], 160, 162
Skink, legless, 30, 170
Slow worm, 226
Snake, Aesculapian, 325, 343
American hairy, 222-225
amphicephalous, 310-319
Arizona flying (=Tl'iish naat'a'í), 180-182
arrow, 181
Australian tree, 108
Balkan whip, 294
barred (western) grass, 40-41, 118, 263-264, 266, 342-343, 361
bipedal, 235, 239, 245
black (Argentina), 251-256
black (Thailand), 105-106
blind burrowing, 53, 55
blow, 365-367
boss, 157-159
brimstone, 368
Bulgarian flying, 184-185
bull-, 158, 258-259
Caribbean crowing crested mystery, 70-73
Carthage giant, 142-143
Caspian whip, 293-294
Congo giant mystery, 148-150
corn, 270-271
Dahl's whip, 294
dicephalous (=bicephalic, two-headed), 113-121, 365
dicephalus dipygus (=anakatadidymus), 118
dog-faced water, 107
eastern black rat, 118
eastern grass, 15, 123, 343
egg-eating, 270

Snake (cont.)
  Egyptian flying, 177, 192-194
  European cat, 36, 38, 43
  flying, 79, 177, 182, 292
  flying mystery, 79, 177-194
  four-striped, 42
  French flying, 183-184
  garter, 270, 301-303
  giant, 141-164, 347-356
  Glamorgan feathered winged, 185-186
  glass, 368, 370
  grass, 15, 40-41, 115, 118, 120, 123, 211, 263-264, 266-267, 290-292, 341-343, 362-363,
  green, 378-379
  green rat, 292
  hammerhead, 365, 367
  hog-nosed, 366-367
  hoop, 16, 45-55, 296, 315, 374
  horn, 46-55
  Indian crowing mystery, 77
  Indian rat, 257
  Javan giant hairy, 221-222
  joint, 368
  kid, 260
  king, 117
  large (=black) whip, 294
  lined house, 257
  London flying, 189-192
  magenta-headed Australian mystery, 108-109
  Malagasy cat-eyed (=Ant mother), 374-376
  melanistic mystery, 251-256
  milk, 115
  Mocquard's worm, 374
  Montpellier, 38-40
  mud, 52
  mulga (=king brown), 107-108
  Namibian flying, 178-180
  New Zealand, 109-112
  Newbury double-headed, 309-310, 314
  northern triangle-spotted, 295-296
  Palau crowing mystery, 75
  Paraguayan barking, 363-364
  Parker's, 107-108
  Patagonian green, 254-256
  Philippines crowing mystery, 75-77
  pine, 116
  rainbow, 53
  red-naped, 108
  red-tailed pipe, 311
  rhinoceros rat (=green unicorn), 368-369
  rough earth, 310-311
  Russian crested mystery, 78-79
  Samoan crowing mystery, 74-75
  sand, 118
  small-eyed, 108
  smooth, 343, 362-363
  snow, 16, 367, 370-372
  somersaulting (see northern triangle-spotted), 295-296
  Stokes's sea-, 307-308
  sunbeam, 103-104
  telescopic (Bolivian), 16, 358
  tiger water, 101
  Tradescant crested mystery, 77-78
  tricephalic (=three-headed), 120
  unicorn, 367-369
  Vietnamese sharp-nosed, 101-103
  Virgin Mary, 41-43
  water, 116
  western brown, 108
  western (=green) whip, 292-293
  winged mystery, 177-194

INDEX

yellow-bellied sea-, 306
Yugoslavian jumping, 288-290
Snakeling (see Karait), 273-274, 278, 282, 284
Songo, 58, 60
Songwe, 63-64
Speckled Band, 17, 19-34, 280, 282
Squirrel king, 298-299
Sucuriju gigante, 151-154
Swiftlet, cave, 268-269

Taguerga, 44
Taipan, 28, 107-108
Telescopus fallax, 36, 38, 43
Teratoscincus spp., 270-271
Terrapin, American, 270
conjoined, 314
Thamnophis [=*Eutoenia*] *sirtalis*, 270, 301-303
Thaumetopoea pityocampa, 218-219, 229
Tic polonga, 23
Tiliqua rugosa (=*Trachydosaurus rugosus*), 311
Titanoboa cerrejonensis, 16, 156, 164
Tl'iish naat'a'í, 180-182
Toad, 57, 136-137, 258
Tropidolaemus wagleri, 23, 203
Trout, fur-bearing, 225
Typhlops spp., 53, 55
Tzuchinoko, 99-101

Viper, Algerian hairy, 220-221
Central African bush, 92
eyelash, 286
Gaboon, 61, 349-350
hairy bush, 220
horned, 44
hump-nosed, 279
Japanese pit, 101
Mexican horned pit, 286
Mexican jumping, 292

montane pit, 286
nose-horned, 289
Orsini's, 289
rhinoceros, 25-26
Russell's, 23-24
saw-scaled (=little Indian), 23-24, 270, 278-279, 284
scarlet (=small red), 81-97
St Paul's Maltese mystery, 35-39
temple, 23, 26, 203
Wagler's pit, 23, 26, 203
water, 48
West African carpet, 138
Vipera ammodytes, 289
aquatica, 48
berus, 81-82, 90, 92, 94-97, 267, 289, 304, 343, 361, 371
rubra (=*Coluber chersea*), 81-97
ursinii, 289

Water moccasin, 48
Wonambi naracoortensis, 160
spp., 106, 160-161
Woolly bear, 226
Worm, army, 229

Xenopeltis unicolor, 103-104
Xiuhcoatl, 316

Yacumama, 155

Zamenis longissimus, 325, 343

ABOUT THE AUTHOR

Born and still living in the West Midlands, England, Dr Karl P.N. Shuker graduated from the University of Leeds with a Bachelor of Science (Honours) degree in pure zoology, and from the University of Birmingham with a Doctor of Philosophy degree in zoology and comparative physiology. He works full-time as a freelance zoological consultant to the media, and as a prolific published writer.

Dr Shuker is currently the author of 33 books and hundreds of articles, principally on animal-related subjects, with an especial interest in cryptozoology and animal mythology, on which he is an internationally-recognised authority, but also including two poetry volumes. In addition, he has acted as consultant for several major multi-contributor volumes as well as for the world-renowned *Guinness Book of Records/Guinness World Records* (he is currently its Senior Consultant for its Life Sciences section); and he has compiled questions for the BBC's long-running cerebral quiz *Mastermind*. He is also the editor of the *Journal of Cryptozoology*, the world's only existing peer-reviewed scientific journal devoted to mystery animals.

Dr Shuker has travelled the world in the course of his researches and writings, and has appeared regularly on television and radio. Aside from work, his diverse range of interests include motorbikes, quizzes, philately, poetry, travel, world mythology, films and in particular the history of animation, the life and career of James Dean, collecting masquerade and carnival masks, and anything relating to Sherlock Holmes (novels, short stories, literary pastiches and parodies, TV shows, movies, collectabilia).

He is a Scientific Fellow of the prestigious Zoological Society of London, a Fellow of London's Royal Entomological Society, and a member of various other wildlife-related organisations. He is also Cryptozoology Consultant to the Centre for Fortean Zoology, and a Member of the Society of Authors.

Dr Shuker's personal website can be accessed at http://www.karlshuker.com and his mystery animals blog, *ShukerNature*, can be accessed at http://www.karlshuker.blogspot.com

His *Star Steeds* poetry blog can be accessed at http://starsteeds.blogspot.com and his *Eclectarium of Doctor Shuker* blog can be accessed at http://eclectariumshuker.blogspot.com

His *Shuker In MovieLand* film review blog can be accessed at https://shukerinmovieland.blogspot.com

There is also an entry for Dr Shuker in the online encyclopedia *Wikipedia* at http://en.wikipedia.org/wiki/Karl_Shuker and a Like (fan) page on *Facebook*.

AUTHOR BIBLIOGRAPHY

Mystery Cats of the World: From Blue Tigers to Exmoor Beasts (Robert Hale: London, 1989)

Extraordinary Animals Worldwide (Robert Hale: London, 1991)

The Lost Ark: New and Rediscovered Animals of the 20th Century (HarperCollins: London, 1993)

Dragons: A Natural History (Aurum: London/Simon and Schuster: New York, 1995; republished Taschen: Cologne, 2006)

In Search of Prehistoric Survivors: Do Giant 'Extinct' Creatures Still Exist? (Blandford: London, 1995)

The Unexplained: An Illustrated Guide to the World's Natural and Paranormal Mysteries (Carlton: London/JG Press: North Dighton, 1996; republished Carlton: London, 2002)

From Flying Toads to Snakes With Wings: From the Pages of FATE Magazine (Llewellyn: St Paul, 1997; republished Bounty: London, 2005)

Mysteries of Planet Earth: An Encyclopedia of the Inexplicable (Carlton: London, 1999)

The Hidden Powers of Animals: Uncovering the Secrets of Nature (Reader's Digest: Pleasantville/Marshall Editions: London, 2001)

Historic Realms of Marvels and Miracles: Between Myth and Materiality (Chelsea House: New York, 2001)

Ancient Worlds, Ancient Mysteries: Legends of Many Millennia (Chelsea House: New York, 2001)

Lost Worlds and Forgotten Secrets: Riddles of Earth and Beyond (Chelsea House: New York, 2001)

The New Zoo: New and Rediscovered Animals of the Twentieth Century (House of Stratus Ltd: Thirsk/House of Stratus Inc: Poughkeepsie, 2002)

The Beasts that Hide from Man: Seeking the World's Last Undiscovered Animals (Paraview: New York, 2003)

Extraordinary Animals Revisited: From Singing Dogs to Serpent Kings (CFZ Press: Bideford, 2007)

Dr Shuker's Casebook: In Pursuit of Marvels and Mysteries (CFZ Press: Bideford, 2008)

Dinosaurs and Other Prehistoric Animals on Stamps: A Worldwide Catalogue (CFZ Press: Bideford, 2008)

Star Steeds and Other Dreams: The Collected Poems (CFZ Press: Bideford, 2009)

Karl Shuker's Alien Zoo: From the Pages of Fortean Times (CFZ Press: Bideford, 2010)

The Encyclopaedia of New and Rediscovered Animals: From the Lost Ark to The New Zoo—and Beyond (Coachwhip Publications: Landisville, PA, 2012)

Cats of Magic, Mythology, and Mystery: A Feline Phantasmagoria (CFZ Press: Bideford, 2012)

Mirabilis: A Carnival of Cryptozoology and Unnatural History (Anomalist Books: San Antonio, 2013)

Dragons in Zoology, Cryptozoology, and Culture (Coachwhip Publications: Greenville, OH, 2013)

The Menagerie of Marvels: A Third Compendium of Extraordinary Animals (CFZ Press: Bideford, 2014)

A Manifestation of Monsters: Examining the (Un)Usual Suspects (Anomalist Books: San Antonio, TX, 2015)

More Star Steeds and Other Dreams: The Collected Poems—2015 Expanded Edition (Fortean Words: Bideford, 2015).

Here's Nessie! A Monstrous Compendium from Loch Ness (CFZ Press: Bideford, 2016)

Still in Search of Prehistoric Survivors: The Creatures that Time Forgot? (Coachwhip Publications: Greenville, OH, 2016).

ShukerNature Book 1: Antlered Elephants, Locust Dragons, and Other Cryptic Blog Beasts (Coachwhip Publications: Greenville, OH, 2019).

ShukerNature Book 2: Living Gorgons, Bottled Homunculi, and Other Monstrous Blog Beasts (Coachwhip Publications: Greenville, OH, 2020).

This Cryptid World: A Global Survey of Undiscovered Beasts (Herb Lester Associates: London, 2020).

Mystery Cats of the World Revisited: Blue Tigers, King Cheetahs, Black Cougars, Spotted Lions, and More (Anomalist Books: San Antonio, TX, 2020)

Secret Snakes and Serpent Surprises (Coachwhip Publications: Greenville, OH, 2022).

CONSULTANT AND ALSO CONTRIBUTOR

Man and Beast (Reader's Digest: Pleasantville, New York, 1993)

Secrets of the Natural World (Reader's Digest: Pleasantville, New York, 1993)

Almanac of the Uncanny (Reader's Digest: Surry Hills, Australia, 1995)

The Guinness Book of Records/Guinness World Records 1998-present day (Guinness: London, 1997-present day)

GWR Amazing Animals (Guinness: London, 2017)

GWR Wild Talents (Guinness: London, 2018)

CONSULTANT

Monsters (Lorenz: London, 2001)

CONTRIBUTOR

Of Monsters and Miracles CD-ROM (Croydon Museum/Interactive Designs: Oxton, 1995)

Fortean Times Weird Year 1996 (John Brown Publishing: London, 1996)
Mysteries of the Deep (Llewellyn: St Paul, 1998)
Guinness Amazing Future (Guinness: London, 1999)
The Earth (Channel 4 Books: London, 2000)
Mysteries and Monsters of the Sea (Gramercy: New York, 2001)
Chambers Dictionary of the Unexplained (Chambers: Edinburgh, 2007)
Chambers Myths and Mysteries (Chambers: Edinburgh, 2008)
The Fortean Times Paranormal Handbook (Dennis Publishing: London, 2009)
Death Worm: Metamorphosis of the Allghoi Khorkhoi [in Russian] (Salamandra P.V.V.: Moscow, 2014)
Folk Horror Revival: Field Studies (Wyrd Harvest Press/Lulu, 2015)
Tales of the Damned: An Anthology of Fortean Horror (Fortean Fiction: Bideford, 2016)

Plus numerous contributions to the annual *CFZ Yearbook* series of volumes, *Fortean Studies*, and various other annual publications.

EDITOR

The *Journal of Cryptozoology* (CFZ Press: Bideford, 2012-present day)

COACHWHIP PUBLICATIONS
Also Available

*THE ENCYCLOPAEDIA OF NEW
AND REDISCOVERED ANIMALS*

Dr. Karl P.N. Shuker

COACHWHIPBOOKS.COM
Cryptozoology Titles and More

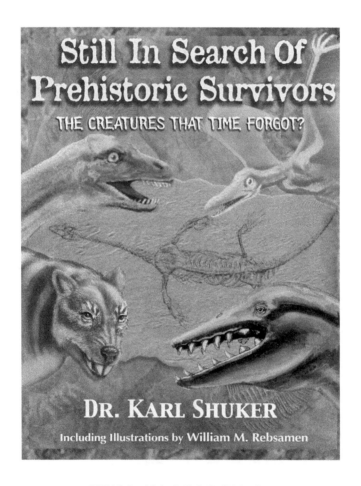

STILL IN SEARCH OF
PREHISTORIC SURVIVORS

Dr. Karl P.N. Shuker

COACHWHIP PUBLICATIONS
Also Available

DR. KARL P. N. SHUKER

Dragons in Zoology, Cryptozoology, and Culture

ShukerNature 1

ShukerNature 2

Living Gorgons, Bottled Homunculi, and Other Monstrous Blog Beasts

Dr. Karl P.N. Shuker

COACHWHIP PUBLICATIONS
Also Available

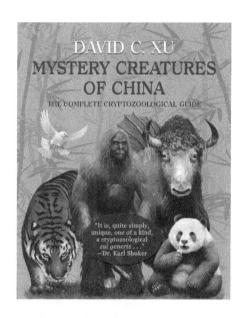

COACHWHIPBOOKS.COM
Cryptozoology Titles and More

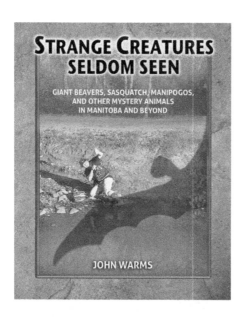

COACHWHIP PUBLICATIONS
Also Available

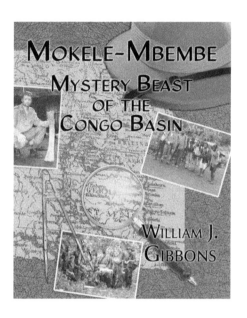

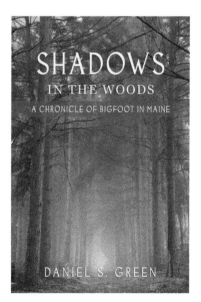

COACHWHIPBOOKS.COM
Cryptozoology Titles and More

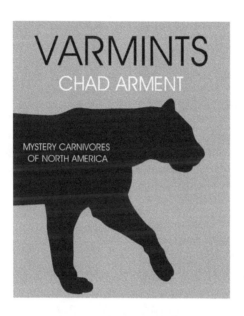

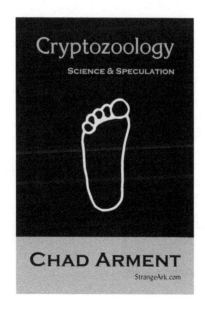

COACHWHIP PUBLICATIONS
Also Available

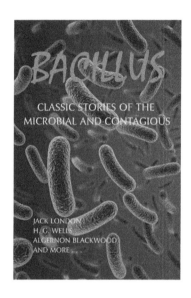

COACHWHIP.COM
Select Titles in Epub

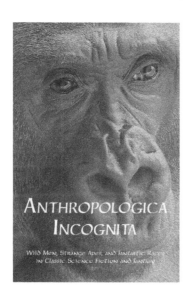

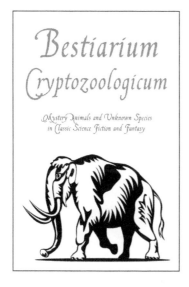

Lightning Source UK Ltd.
Milton Keynes UK
UKHW040652060522
402599UK00001B/16